Content-Based Instruction

in

Foreign Language Education:

Models and Methods

Stephen B. Stryker and Betty Lou Leaver, Editors

Georgetown University Press, Washington, D.C. 20007
© 1997 by Georgetown University Press. All rights reserved.

10 9 8 7 6 5 4 3 2 1   1997

THIS VOLUME PRINTED ON ACID-FREE OFFSET BOOK PAPER

Library of Congress Cataloging-in-Publication Data

Content-based instruction in foreign language education: models and
methods/Stephen B. Stryker, Betty Lou Leaver, editors.
      p. cm.
Includes bibliographical references and index.
1. Language and languages — Study and teaching. I. Stryker, Stephen B.
II. Leaver, Betty Lou.
   P53.C594 1997
   418'.007—dc21   97-6085
   ISBN 0-87840-659-X (pbk.)

Contents

Preface

This book has been compiled for foreign or second language educators who would like to implement content-based instruction (CBI) in their classrooms but who have neither models to follow nor time to develop new ones. Although this volume will be of interest to teachers working in English as a Second Language (ESL) and bilingual education—areas in which content-based models already exist—it is intended primarily for those who teach foreign languages to adult learners.

We anticipate that our readers have already given some thought to the potential of content-based instruction and are searching for practical models and specific methods for their own classrooms. Perhaps readers have had their interest piqued by publications such as *Content-Based Second Language Instruction* (Brinton, Snow, and Wesche 1989) or *Language and Content* (Krueger and Ryan 1993), which present theoretical and linguistic arguments in support of CBI. The latter volume, collected papers from a 1991 conference of the Consortium for Language Teaching and Learning at Brown University, includes a few actual "case studies" of CBI. Another edited volume, *Languages Across the Curriculum* (Straight 1994), a collection of essays on the foreign languages across the curriculum (FLAC) variation of CBI, addresses broad policy issues and offers some program descriptions. However, as Richard Jurasek observes, those volumes do not reveal much about what actually happens in the classrooms; pedagogical concerns were not their central focus (in Straight 1994, 137).

This volume does focus on the pedagogical concerns of CBI. Our objective is to give language educators concrete and practical ideas for implementing CBI, not to expound on all the reasons why theory suggests that we do so. We and our colleagues present eleven case studies of successfully implemented models of CBI. Each chapter describes a CBI course or program that was actually implemented and evaluated. The nine foreign language models include programs in Arabic, French, Indonesian, Italian, Russian, Serbo-Croatian, and Spanish; the two FLAC programs encompass more than a dozen other languages. Students' language proficiencies range from beginning to advanced levels. There are single-teacher models and multi-teacher models in a broad variety of settings that include the Foreign Service Institute (FSI), the Defense Language Institute (DLI), the Monterey Institute of International Studies, Columbia University's Center for International Studies, Ohio University, SUNY-Binghamton, the University of Utah, and the University of Minnesota. Taken as a whole, this collection represents a broad overview of CBI in foreign language programs for adults during the last decade. We are confident that teachers and curriculum developers in all areas of foreign language education will benefit from the ideas presented in these case studies. We are especially pleased to present models in some less commonly taught languages such as Arabic, Indonesian, Russian, and Serbo-Croatian.

In compiling this volume, we have sought out pioneers and leaders in the field and asked them to include sufficient detail about CBI modles that they use so that other foreign language educators could adapt these models (or portions thereof) to their own classrooms. Although many contributors have included detailed appendixes listing sources and materials, space has not permitted us to include all supporting information in each case. Consequently, readers who are particularly interested in more information about any one of the models are invited to contact the authors directly. Addresses are provided in the biographic section at the end of each chapter. Readers might note that the Consortium for Languages Across the Curriculum maintains a web site at http://www.language.brown.edu/lac.

We have divided this book into six parts. Part One is an introductory chapter in which we elaborate upon the definition and characteristics of CBI that we first presented in *Foreign Language Annals* (1989) and trace the evolution of contemporary CBI from immersion programs in the 1960s to foreign language and FLAC classrooms in the 1990s.

Parts Two, Three, and Four group the curriculum models according to the levels of foreign language proficiency as defined by the American Council on the Teaching of Foreign Languages (ACTFL). Part Two presents three models aimed at *Novice* levels; Part Three presents three models for *Intermediate* levels; and Part Four presents three models for *Advanced* levels. In these three parts, we and our colleagues present detailed descriptions of successful CBI courses or programs for adult learners. Each contributor describes the setting, objectives, curriculum design, evaluation procedures, materials and teacher preparation. Appendixes in some of the chapters provide program evaluation data, model syllabi, sample lessons and activities, and lists of materials. Part Five is dedicated to two case studies of the FLAC variation of CBI.

In Part Six we discuss the pros and cons of CBI in light of the combined experiences of our contributors, and we attempt to summarize and evaluate from our own perspective some of the central issues involved with CBI.

The bibliography at the end of this volume combines the general references from all thirteen chapters. To this list we have added many other sources that we believe the CBI researcher will find useful.

The proficiency chart in Chapter One comes from the American Council on the Teaching of Foreign Languages (ACTFL). We thank ACTFL for permission to reproduce the chart here.

We would like to acknowledge the contributions of H. David Argoff, Gary Crawford, and Candice Hunt of the Foreign Service Institute and Martha Nyikos of Indiana University, who commented on early drafts. We thank Karen Willetts of Montgomery County Public Schools for her encouragement to write this book in the first place.

Layout graphics and formatting on Adobe Pagemaker was accomplished by Carl Leaver. Computer and editing assistance was provided by Shawn Leaver, David Robbins, Heidi Whitehouse, Veronica Cervantes, and Bayard Stryker. Valuable editorial and research assistance was provided by Shirley Richberger Butler. We are especially grateful for the support of the English Department of California State University, Stanislaus, and the staff of the American Global Studies Institute. We also owe Earl Stevick and A. Richard Evans a debt of gratitude for their practical advice.

Stephen B. Stryker
Betty Lou Leaver

This book is dedicated to our families whose patience and support for nearly a decade helped make this book a reality: Christine Stryker, Bayard Stryker, Alexis Stryker, Chloe Stryker, Carl Leaver, Echo Leaver, Fawn Leaver, Shawn Leaver, Shenan Leaver, and Brian Martinez.

Part One

Introduction

1

Content-Based Instruction:
From Theory to Practice

Stephen B. Stryker and Betty Lou Leaver

Learning a second language has been compared to learning to ride a bicycle, learning to play tennis, or learning to play a musical instrument. In spite of broad recognition that the best way to learn these skills is by *doing* them, not just by studying about them or performing exercises and drills, our traditional foreign language classes resemble music classes in which all of the learners' time is spent practicing scales and studying theory, and they are not permitted to play any real pieces until they are proficient enough to give a recital. Content-based foreign language instruction, on the other hand, encourages students to learn a new language by playing real pieces—actually *using* that language, from the very first class, as a real means of communication. Furthermore, the philosophy of content-based instruction (CBI) aims at empowering students to become independent learners and continue the learning process beyond the classroom. After all, the ultimate goal we foreign language teachers should have for our students is that they spread their wings, leave the nest, and soar off on their own toward the horizon. CBI is a way of showing our students how to can fly.

CBI, as demonstrated in the following chapters, is a truly holistic and global approach to foreign language education. CBI can be refreshing and liberating for both teachers and students, offering an alternative to the tedium and boredom so often associated with the piecemeal, bottom-up approaches of linguistically driven curricula. More a philosophy than a methodology, there is no singular formula for CBI. Some of the most common models, implemented by increasing numbers of second and foreign language educators worldwide, include sheltered content courses, adjunct courses, theme-based and area studies modules, Language for Special Purposes (LSP), discipline-based instruction, and foreign languages across the curriculum (FLAC). All of these variations of CBI, in myriad combinations, are illustrated in the following chapters.

The term "sheltered content," once an erudite term used in second language acquisition, has become a mantra in many public school systems in the United States (especially in California) that encompasses specially designed math, science, history, English, and social studies courses for K-12 second language learners. In a sheltered class, the teacher uses special methods and techniques to "shelter subject matter," i.e., make the content more accessible to second language learners. In this general sense, all the authors in this volume use sheltered methods and techniques in their foreign language classrooms.

"Adjunct courses" have appeared in many secondary and postsecondary settings as a means of connecting English as a Second Language (ESL) classes, often offered in a language institute on or near campus, to content classes in the regular academic program. Several authors of the chapters that follow, especially in FLAC, use a variation of the adjunct model to make connections between the study of a foreign language and the study of a particular subject matter. Just as sheltered content approaches can make connections that stimulate students' interest, adjunct courses can enhance students' self-confidence with a feeling of using the new language to accomplish real tasks.

"Theme-based approaches," which have existed for a long time in foreign language education, are often supplementary activities that interrupt the systematic study of grammar with readings and activities on topics such as food, music, dating, and the family. In CBI, these kinds of themes often take on a central role in the curriculum. The content modules described by several of the contributors are, in a sense, expansions of the theme-based concept, but in these cases the entire course is designed around in-depth study of topics such as a country's economy, political system, family structure, or the role of women in the society. Instead of being add-ons to a course based on the study of grammar, the study of grammar in these courses becomes linked to, defined by, and dependent upon the topics.

Language for Special Purposes (LSP) courses, currently very common in ESL and English as a Foreign Language (EFL) classes around the world, are now offered in many foreign language programs as well. For example, the courses at the Foreign Service Institute (FSI) and the Defense Language Institute (DLI) described in this volume have strong elements of language for special purposes in that the content is aimed at preparing students for specific positions in overseas assignments—a diplomat in Mexico City or a military peace keeper in Bosnia.

The content of LSP courses is relatively easy to determine depending on what those "special purposes" are; however, in academic foreign language programs determining content is less clear cut. Content is frequently decided arbitrarily by the teacher and is usually based on academic tradition. Literature, the most common of the "content" courses offered in intermediate and advanced foreign language programs, can be combined with elements of LSP. One such successful combination of LSP with the study of literary academic subjects is presented in Klahn's Contemporary Mexican Topics Course in Chapter 9.

FLAC programs, an innovation started in the 1970s and now implemented in dozens of universities in the United States, incorporate the use of a foreign language as a research tool in selected courses across the entire university curriculum. This approach has students using their foreign language ability to read primary sources for information and, as such, helps students to make meaningful use of their language skills while enriching their cross-cultural knowledge. Two successful programs in FLAC are presented: Straight's program at SUNY-Binghamton in Chapter 11 and Shaw's courses at the Monterey Institute of International Studies in Chapter 12.

Experience in foreign language classrooms has convinced us that content-based approaches such as these have the potential to enhance students' motivation, to accelerate students' acquisition of language proficiency, to broaden cross-cultural knowledge, and to make the language learning experience more enjoyable and fulfilling. Moreover, students who experience a well-organized content-based program are more likely to become autonomous, lifelong learners—to develop the wings they need to fly on their own.

What Is CBI?

As we originally suggested in our article in *Foreign Language Annals* (Leaver and Stryker 1989), CBI can be at once a philosophical orientation, a methodological system, a syllabus design for a single course, or a framework for an entire program of instruction. CBI implies the total integration of language learning and content learning. It represents a significant departure from traditional foreign language teaching methods in that language proficiency is achieved by shifting the focus of instruction from the learning of language *per se* to the learning of language through the study of subject matter.

We see a CBI curriculum as one that 1) is based on a subject-matter core, 2) uses authentic language and texts, and 3) is appropriate to the needs of specific groups of students. All three characteristics are essential for success. We will first look at what is meant by "subject-matter core."

Subject-matter core

The fundamental organization of the curriculum is derived from the subject matter, rather than from forms, functions, situations, or skills. Communicative competence is acquired during the process of learning about specific topics such as math, science, art, social studies, culture, business, history, political systems, international affairs, or economics.

Over the last few decades there has been a movement in language education away from studying *about* language toward a focus on using a language as a tool to communicate. Yet in actual practice, most foreign language courses and texts, including some that call themselves communicative, continue to follow a grammatical-structural or skill-based orientation. Foreign language curricula in too many instances continue to use bottom-up approaches that focus on form rather than top-down approaches that focus on meaning. In our experience, bottom-up approaches rarely spark student interest and motivation and have often created frustration and anxiety. In other words, many disenchanted learners leave the nest before they ever learn to fly.

Swaffar (in Krueger and Ryan 1993) distinguishes between the top-down approach of CBI, in which students are asked to look first at the overall meaning of whole works before attending to the sentence level operation of vocabulary and syntax, and the bottom-up approach of traditional language instruction, which focuses mainly on the words and syntactic structures within sentences. Language-based courses, according to Swaffar, assume that language must be mastered before content can be understood, whereas content-based courses assume the reverse: " . . . students must think about what content means in order to know what they are looking for in language" (185). Thus, attention is shifted from learning language *per se* to learning language through content.

Contrary to some popular thinking that a focus on content knowledge requires a sacrifice of linguistic skill, our experience in CBI classrooms indicates that linguistic development need not be ignored nor taken for granted. In CBI courses there is constant interplay between language and content. Richard Jurasek provides an excellent summary of this central assumption:

> A student's exposure to meaningful subject matter phrased in the second language yields content mastery and linguistic mastery. This is a long way from the not-too-distant past when foreign language teaching was basically content-free—class time was filled with

manipulation of linguistic forms and discussion of correct usage. Since those bad old days, program designers and researchers have been modeling the ways content-focused and use-oriented programming can motivate, facilitate and recontextualize undergraduate foreign language learning (in Krueger and Ryan 1993, 85).

We consider content mastery and linguistic mastery, believed by many to be strictly sequential, to be synergistic. Brinton, Snow, and Wesche, in describing the ascendancy of CBI in the teaching of English as a second or foreign language, propose that ". . . content-based instruction aims at eliminating the artificial separation between language instruction and subject-matter classes which exists in most educational settings" (in Oller 1993, 137).

Unfortunately, this artificial separation between language instruction and subject- matter classes remains an obstacle in many, if not most, foreign language settings. The reasons stem from a combination of cultural factors— insular social values, a lack of perceived need for integration of language and content, old teaching habits based on false assumptions, and an educational bureaucracy mired in the past. While research and experience indicate the advantages of a content-driven curriculum in foreign language classrooms, teachers' unfamiliarity with second language acquisition processes reinforces false assumptions, such as the idea that the study of language equates to the study of grammar, that meaning should be communicated through translation, that the study of culture equates to the study of literature, or that students must be "fluent" before they are ready to study real content. Our educational bureaucracy, not interdisciplinary by nature, perpetuates the separation of language and content.

In sum, the implementation of a subject-matter core in a foreign language curriculum raises a number of issues that CBI teachers must consider:

- How can we build the necessary interdisciplinary foundation?
- How do we achieve the desired balance between language and content?
- Which subjects do we select and how do we sequence them?
- Who will teach the course, a language teacher, a content specialist, or both?
- How do we define and evaluate student learning outcomes?

These are some of the key questions that will be addressed by the authors of the following chapters, and we will discuss these issues in more detail in the final chapter. Next, we look at the second criterion for CBI.

Use of authentic language and texts

The core material—texts, videotapes, audio recordings, and visual aids—are selected primarily from those produced for native speakers of the language. Learning activities focus on understanding and conveying meaningful messages and accomplishing realistic tasks using authentic language.

One of the major characteristics of CBI is the extensive (though not necessarily exclusive) use of materials taken directly from the culture being studied. Depending on the language, the decision to use a subject-matter core may require the use of authentic texts exclusively. In some cases, the only textbooks available for teaching selected subject matter (e.g., mathematics, physics, history) are those produced for native speakers of the language. Therefore, CBI teachers can find themselves routinely working with materials that are, in the traditional view, far beyond the current linguistic expertise of their students. In such a case, the important issue is not so much what those texts *are* but what the teacher *does* with them.

If the teacher knows how to effectively "shelter" the texts, making them accessible to the students at their level of proficiency, most students can benefit from the use of authentic materials in any content area, even if their linguistic skills are minimally developed. Bernhardt (1986), posing the rhetorical question of whether there are "proficient texts" or "proficient readers," suggests that the idea of "graded texts" should be replaced by "graded activities." An important part of sheltering content is knowing how to grade activities and utilize a broad variety of teaching strategies; among these are using context effectively, recycling or spiraling information, exploiting students' background knowledge and schemata, using peer work, and teaching coping strategies. Such expertise is more likely to be found in a language teacher than in a subject-matter specialist, including specialists in literature.

Language teachers who lack expertise in sheltering content tend to avoid using authentic texts because they fear that students will be overwhelmed and frustrated by the material. Often, teachers believe that some grammatical features and vocabulary are inherently easier and must be learned first (e.g., the dative case before the genitive case or indicative before subjunctive). In actuality, graded language texts often present students with even more frustrating experiences than some authentic texts. The artificial language of foreign language texts does not provide students with models of how people really communicate in the foreign language. Such artificial language lacks natural redundancy, depriving students of multiple cues for comprehension. Rarely do graded language texts lead efficiently to language proficiency gain.

If the teacher carefully selects the content, students will study topics for which they already possess schemata (i.e., the relevant linguistic, content, and cultural background knowledge). Using content and context together to understand messages, students develop coping mechanisms for dealing with unknown language in other contexts, ultimately fostering the development of foreign language proficiency.

In the following chapters the contributors to this volume relate how their students gained proficiency through the use of texts and activities that traditional foreign language teachers would eschew. In these cases, the effective use of authentic language and texts has been a powerful force in propelling students to higher levels of foreign language proficiency. When students successfully negotiate the meaning encountered in authentic written or spoken language, they experience increased self-confidence, which in turn leads to gains in motivation and achievement. They also develop learning strategies for coping with unknown vocabulary and grammar and handling unpredicted situations in the environment in which the foreign language is spoken.

Some of the specific questions related to the use of authentic input that will be addressed in the following chapters are the following:

- What are the appropriate authentic materials and how can we obtain them?
- How do we provide students with authentic spoken input?
- What are the appropriate activities and tasks to exploit this authentic input?
- How do we incorporate student schemata?
- What is the role of students' first language in coping with authentic language and texts?

We now look at the meaning of the third criterion for CBI.

Appropriate to the needs of specific students

The content and learning activities correspond to the linguistic, cognitive, and affective needs of the students and are appropriate to their professional needs and personal interests.

A CBI curriculum must initially correspond to students' needs and remain highly fluid and flexible. A CBI program is dynamic and constantly changing. Although we often have to make initial guesses concerning the topics and the materials that will be most appropriate for a particular group of students, an ongoing assessment of students' outcomes should inform teachers in the continuing choice of subject matter, the selection of authentic texts, and the effectiveness of certain activities. Carefully monitoring student reactions alerts teachers to the linguistic, cognitive, and affective needs of the students and assists them in making the necessary adjustments in the program.

Monitoring students' linguistic development is especially important. Due to differences in schemata, individual students will find some linguistic features salient and others less so, resulting in student A learning a different set of grammar rules and vocabulary than student B. To ensure that all students are able to learn from the materials presented, teachers need to be aware of what items have and have not been acquired and by which students. Some students in CBI programs are comfortable using schemata to induce meaning, i.e., guessing. Others, who have a lower tolerance for ambiguity, possess fewer strategies for coping with unknown language and feel a greater need for confirmation of their hypotheses by authority—a teacher, a grammar reference book, or a dictionary. They often prefer to memorize. Sometimes, students do not feel that they are learning "unless it hurts" (Maly 1993, 40).

On a cognitive level, there are dozens of learner profiles (i.e., the aggregate of learning style variables within an individual student). These include such variables as whether students learn better through sight or sound, prefer to induce or deduce, focus on the whole or on the parts, look for differences or similarities, and process information sequentially or in parallel. There are limitless cognitive variables in a classroom. Each learner profile is associated with its own set of learning strategies, and each learner reacts differently to any given set of teaching strategies. Teachers who understand teaching strategies and learner profiles have a distinct advantage in helping to make authentic content materials accessible to all students in the classroom. One basic strategy for covering a broad spectrum of learning styles is to vary the presentation. Mohan (1986) recommends using a combination of "expository approaches"—lectures, readings, presentations and discussions—and "experiential approaches"—role plays, workshops, simulations, field trips, demonstrations, and interaction with native speakers. The contributors to this volume, recognizing the importance of varying the presentation, describe a broad variety of ways in which differing learner profiles can be accommodated within one classroom.

Affective variables (i.e., students' feelings and emotional reactions) play no less crucial a role. While most students in a CBI class respond enthusiastically when they feel a sense of achievement in working with real-life materials and real-life issues, students who feel frustrated can lose their motivation. Some students feel more comfortable working alone while others need peer support. Some students want praise for their efforts while others want praise for their accomplishments. Some students are angered by overt correction while others are frustrated by the lack of it. An astute teacher will constantly assess and adjust to the affective needs of students and try to maintain what Krashen (1982) refers to as a "low affective filter."

There are benefits in giving students a voice in determining the curriculum in CBI. Participation in choosing topics and activities has been found to be highly motivating and has resulted in a course changing direction in order to better meet the needs of students. Furthermore, student-generated themes and activities create an atmosphere in which the students take responsibility for their own learning and the teacher becomes more of a "manager of student learning" (Maly 1993, 11).

Some of the specific questions regarding student needs that will be addressed in the following chapters are:

- How do we make an accurate needs assessment?
- How do we ensure that students are cognitively, linguistically, and affectively prepared for the program?
- How can we accommodate the widest possible range of learner profiles?
- How do we deal with error correction to maximize learning and motivation?
- How can we use student input to ensure ongoing evaluation and adjustment?

Variations on the Three Criteria for CBI

The questions above, as well as those posed earlier concerning subject-matter core and authentic materials, are answered by the contributors to this volume in vastly different ways. For example, sometimes the subject matter may be delivered in a mixture of the native language and foreign language, while other times information may be "recycled" in the foreign language after initial exposure in the students' native language. The texts may not always be "authentic" in the strictest sense: they may be abridged or edited for beginning language learners. Some programs may place greater emphasis on meeting the academic needs of students, others on meeting linguistic or affective needs. Sometimes the subject matter may be systematically augmented by explicit grammar lessons. In short, there are many ways that these components can be successfully combined, depending on the setting, the needs of the students, the objectives of the program, the availability of materials, and most importantly, the preparation and disposition of the faculty. The models presented in subsequent chapters, each unique, demonstrate the many combinations that are possible under the broad umbrella of CBI. In our retrospective chapter (Chapter 13), we look back on all eleven case studies and discuss these variations, point out similarities and differences, and discuss some of their implications.

In order to fully appreciate these CBI models, we feel it would be useful to review CBI theory and practice in the larger context of second and foreign language education over the last few decades. In the following sections of this introduction we will discuss CBI and the new paradigm, the development of CBI in ESL and immersion programs, and, finally, the emergence of CBI in foreign language settings.

Communicative Competence, the New Paradigm, and CBI

In the broadest sense, CBI is part of what has been termed a "new paradigm" in language education. This new paradigm centers on the concept of fostering our students' "communicative competence" in the foreign language, that is, the ability to communicate with native speakers in real-life situations—authentic interpersonal communication that cannot be separated from the cultural, paralinguistic, and nonverbal aspects of language (Spolsky 1978). This concept is especially relevant to CBI since, in order to prepare our students to live and work in a new culture, we must create a direct link between the classroom and the culture being studied. This cannot be accomplished effectively in a program that focuses primarily on grammatical competence.

Canale and Swain (1980) elaborated four specific components of communicative competence: grammatical, discourse, sociolinguistic, and strategic competencies. The first two categories, grammatical competence and discourse competence, describe language *usage*. *Grammatical* competence includes knowledge of language structure—the phonemes, the morphemes, and the rules of syntax. *Discourse* competence includes the ability to successfully link sentences for communicative or rhetorical purposes. The second two categories, sociolinguistic competence and strategic competence, describe language *use*. *Sociolinguistic* competence includes the ability to use language appropriate to a given situation including the appropriate choice of register and knowing when to say or not to say something. *Strategic* competence refers to the ability to use inference, paraphrasing, and repetition to cope with situations in which language or comprehension is lacking.

Traditional bottom-up foreign language approaches place primary emphasis on grammatical and discourse competence—language *usage*. CBI programs typically place primary emphasis on sociolinguistic and strategic competence—language *use*. CBI is especially suitable for facilitating the development of all four language skills (listening, speaking, reading, and writing) while simultaneously focusing on the functional *use* of language in authentic settings.

In a summary of "Communicative Language Teaching," H. Douglas Brown (1994, 245) describes four characteristics shared by various communicative approaches. These four characteristics, listed below, provide an excellent summary of the pedagogical precepts of "the new paradigm"—and of CBI.

1. Classroom goals are focused on *all* of the components of communicative competence and not restricted to grammatical or linguistic competence.
2. Language techniques are designed to engage learners in the pragmatic, authentic, functional use of language for meaningful purposes. Organizational language forms are not the central focus but rather aspects of language that *enable* the learner to accomplish those purposes.
3. Fluency and accuracy are seen as complementary principles underlying communicative techniques. At times fluency may have to take on more importance than accuracy in order to keep learners meaningfully engaged in language use.
4. In the communicative classroom, students ultimately have to *use* the language, productively and receptively, in *unrehearsed* contexts.

In her discussion of discipline- and content-based approaches and the change of paradigm, Claire Kramsch (in Krueger and Ryan 1993) observes that foreign language study has become more than a mere linguistic enterprise but ". . . also a social, cultural, historical adventure, because it is the study of *language as social practice.*" She observes that in this new paradigm for foreign language teaching " . . . the traditional distinctions between language and literature, big 'C' culture and little 'c' culture, competence and performance, general education and vocational training, are not as clear-cut as they used to be, even though academic structures have often remained the same" (204). Kramsch identifies four general advantages to discipline-based approaches: 1) diversification of sources of knowledge by drawing from fields such as linguistics, sociology, anthropology, etc., 2) use of a variety of discourse forms rather than just the traditional discourse of the foreign language classroom, 3) diversification of the purposes of foreign language study both as a tool for general education and for specific professional purposes, and 4) the enhancement of the theoretical dimension of foreign language study as a subject matter (208).

Two prominent champions of teaching second and foreign languages through subject matter are Stephen Krashen and Tracy Terrell. In describing their "Natural Approach" to teaching foreign language, Krashen and Terrell (1983) differentiate between language *learning*—gaining the knowledge of language rules consciously and critically through classroom activities—and language *acquisition* —the subconscious ability to use the language communicatively as a result of sufficient "comprehensible input." They recommend content activities as an effective means of providing students with comprehensible input in the classroom and base their claim, in part, on the success of the Canadian immersion models in which children achieve proficiency and literacy in a foreign language by learning subject matter such as mathematics, science, and history in the target language. They claim that the success of such programs is due to their focus "on the message and not the form" (124).

Krashen (in Oller 1993) argues that "sheltered subject-matter teaching," which he calls SSMT (and we are calling CBI), is the most effective way to teach a foreign language. He anticipates strategies described in later chapters of this volume when he observes:

> Implementation of SSMT requires some planning and effort, but it is not as hard to do as some exotic language teaching methods. One possibility is to move toward SSMT gradually, beginning with short modules as part of traditional intermediate classes. As these modules are developed and introduced into the curriculum, the language courses will take on the character of content-based second language classes and second language medium classes (148).

Ian Martin (in Anivan 1990) echoes Krashen's view that "thematic modules" offer a good way to initiate a CBI approach. He started a CBI program in his ESL program in Toronto by introducing thematic modules into existing courses. This approach allowed teachers to experiment with only minimal changes to the existing programs, obviating the need to design whole new courses. He proposes that the modular format is ideally suited to CBI curriculum because the modules are self-contained and, therefore, flexible, movable, and relatively inexpensive to implement since elaborate interdisciplinary collaboration is not required.

Several of the contributors to this volume utilize modules similar to those described by Krashen and Martin. The "thematic module" approach is used by Sternfeld (Chapter 3, Italian), Ryding and Stowasser (Chapter 5, Arabic), Stryker (Chapter 8, Spanish), Klahn (Chapter 9, Spanish) and Chadran and Esarey (Chapter 10, Indonesian).

In the following section, we turn our attention to the development of CBI in "immersion" bilingual programs and in programs for English as a Second Language in public schools—developments that have had a significant impact on CBI in foreign language education.

CBI in K-12 Immersion and ESL Classrooms

In "immersion programs" and "sheltered English" classrooms, CBI serves as either a component of a curriculum or as the organizational framework for an entire curriculum. Contemporary CBI gained prominence in the 1960s with experiments in elementary and secondary education in the former Soviet Union and Canada. In the former Soviet Union, experimentation with content-based instruction was carried out at a large number of special secondary foreign language schools where all subjects were taught in the foreign language. These programs began in the early 1960s but disappeared by the mid-1980s, when staffing of such schools became impossible because of increasing demand and an inadequate number of qualified teachers (Garza 1987; Nikonova 1968; Star Mountain Inc. 1991).

In Canada in the early 1960s, CBI served as the methodological cornerstone of second language "immersion" programs for K-12 students. The immersion programs, most notably the St. Lambert Experiment in Montreal (Lambert and Tucker 1972), were influential in bringing CBI methodology to the attention of second and foreign language educators everywhere. Similar to the Russian model in concept, the Canadian immersion model started kindergarten students learning all subject matter in the foreign language. Designed primarily to teach French to English-speaking children, these programs enjoyed success, publicity, and, ultimately, emulation (Swain 1975; Hart, et al. 1977; Cummins 1989). The Canadian model was adopted for similar programs in the United States. One of the early examples was the Culver City Experiment (Cohen 1976). By the mid-1990s there were scores of immersion programs in the United States, most of them serving Spanish-English bilingual communities.

In the U.S. public education system, where the need to integrate language and content learning is essential, content-based sheltered English courses are proving successful for students who enter K-12 classes with little or no English proficiency, especially for students who are preparing to enter English-only classes. The State of California, for example, in an effort to deal with an onslaught of over one million students who do not speak English as their native language (1996 statistics), has officially embraced sheltered content courses, or "specially designed academic instruction in English (SDAIE)," as the most efficient approach for transitioning children who speak English as a second language into English-only classrooms.

Theories and models to support CBI in ESL and bilingual settings are now common. Brinton, Snow, and Wesche (1989) describe three models for CBI at multiple levels: 1) *Theme-based courses* are organized as a series of modules in which the language teacher teaches both subject matter and language; 2) *Sheltered instruction* is specially designed subject matter teaching given to a group of second language learners by a content specialist; and 3) *Adjunct instruction* requires that students be enrolled concurrently in a language course and a content course that are linked through collaboration between the two teachers. These three models have become almost commonplace wherever English as a Second Language and English as a Foreign Language are taught.

Chamot (1986), who labels her CBI instructional model the Cognitive Academic Language Learning Approach (CALLA), sets three goals for instruction: 1) to meet the academic needs of elementary and secondary English language learners, 2) to provide a bridge between ESL and mainstream education, and 3) to provide instruction based on a cognitive model of learning.

Nunan (1989) suggests "task-based instruction" to enhance a CBI curriculum. Task-based activities focus the students' attention on meaning rather than form. He distinguishes between "pedagogic tasks" that are aimed at formal language-learning (such as following the teacher's instructions to make a drawing) and "real-world tasks" that are more authentic (such as filling out a job application). The "real-world task" is related to something that the students will have to do with the language. He suggests the use of three types of tasks to stimulate student interaction: information gaps (e.g., find out what is missing in two pictures), reasoning gaps (e.g., find what is wrong with a picture), and opinion gaps (e.g., rate your favorites and tell why). Task-based instruction has been combined with CBI very successfully in ESL and EFL programs to pair students to exchange information and to solve problems—that is, negotiate for meaning.

One of the major recurring themes in the chapters ahead is the importance of connecting what goes on in CBI classrooms to "real-world tasks." Corin, in Chapter 4, is particularly articulate on the topic of how successfully task-based and content-based approaches can converge.

CBI in Adult ESL and EFL Programs

Paralleling the development of CBI in K-12 schools is an increasing use of CBI frameworks in postsecondary ESL and EFL settings. Snow and Brinton (1988a) have developed an "adjunct model" of CBI language instruction in ESL courses. In this collaborative model, ESL courses at the University of California at Los Angeles (UCLA) are linked with introductory-level content courses in anthropology, computer science, geography, political science, psychology, and social science. Students spend twelve to fourteen hours per week in an ESL class and eight hours in content classes. The ESL and content instructors coordinate lesson assignments. By sharing content and coordinating assignments, the ESL teachers can concentrate on the language and cognitive skills, as well as on the knowledge needed by the students to perform well in their content courses. "The perspective taken," write Snow and Brinton, "is a reciprocal relationship between language and content. Students must be given opportunities to 'learn to write' and 'learn to read,' but must also be allowed to 'write to learn' and to 'read to learn' in order to fully participate in the educational process" (4).

Adamson (1993), in his discussion of content-based approaches in college-level ESL courses, describes his success with "precourses." He argues that adjunct courses alone frequently tend to create a "submersion" environment in which none but the most linguistically advanced and cognitively well-prepared students can survive. He also points out that adjunct courses require extensive (and often impractical) collaboration and cooperation between content and language teachers. His "precourse" combines elements of both adjunct and theme-based approaches that are more appropriate for a single-teacher course. In this model, "students enrolled in a theme-based course join a regular content course for less than a full semester and are tutored in the content subject and in academic strategies by their ESL teachers" (96). This is one of many ESL models at the college level that establishes a connection with regular university courses. Connections such as these have become part of an interdisciplinary movement that has produced several collaborative experiments, including the FLAC programs that are described in Chapters 11 and 12.

Content-based models are becoming increasingly common in EFL settings as well. Johnston (1991) describes CBI courses at Temple University's Japan campus that are offered to Japanese students preparing for study in the university's English-language academic program. The CBI courses include sheltered content courses in geography, history, literature, art, biology, and psychology. These courses were developed, scheduled, and taught by the English instructors themselves. The instructors also conducted the needs assessment, collected and selected authentic materials and texts, designed tasks and activities appropriate to the students' proficiency levels, and evaluated the outcomes. This huge effort gives testimony to the extraordinary faith and dedication of a group of teachers who were "true believers."

In 1989, the Language Centre for Finnish Universities in Tampere, Finland, undertook an experiment teaching history in English. In order to accomplish this, a historian was paired with a language teacher. While student reaction was positive, teachers wrestled with the same questions that we wrestle with in this volume: What is the right mix of content and language in teaching a history course? Which is primary and which is support? Given the positive initial experience, the experiment was expanded to include the department of literature (Kurki-Suonio 1990).

Crandall and Tucker summarize several program models now common in ESL and EFL settings. These include English for Specific Purposes (ESP), English for Academic Purposes (e.g., Adamson and Johnston, cited above), Vocational English, and, more recently, English for Foreign Student Assistants. Crandall and Tucker identify three basic approaches: 1) integrated language/content instruction by a language teacher, 2) integrated instruction taught by a content teacher, and 3) parallel courses. They suggest, as an ideal CBI program, the combination of all three, and they cite the example of an EFL program in Honduras developed by the Center for Applied Linguistics. In that program, designed for students preparing to enter universities in the United States, math and science courses are taught by bilingual instructors who begin with Spanish and integrate progressively more English over a period of three trimesters, ending up with all-English instruction. Simultaneously, English teachers are introducing more and more content into their courses, using both sheltered content and parallel courses. Of course, such a program requires considerable planning and cooperation across the disciplines (in Anivan 1990, 86-87).

An EFL program recently developed by the American Council for Collaboration in Education and Language Study (ACCELS) in Tashkent, Uzbekistan, takes full advantage of contemporary experience and research in CBI, and develops some new aspects of its own. Taught by a team of foreign language teachers who rely on the knowledge of the students themselves as a source of content expertise, the ten-month (700-hour) intensive English course for Ministry of Justice officials aims at taking beginners to an ILR level-3 (professional proficiency) via a content-based curriculum. The curriculum is based on a comparative study of American and Uzbek history, geography, culture, government, and administration of justice. Students acquire English language skills through the study of authentic materials, interaction with American expatriates, research, and preparation of studies and reports. Evaluation procedures consist of "prochievement tests" (which combine language proficiency and content achievement), graded projects, and the Test of English as a Foreign Language (TOEFL). Based on the success of the Ministry of Justice course, the ACCELS country director selected CBI as the curriculum design for the American Language Center, opened in May of 1997.

In summary, many ESL, EFL, and immersion educators have adopted CBI as a preferred methodological framework. They have already moved beyond theory to the institutionalization of CBI. A few crossover ESL/EFL educators have carried these ideas into foreign language settings (Tracy Terrell, for example), but a large part of the foreign language teaching community remains mired in structural, grammar-translation, audiolingual, or literature-based approaches. The need for change has been apparent to many foreign language educators. Following a seminar on content-based language instruction conducted by the Center for Language Education and Research (CLEAR) at UCLA, Crandall and Willetts (1986) noted that "the successes of content-based instruction as evidenced in immersion programs and in sheltered English programs need to be carried further into other more traditional foreign language programs." We, of course, wholeheartedly endorse this view. We, as well as our contributors, would like to see CBI more fully integrated into foreign language instruction.

CBI in Foreign Language Programs

CBI models and methods have already appeared in many foreign language settings, including university programs and major language institutes. Successful university language department programs include courses in French at the University of Ottawa, business courses in French at Drury College, political studies courses in Russian at George Washington University, a Greek mythology course in French at Northern Arizona University, a scientific-technical program in French at Napier College in Scotland, a Russian course at the Caspian Naval Academy in Azerbaijan, English courses in China and Hungary, and German courses at the University of Kiev. Several successful CBI models in higher education are described in Krueger and Ryan (1993), including the program in economics and international business at Eastern Michigan University, the international engineering program at the University of Rhode Island, Russian courses at Harvard University, and a course in anthropology in Japanese at Brown University.

Language for Special Purposes (LSP) courses are usually taught entirely in the foreign language, as is the case at Eastern Michigan University's World College, mentioned above, which specializes in teaching LSP courses in the area of international business. World College has done much to bring CBI to the attention of foreign language educators and business leaders through its annual conferences on teaching foreign languages for business and the professions.

Along similar lines, Clemson University has a Language and International Trade Program in which the curricular model is a cross between LSP and language department CBI courses. Students major in a foreign language plus some technical specialty. A second year Spanish class focuses on economic/political/social characteristics of areas where the language is spoken, and an upper division course on current events in a foreign language is planned. These latter two courses are taught by a faculty member with a joint appointment as professor of languages and professor of political science (Morris 1997).

CBI courses developed entirely within a foreign language department (i.e., without collaboration with another discipline) are somewhat different. These, like the LSP courses, are usually single-teacher models, although in some cases they may include four-handed instruction (i.e., two instructors teaching together in one classroom). In single-teacher models the instructor is usually an experienced language teacher who uses a variety of sources to develop the required content knowledge. An excellent example of the academic, single-teacher model is presented by Vines in Chapter 6 of this text. In the mid-1980s she designed "French for Journalism" courses that are still being offered at Ohio University. Vines describes her efforts to develop the necessary content expertise by attending conferences and workshops and through extensive reading. Other single-teacher language department models in this volume include the Basic Russian Program described by Leaver in Chapter 2, the Mexico Program described by Klahn in Chapter 9, and the Italian course described by Sternfeld in Chapter 3.

Using both single-teacher and collaborative models, the Foreign Service Institute (FSI), the training school of the United States Department of State, began to experiment with CBI in the early 1980s. Collaborative models, which pair a language instructor with a content specialist, are especially appropriate at the FSI where there are two parallel programs, one in the

School of Language Studies and one in the School of Area Studies. The goal of the FSI experiments was to integrate the area/culture studies programs and the language programs in such a way that the students, United States government officials and diplomats, would be able to "hit the ground running" at their overseas posts. Four of those programs are described in this volume.

The earliest all-CBI program at the FSI was in Russian (Leaver, Chapter 2), while later programs were implemented in Arabic (Ryding and Stowasser, Chapter 5), Indonesian (Chadran and Esarey, Chapter 10) and Spanish (Stryker, Chapter 8). Not only did these programs successfully integrate language and content, all of them significantly improved student foreign language proficiency. In the cases in which program entry and exit testing was done, students' proficiency scores (as measured by the oral proficiency interview) showed significant increases in relatively short periods of time.

CBI came later to the Defense Language Institute (DLI), the military language school in Monterey, California. In the early 1990s, several language departments, including German, Russian, Czech, and Ukrainian, experimented with both single-teacher and multi-teacher approaches. The latter three combined a content-based program with task-based methods. Some of the most interesting of the CBI courses at DLI were the multi-teacher "conversion" courses designed to teach a third foreign language to students who already knew a related second language. One such course, designed to convert Czech or Russian to Serbian and Croatian, is described by Corin in Chapter 4.

The FSI and DLI programs, although taught in highly intensive, specialized settings, provide viable models for the design, implementation, and evaluation of CBI programs in other settings, as well as interesting insights into the foreign language acquisition processes of adult students, which we discuss in our final chapter.

Foreign Languages Across the Curriculum (FLAC)

The basic idea behind FLAC is that students study an academic subject, or portions thereof, in a foreign language as a part of their regular university curricula. According to Straight (1994 and in Chapter 11 of this volume), the key characteristic of FLAC is that a foreign language is used as the medium of instruction and learning irrespective of the subject matter that is taught. Frank Ryan, a proponent of FLAC programs, argues that ". . . theories of the nature of language and of communicative competence acquisition both lead to the conclusion that an LAC situation provides all of the necessary conditions for language acquisition" (in Straight 1994,

47). Most FLAC programs are designed for students who have already achieved a minimum proficiency in a foreign language and desire to maintain or further develop their language skills. In a discussion of the FLAC program at the University of Minnesota, Klee and Metcalf identify four discrete objectives: 1) to demonstrate to undergraduates the benefits of acquiring a foreign language, 2) to hone students' analytic and critical abilities in the foreign language, 3) to encourage continuing development of students' language skills, and 4) to provide opportunities for faculty to utilize their foreign language abilities in the humanities and social sciences (in Straight 1994, 104).

FLAC programs require collaboration between a content teacher and a language teacher. One of the major goals in FLAC, in the words of Lambert (1994), is to "deghettoize" the language departments by putting faculty in contact with their colleagues in other departments. In Chapter 12 Shaw describes five different models for such collaboration at the Monterey Institute for International Studies.

FLAC courses have been called area studies-foreign language integration courses or interdisciplinary courses. Straight calls them "language-based content courses." Such courses frequently use multi-teacher models. The relationship between the teachers in a multi-teacher course can take many forms, from an adjunct model to a model in which the content specialist works very closely with a language teacher and acts as a source and guide for the students. In response to the logistical challenge (and, of course, the added expense) of having a language teacher work with a content teacher, Straight hired and trained a cadre of international graduate students who acted as language resource specialists.

Jurasek, who pioneered one of the first FLAC programs at Earlham College in 1982, describes FLAC as the intersection of content teaching and foreign language teaching located outside of the foreign language department curriculum. He mentions, among nineteen programs, those at SUNY-Binghamton, Brown, Carnegie Mellon, Earlham, Minnesota, Ottawa, St. Olaf, and the University of California at Santa Cruz. Some of these programs are broadly described in Krueger and Ryan (1993) and in Straight (1994); however, as Jurasek points out, these texts do not reveal details of what happens in the actual classrooms. He calls for the production of "dedicated handbooks that describe successful skill-using activities, how-to cookbooks at the syllabus-, classroom- and text-levels" and workshops on what works and what does not (in Straight 1994, 138).

Our goal in compiling this volume has been to provide precisely such a "dedicated handbook." Three of the contributors to the above-mentioned volumes, Klee, Shaw, and Straight, describe their programs in subsequent chapters, providing detailed information regarding the design, content, methods, and evaluation procedures.

Testing Issues in CBI

One of the major challenges in CBI is how to evaluate the outcomes, especially the growth in students' oral proficiency skills—a central goal in most of the foreign language models presented in subsequent chapters.

Communicative language teaching and learning require communicative language testing. Testing for communicative competence—measuring those four characteristics described by Canale and Swain—cannot be accomplished by traditional pen and pencil tests and certainly not by discrete-point grammar tests. If we agree with Spolsky that proficiency means the ability to communicate with native speakers in real-life situations, then a "proficiency test" must involve such spontaneous interactions. The oral proficiency interview was developed to accomplish this goal. Since most of the programs described in this book use the FSI, ACTFL, or Interagency Language Roundtable (ILR) oral proficiency interview as the major instrument in the evaluation process, we think it would be useful to explain how the process works and what the ratings mean.

The oral proficiency interview, first developed at the FSI in the 1950s, introduced the idea of scoring a student on a proficiency scale based on a one-on-one personal oral interview in which no writing is involved. That FSI prototype has evolved, over the decades, into the Interagency Language Roundtable (ILR) test, a broadly accepted procedure for conducting an oral proficiency interview and a reading test and awarding scores in both speaking (S) and reading (R) skills. The ILR scale ranges from "zero" (no proficiency) to "five" (native-speaking proficiency), with half-point increments, designated as "plus," along the five-point scale.

The ILR testing procedures continue to be used by all agencies of the federal government. Due to the nature of the ratings and the time and expense of administering the tests, which often take over one hour to complete, the oral proficiency interview and reading tests were not particularly suitable for academic settings.

The American Council on the Teaching of Foreign Languages (ACTFL), working with the Educational Testing Service (ETS), adapted the ILR concept and created an oral proficiency test and scale that are more suitable for academic settings. Figure 1 compares the ILR and ACTFL scales.

ILR	ACTFL
5 Functionally Native Proficiency	Superior
4 Advanced Professional Proficiency	Superior
3 General Professional Proficiency	Superior
2 Limited Working Proficiency	Advanced High
2 Limited Working Proficiency	Advanced
1 Elementary Proficiency	Intermediate High
1 Elementary Proficiency	Intermediate Mid
1 Elementary Proficiency	Intermediate Low
Memorized Proficiency	Novice High
0 No Proficiency	Novice Mid
0 No Proficiency	Novice Low

Fig. 1 The ILR and ACTFL Proficiency Scales

Figure 1 illustrates how the ACTFL expanded the lower end of the ILR scale (0 to 1) to reflect student achievement in academic foreign language classrooms and suggest more positive linguistic levels of proficiency, i.e., "Novice Low," "Novice Mid," and "Novice High" levels (rather than the label "0+" used in the ILR scale). ACTFL uses four basic levels of proficiency. *ACTFL-Novice* refers to students who have had no prior experience with a foreign language and would be considered at ILR levels of 0 and 0+. *ACTFL-Intermediate* refers to students who have basic survival skills and would be considered at ILR levels of 1 and 1+. *ACTFL-Advanced* refers to students who have basic communication skills and would be considered at ILR levels of 2 and 2+. Finally, *ACTFL-Superior* refers to students who are functional in the language and would be scored at an ILR level 3 or above.

At each level of the ACTFL scale, *functions, context, content,* and *accuracy,* are measured. Figure 2 describes each level and gives definitions in each of the three categories.

Global Tasks/Functions	Context	Content	Accuracy	Text Type
SUPERIOR Can discuss extensively by supporting opinions, abstracting and hypothesizing	Most formal and informal settings	Wide range of general interest topics and some special fields of interest and expertise; concrete, abstract, and unfamiliar topics	Errors virtually never interfere with communication or disturb the native speaker	Extended discourse
ADVANCED Can describe and narrate in major time/aspect frames	Most informal and some formal settings	Concrete and factual topics of personal and public interest	Can be understood without difficulty by speakers unaccustomed to non-native speakers	Paragraph discourse
INTERMEDIATE Can maintain simple face-to-face conversation by asking and responding to simple questions	Some informational settings and a limited number of transactional situations	Topics related primarily to self and immediate environment	Can be understood, with some repetition, by speakers accustomed to non-native speakers	Discrete sentences and strings of sentences
NOVICE Can produce only formulaic utterances, lists, and enumeration	Highly predictable common daily settings	Common discrete elements of daily life	May be difficult to understand, even for those accustomed to non-native speakers	Discrete words and phrases

Fig. 2 ACTFL Assessment Criteria: Speaking Proficiency.
Source: *ACTFL Oral Proficiency Interview Tester Trainer Manual,*
Kathryn Buck, ed., 1989.

Many of the contributors to this volume have used the ILR or ACTFL tests in designing and evaluating their CBI programs. Since these tests measure only global listening, speaking, and reading skills, other means must be used to test for writing skills and content knowledge. In those programs in which only the ILR tests were used to measure outcomes (i.e., the FSI and DLI programs), there was no formal measure of students' content knowledge or of foreign language writing ability. This reflects the special circumstances at the FSI and the DLI where only oral and reading skills are measured and writing is not a required skill. The content learning is seen as a secondary (though highly desirable) objective and as a vehicle to speed up language acquisition.

However, in most settings, an ILR or ACTFL test is not adequate; there is a need to measure growth in content knowledge and in writing. FLAC programs, of course, already have content exams in place and, unlike foreign language programs, are not usually concerned with measuring linguistic development.

Some CBI instructors are exploring the possibility of testing both content and language through "proficiency-based achievement tests," which combine both the language proficiency and content achievement components (Campbell 1996). A standard technique in proficiency-based achievement tests is to measure students' knowledge of subject matter using standard oral and reading proficiency testing techniques. This combination was implemented in an experimental basic Russian course at the DLI where, after five weeks of studying the history of Russia, students took a multiple choice test on Russian history; their grades were based on answering the history questions correctly. Implicit in the accomplishment of this task was not only the knowledge of the historical events but also the language proficiency required to understand the content questions and test organization. In a strategy suggested by students at the DLI, Czech instructors in a content-based course gave students two sets of grades on their achievement tests: a grade for content and a grade for language.

The challenge of measuring both proficiency and achievement in a CBI foreign language curriculum is addressed creatively—and very comprehensively—by Klee and Tedick in Chapter 7. In addition to the ACTFL oral proficiency test, they designed an "assessment battery" that measures reading, writing, listening, and grammar, all within the context of an academic theme.

Funding CBI

Among the challenges mentioned by experimenters in CBI and FLAC, including all the contributors to this volume are the special personnel considerations and large amounts of preparation and maintenance. We should point out that many of the programs described in this volume were funded initially by special grants and that some of the programs have been either eliminated or scaled-down because of the expenses involved. Several major foundations sponsored these experiments. For example, the Pew Memorial Trust funded experiments at the Monterey Institute of International Studies. The National Endowment for the Humanities (NEH), the Fund for Improvement of Post-Secondary Education (FIPSE), and the United States Information Agency (USIA) have helped fund the experiments at SUNY-Binghamton.

Most of the programs described in this volume are still ongoing in 1997. Once established, some of them have required no extraordinary funding to maintain. These issues are discussed by the individual authors in their chapters. We comment at greater length on funding and administrative support in our final chapter.

Summary

The eleven case studies that are described in subsequent chapters were undertaken by "true-believers" who responded to a compelling need to prepare their students to move from the classroom directly into a new cultural environment. Many of the students involved in these programs went on to live, work, or study overseas. These CBI programs helped them to develop the language skills and the cultural knowledge to get off to a good start in their international careers—the wings to fly from the nest and soar on their own.

The programs you will read about represent a broad variety of settings that include two United States government institutions (the Foreign Service Institute and the Defense Language Institute), an institute for graduate professional studies (Monterey Institute of International Studies), and five universities: Columbia University, SUNY-Binghamton, the University of Utah, the University of Minnesota, and Ohio University. The authors describe their curricula in considerable detail and speak frankly about the special challenges in developing, maintaining, teaching, and evaluating their programs. Each author addresses the key questions we have raised in this chapter concerning subject matter, authentic materials, and student need, and these questions will return to guide our discussion of the pros and cons of CBI in the final chapter.

The overall success of these eleven programs demonstrates that CBI can be implemented effectively in a variety of ways with positive results when there is adequate administrative support and a passionate commitment to CBI philosophy on the part of the teachers. We hope these case studies will provide models and methods for others to emulate, as well as stimulate thought concerning the foreign language teaching and learning process.

∾ ∾

Stephen Stryker, Professor of English, TESOL Director, and Adjunct Lecturer in Spanish at California State University, Stanislaus, was Head of the Spanish Language Training Section at the Foreign Service Institute in Washington, D.C., from 1984 to 1990. Address: Department of English, CSU, Stanislaus, 801 W. Monte Vista, Turlock, CA 95382. (E-mail: stryker@toto.csustan.edu)

Betty Lou Leaver, President of the American Global Studies Institute in Salinas, California since 1993, served as Dean of the School of Central European Languages and Dean of the School of Slavic Languages at the Defense Language Institute from 1989-1993. From 1983 to 1989 she was Russian Language Training Supervisor at the Foreign Service Institute. Address: AGSI, 2 Rex Circle, Salinas, CA 93906. (E-mail: leaver@aol.com, leaver@glasnet.ru)

Part Two

CBI at Novice Levels of Proficiency

2

Content-Based Instruction
in a Basic Russian Program

Betty Lou Leaver

Editors' Note: Since the eighteenth century, Russians have experimented with various forms of CBI. It is appropriate, then, that the Russian program was among the first to implement CBI at the Foreign Service Institute The Basic Russian Program, designed to take students from ILR level 0 to level 3 in forty-seven weeks of intensive study, proved to be an ideal setting for experimentation with CBI. Leaver describes a two-stage implementation process: textbook supplementation and textbook development. The former proved highly successful and demonstrated that CBI can be used successfully at elementary levels of foreign language proficiency, even in languages considered "difficult." The latter was less successful. The author concludes that perhaps the CBI textbook project should have been an effort to replace the textbook with authentic materials and subject matter textbooks from Russia. The use of authentic materials to the near-exclusion of textbooks has subsequently been found to be successful in other foreign language programs, including programs in Slavic languages. General references for this chapter are located in the bibliography at the end of this volume.

The Foreign Service Institute

The Foreign Service Institute (FSI) is the training arm of the U.S. Department of State. It consists of three schools—the School of Language Studies, the School of Area Studies, and the School of Professional Studies, as well as two centers—the Center for Foreign Affairs and the Overseas Briefing Center. The School of Language Studies trains students to proficiency levels in speaking and reading that are set by the posts at which the students will be working. Most students are required to reach levels that the FSI labels as Speaking (S) -3 and Reading (R) -3, described as "minimal professional proficiency." The FSI levels, now more widely known as the Interagency Language Roundtable (ILR) levels, are discussed in Chapter 1.

FSI students attend class for up to thirty hours a week, for periods ranging from six weeks to forty-seven weeks, depending on the exit proficiency level required and the established difficulty level of the language. Classes are relatively small, typically three to six students per class. The language instructors are all "educated native speakers" (ILR-5) of the languages they teach. Most are immigrants; some are second-generation (or "heritage") speakers.

The Russian Section

The Russian section has traditionally been one of the largest at the FSI, occupying an especially important political position during the 1980s—the last days of the Cold War before the fall of the Berlin Wall. As a result, while resources were usually scarce, there was administrative support for innovation and creativity in Russian language teaching.

The Russian Section was one of the first foreign language departments at the FSI to implement elements of content-based instruction in a beginning program. Three principal reasons why the seeds of CBI found fertile ground there were: 1) student need and readiness, 2) the unique disposition and skills of the instructors, and 3) the importance of Russian in the international community.

The students, who would soon find themselves living and working overseas, needed to learn a great deal of sociopolitical and cultural information to function successfully at their posts. In 1984, the year that the Russian Section undertook course revisions, there were many Russian instructors who were skilled and experienced in the use of CBI. Philosophical agreement and enthusiastic mutual support existed among many of the language training supervisors (including three other contributors to this volume—Esarey, Stryker, and Ryding), and there was strong administrative support in both the School of Language Studies and the School of Area Studies for the concept of integration of area and language studies. Consequently, it is not coincidental that the CBI program in Russian, as well as the other FSI programs described in this volume, were initiated during this period.

The Rationale

A new Basic Russian Program, a forty-seven-week course aimed at taking students from an ILR level 0 to level 3, was completed in 1983. Although this curriculum was already proficiency-oriented, the needs of the students and the disposition of the faculty facilitated a strong movement in the direction of content-based instruction. As most of the Foreign Service

Officers posted to the USSR were seasoned officers—mid-career and senior political officers, economic officers, cultural attachés, general services officers, security officers, and military attachés—they had accumulated a wealth of experience, expertise, and knowledge. Most were proceeding to sensitive diplomatic positions that would require them to utilize that expertise. CBI was recognized as an ideal method to capitalize on those students' sophisticated professional schemata. A majority of the students had learning style profiles that did not match the generally inductive Notional-Functional and Natural Approach orientations of their course materials. Most students had well-developed analytic and deductive skills (as opposed to synthetic and inductive skills), and it was felt that CBI could foster a productive application of these skills to analyze content. Another factor favoring CBI in the Russian Section was the content limitation of the curricular materials, especially for study beyond the 2+ level. At the time that the CBI supplementation began, only about 50 percent of the students routinely reached the S/R-3 level required for their positions in Moscow and Leningrad. CBI was seen as a possible vehicle to accelerate students from an S/R-2+ level to the S/R-3 level needed for adequate job performance.

Designing the Curriculum

CBI in the Basic Program in Russian was implemented in two stages. The first stage was "textbook supplementation," and the second was "textbook replacement." Even as the textbook supplementation project got under way for the beginners, the Russian Section undertook the development of an entirely content-based Advanced Course for students already at level 3 or 3+ who needed to increase their proficiency to even higher levels. The development of a curriculum for the advanced students had a very positive impact on the Basic Program. The Advanced Course had a "trickle-down" effect on the development of the content-based components of the Basic Program, in large part due to daily contact between students and instructors and activities in which all the students of the Russian Section participated. In some cases, talented beginners were actually able to enter the Advanced Course near the end of their first year in the Basic Program.

Scope and Sequence of the Program

Given the experience and needs of Foreign Service Officers, most of the new CBI curriculum was designed around the study of political, economic, military, and cultural, themes or professional concerns such as security, general services, cultural and scientific exchanges. Other topics were specific to the individual needs of students. The themes of Soviet life and world view permeated the entire program.

The initial CBI effort in Russian concentrated on job-oriented Language for Special Purposes (LSP) modules offered in the last twelve weeks of the Basic Program in an effort to "top off" students' training with a final push toward level 3 (as was the case in the Arabic, Indonesian, and Spanish models described in later chapters). As a result of the success of the modules in the final twelve weeks, CBI was added to the beginning and middle of the program, and the goal became the design of a fully content-based program from start to finish. This led to Stage Two, the development of a CBI textbook.

Faculty and Materials

In spite of much moral support from the administration, early efforts at course supplementation with CBI were largely unfunded. Faculty devoted extra time, including weekends and evenings, to preparing materials in time for an early 1984 launch.

Fortunately, the twenty-four Russian language and culture instructors brought a wealth of knowledge and experience to the task of developing a CBI program. Many had been content teachers or successful professionals in the Soviet Union and had turned to language teaching when they emigrated to the United States. For example, one instructor, a high-ranking Soviet Army officer, had taught at a military academy, another had been a docent at a museum, and yet another was a professional actress. Many of those who were language teachers by profession had received training or had experience in CBI in Russia, where CBI had been a typical feature of the "special foreign language schools" (described in Chapter 1). Thus, the teachers were generally inclined to embrace the CBI philosophy and to find creative ways to include it in their classrooms.

Materials came from a number of sources. In the mid-1980s, obtaining authentic materials from the Soviet Union was very difficult. Nevertheless, FSI graduates who were stationed in the former Soviet Union supported the plan to develop a CBI curriculum. Many purchased materials out of their own pockets; others found ways to use official budgets to obtain materials. Nearly every week during the 1980s, newspapers, magazines, pictures, and assorted realia arrived by the "State Department Pouch," along with letters wishing the section well in its CBI endeavor.

In 1986 an unrelated development facilitated access to authentic video materials. Spearheaded by the enthusiasm of Richard Robin, a professor at George Washington University (GWU), the FSI, the Office of Training and Education, and GWU joined together to establish the Listening Comprehension Exercise Network (LCEN). This network provided Russian teachers across America with exercises to accompany Satellite Communications for Learning (SCOLA) broadcasts. These broadcasts became additional tools for teachers to use as they struggled to find enough authentic materials to meet the demands of course supplementation. (SCOLA has become a major source of materials for foreign language instructors worldwide. For information on SCOLA, see Appendix A of Chapter 4.)

Even the Soviet embassy in Washington helped supply authentic materials. Every Thursday, after embassy personnel had finished watching the latest movies from home, the cultural attaché would make them available to the FSI. (This was a service of the Soviet embassy of which a number of local universities also took advantage, although in the cloak-and-dagger days of the Cold War, it is not clear why Soviet embassy personnel were willing to help the U.S. Department of State.)

Soon after the materials arrived, teachers prepared them for use in the courses. They wrote booklets to accompany a "monolingual language training" (MOLT) program, additional job-oriented LSP modules, and supplemental reading materials for the early stages of language acquisition. Between 1984 and 1986 twenty-five content-related booklets of authentic materials were completed, most of them prepared with little administrative support in either dollars or time. These included eleven MOLT booklets, eight LSP booklets, *Mark Smith's Diary*, a set of area studies exercises and readings, and four reading books.

With limited time and resources to edit and field-test these materials, once again friends came to the rescue. Faculty at Harvard University and Columbia University offered to field-test the materials with their own students. In most cases, students at these universities used the materials before the FSI students were ready for them. Useful comments and suggestions from the Russian faculties there facilitated revision of the materials before their use with FSI students.

Implementing the CBI Curriculum

Stage One: Textbook Supplementation

The CBI initiative in Russian was launched piecemeal, relying on the good will of students and extra efforts of the faculty. During the first year of development, the sequence of the supplementation matched student proficiency level step-for-step, beginning with the Monolingual Language Training (MOLT) modules, the writing of *Mark Smith's Diary*, the Special Courses (or LSP modules), and the professional conference. The following year the area studies modules and a series of reading books on content topics for the entire duration of the program were introduced.

Monolingual Language Training (MOLT) Modules: The MOLT lessons were extended role plays lasting a total of three hours over a three-day period. The MOLT instructor, a former actress, played a variety of roles very convincingly. Other instructors would occasionally assist. The first role plays were modifications of the notional-functional themes of the textbook (such as buying theater or airline tickets) but these were integrated into larger contexts (such as taking a train trip across Siberia) and combined with content themes (such as meeting educators on the train and comparing Russian and American educational systems). Later, as students became accustomed to dealing with real content, the themes became more academic or professional, dealing with topics such as "comparative political systems." In these scenarios students played the roles of American diplomats and conveyed information about life in America, American values, and American institutions to their Russian counterparts, played by Russian instructors.

Mark Smith's Diary: Cross-cultural information was imparted via diary entries of Mark Smith, an imaginary American diplomat living and working in Moscow. The diary consists of Mark Smith's written records of ongoing conversations with his Russian friend, Nikolai. They share their cross-cultural observations, comparing and contrasting differences in Soviet and American reactions to events. For example, the two exchange commentaries on daily interpersonal interactions (e.g., why someone didn't smile back: Russians don't smile at strangers; why Mark's wife offended her pregnant Russian friend by giving her a baby gift: a gift before the birth of a baby is a bad omen); differences in Soviet and American "values" (e.g., the concepts of government or of mental illness); and cultural imagery (e.g., the word *border* suggests the image of a wall or stop sign to a Russian but suggests the image of a passport or a line to be crossed to an American). Initial diary entries were in English with a few Russian words and phrases added. By lesson twelve, the entries were only in Russian. (Mark Smith became proficient in Russian after a twenty-three-lesson stay in Moscow!)

Mark Smith's Diary was originally intended as a consciousness-raising activity designed to make students more sensitive to cultural and linguistic differences between the Soviet Union and the United States. It turned out to be a major feature of the program and was very popular among the students.

Individual teachers used the materials in unique ways. Some teachers used the materials as a basis for further classroom discussion. Others took a more elaborate approach and reenacted the contents in some way. Still other teachers used the contents as a springboard for students to interview native speakers who had emigrated to the United States about these topics.

Mark Smith's Diary has been made available to the public through the ERIC Clearinghouse on Languages and Literature and through serialization in the American Council of Teachers of Russian's *ACTR Letter.* Of course, Russia has changed immensely since 1990, and *Mark Smith's Diary* has not been updated to reflect the changes. (A sample lesson from *Mark Smith's Diary* is in Appendix A.)

Language for Special Purposes seminars: Language for Special Purposes (LSP) modules, called "spetsseminary" (special seminars) by the Russian students, the third element of CBI to be added after MOLT and *Mark Smith's Diary,* started toward the end of the Basic Program, when most students were at a level 2 or 2+. For two hours per day during the final three months of the program, students were enrolled in a special seminar dealing with the professional area in which they would be working in Russia. Six special seminar modules were developed for the end of the program: military affairs, political affairs, economics, security studies, general services, and consular affairs. These modules encompassed a total of one hundred classroom hours of study and were based primarily on authentic materials. Each special seminar was unique—based on the specific needs of the students in the seminar. Special seminars were similar only in the number of hours assigned and the use of a booklet with the activities and authentic materials. Some seminars used Natural Approach techniques that focused primarily on getting messages across and understanding. In other seminars, focused more on accuracy of expression, teachers used more traditional methods. Some seminars used newspaper articles while others incorporated popular books, role plays, authentic documents, and, occasionally, traditional situational dialogues.

The political affairs and economics seminars were based on readings of authentic texts from multiple sources. One frequent task was to make comparative analyses of what Russian sources stated and what American experts believed. Economic topics included both microeconomics and macroeconomics. Political topics included political structure, key players, and political action. In addition to newspapers, both seminars incorporated television broadcasts and documentaries.

The consular seminar, using documents sent from the American embassy in Moscow or consulate in Leningrad, was based on role plays in which students performed the kinds of tasks expected of consular officers in Russia, such as handling complaints or dealing with bogus documents. In designing the consular seminar, the course developers also had access to useful materials from the generic Consular Officer Course taught in the FSI School of Professional Studies.

The military special seminar used two "textbooks." The first was a manual handed out to Russian inductees into the Soviet Army. An "easy read" (written at a *Reader's Digest* level), it presented anecdotes about enlisted men who had performed great, unsung war deeds and described the various branches of the armed forces and how they were organized. The second "textbook" was much more challenging—a book well-known in Russia on battle tactics and strategies, written by a high-ranking official working in the Russian Ministry of Defense. In later years, the seminar incorporated several video tapes made by a former Soviet Army officer who taught at the U.S. Army Russian Institute in Garmisch, Germany. Popular Russian films with military themes also were used as "authentic input" for part of the program.

The security and general services special seminars were the most traditional in format and were linguistically oriented. Because security officers and general service officers had to use language accurately in order to perform their jobs adequately, emphasis was placed on precise usage of vocabulary and accuracy in sentence and grammar structure. Thus, these two seminars had the structure of traditional courses, although the content was, indeed, specific subject matter. The general services seminar was conducted in three phases. First, students learned to use the documents associated with their work, supplied by the American embassy in Moscow and the American consulate general in Leningrad. Second, students participated in a series of role plays associated with general services situations. Third, students developed linguistic knowledge and skills, using a core dialogue as the point of departure. (Appendix B contains sample lessons.)

These LSP modules were developed with the assistance of various departments of the American Embassy in Moscow and the American consulate general in Leningrad. As the Russian Section received comments on the effectiveness of the particular topics in the modules from Embassy and Consulate personnel, the teachers modified the content to more closely match the diplomats' needs. The modules were subsequently field-tested and revised as needed. The revision of these modules was an ongoing process as the needs of the embassy and consulate changed, with diplomats sending samples of their work to the Russian Section, providing new documents, and other useful materials to aid in the process of revision. (Needless to say, Gorbachev's policies of *glasnost* (openness) and *perestroika* (rebuilding) engendered much revision in all of the Russian Section's materials in the late 1980s.)

In recent years, the time and duration of study allotted to these special seminar modules has been expanded (Bernhardt 1994). (Unfortunately, the LSP modules are the only components of the original Russian CBI experiments that still thrive today.)

Area Studies: During the Basic Russian Program the students attended three hours per week of area studies instruction given in English in the FSI School of Area Studies. The topics encompassed political, economic, military, cultural, and foreign policy issues. Two years into the supplementation process, a handbook was prepared in Russian to accompany the weekly topics presented by the School of Area Studies. Each lesson in the booklet contained a reading on the topic that was understandable yet challenging to the average student. In addition, each lesson contained an intensive reading assignment, usually taken from authentic sources, that provided new information and represented a linguistic challenge for most students. The most capable students often incorporated this information into their own speaking and writing; the less capable students used them to find specific pieces of information and learn the most important concepts associated with the topic. In all, there were twenty lessons, each lasting about two weeks.

In addition to the material presented in the area studies courses, teachers developed their own area studies activities. For example, teachers showed videos, found newspaper articles on the same topics, and conducted in-class discussions. Occasionally, field trips were taken, such as one to the Hillwood Museum in Washington, D.C., in conjunction with the lesson on Art and Architecture; there, a tour was conducted entirely in Russian by Russian-speaking museum personnel. Teachers also worked in teams of two or three to conduct debates or simulations, for example, leading a debate on the role of Kievan Rus' (Kiev, Ukraine, was the seat of the first Russian government) in Russian history from the point of view of three different religious persuasions. Such presentations began in the very first weeks of Russian instruction. Student activities associated with these presentations took a variety of forms, including writing an analysis (in-depth if written in English or in outline form if written in Russian), reenacting the presentation with classmates, or arguing for their own interpretation, depending on their level of proficiency at the time.

In the early weeks of the program, in order to make area content more accessible to students, teachers used a form of "scaffolding" by relating information to students' schemata (see a fuller description of scaffolding by Ryding and Stowasser in Chapter 5). An example of this scaffolding-building process is the students' first geography lesson, taken from lesson 1 (see Appendix C). In this lesson, students learned geographic terms (continent, mountain, river, city, capital, etc.) in Russian as they described familiar American topographical features and the location of American cities on a map of North America. They later moved on to Russian geography and the location of Russian cities and terrain features. In this way new vocabulary and information were introduced in a familiar context.

Supplemental Reading Packets: Separate from the area studies booklet, the Basic Program textbook was supplemented by reading packets that contained authentic articles on political affairs, economics, human rights, social welfare, and other current topics. These reading packets were thematically organized in order to develop vocabulary and structure through extensive exposure to authentic materials. At very low proficiency levels (0/0+), students were given sorting and identification tasks. For example, on the first day of class, students received a collection of a dozen or more articles containing many cognates. Their task was to sort these into categories such as "kosmos," "meditsina," "politika," "sport," and "ekonomika." As they progressed through the program (0+/1) they graduated to skimming, scanning, and "gisting" (i.e., grasping only the general idea or gist of the article), often comparing Soviet and American articles on the same event and analyzing the differences in reportage and interpretation. This type of exercise not only provided background information in English (a bit of a "cheat sheet") but also gave students an insight into the Russian ethos. Toward the end of the program they were asked to analyze texts in greater depth, identifying elements that were culturally loaded or ambiguous, specifying the underlying simple structure of linguistically complex passages, and for students who would be posted to positions requiring translation skills, proposing alternative translations of culturally or linguistically complex materials.

The Conference: "The conference," in which all students participated, served as a capstone activity at the end of the year-long program. Both Basic Program and Advanced Course students presented papers in Russian on area studies topics of their own choice. The criteria for selecting a topic was that it dovetail with those studied in the School of Area Studies and that it represent the same sophisticated level of thinking that students were capable of in English. Papers ran fifteen to twenty minutes in length, followed by ten to fifteen minutes of answering questions from an audience composed of teachers, other students, and invited guests.

In addition to individual papers, the conference featured debates and roundtables that focused on current issues such as *perestroika*, an analysis of Gorbachev's first days in office and their significance for the future, and the outlook for improvement in Soviet-American relations. Roundtable topics were announced only two or three days in advance of the conference. Although students routinely discussed these topics in their classrooms, there was no advance preparation of position papers specifically for the roundtables. Students from the Advanced Course and those students from the Basic Program who had reached at least ILR S-3+ proficiency by the time of the conference conducted the hour-long roundtable, at which they extemporaneously discussed the chosen topic. Sample paper presentations and debate topics are listed below.

Sample Paper Presentations
- "Scientific and Cultural Contacts Between the United States and the Soviet Union"
- "The Current Status of Sino-Soviet Relations"
- "Perestroika in the Economics Sphere"
- "The Struggle for Human Rights in Russia"
- "The Influence of American Policy Towards Refugees on Soviet-American Relations"
- "Differences in Soviet and American Social Values"

Sample Debate Topics
- "Should Cultural Contacts Between the U.S. and Russia Be Expanded?"
- "Is the Party Apparatus Yielding Power to the KGB or Armed Forces?"
- "Should NATO Modernize Its Forces in Europe?"
- "Can a Policy of Economic Sanctions Be Effective?"

The deans of the Schools of Language Studies and Area Studies hosted the conference and shared responsibility for opening and closing remarks, usually speaking in English. Students acted as Russian interpreters— sometimes receiving the texts in advance, often not. Most of the outside guests were speakers of Russian; non-Russian-speaking guests were paired with student interpreters. Conference participants from the outside learned new information or gained new insights from students' presentations.

As a capstone to their training in the School of Area Studies, Basic Program students were required to write a ten-page term paper on some aspect of Russian history or politics. Students were given the option of writing those papers in Russian. Most students worked long hours to polish their conference presentations for this purpose, and teachers worked with students to ensure a literate product. One student subsequently published his Russian language paper—an analysis of actual Soviet military capability versus Soviet rhetoric on the topic.

Testing:

No formal tests were given during the Basic Program. Approximately once every three months an interim oral proficiency interview was administered to ascertain whether students were "on track" to the required end-of-training proficiency level (typically a level 3 in speaking and reading). If specific deficiencies were discovered during the interim tests, students were "tracked" (put into a special skill-building class one hour a day) for work specifically in the deficient area. Examples of "tracking" included vocabulary enrichment, focus on structural accuracy in speaking, improvement of listening comprehension skills, and enhancement of discourse competence.

Stage Two: Textbook Development

By 1986 the Basic Program was supplemented by elements of CBI from the very first week of class, and by 1988 as much as one-third of the daily work was based on supplemental CBI materials.

In 1987, encouraged by favorable comments of students and embassy officials and having observed significantly improved end-of-training scores, the administration of the North and East European Languages Department decided to move forward with full-day implementation of CBI from the first day of class. This was to be realized through the preparation of a new "Basic Program CBI Textbook." The topics for the CBI lessons were to be based on area studies topics. The twenty supplemental area studies lessons and *Mark Smith's Diary* lessons were to form the core of the textbook.

Unfortunately, in spite of favorable student response and documented proficiency gains in students who field-tested the first five lessons, all twenty lessons were never completed. The project was significantly underfunded and understaffed. Growth pains caused by a dramatic increase in the student body and the hiring of a number of new instructors created a need for faculty development without adequate time or resources to train new faculty concurrently with the development of a new textbook. In addition, personnel changes in administration created waning support for nontraditional programs.

More importantly, as portions of the CBI textbook were completed, the course developers themselves began to question the viability of a "CBI textbook." The materials that were being put into the textbook would clearly become obsolete and have to be replaced periodically; finding "authentic materials" that would not quickly become dated was very restrictive. In addition, trying to meet the needs of individual groups of students required introducing specific materials that reflected their interests and learning styles. The strong emphasis on teaching to students' learning styles, which had become the norm in the Russian Section, meant that even with a CBI textbook (i.e., one that was subject-matter based and used authentic materials), teachers were still supplementing and adapting lessons in order to meet the learning needs of specific groups of students. No two groups of students received exactly the same instruction, because no two groups of students had exactly the same learning needs. A key question arose: Why are we writing a CBI textbook, if, in order to implement a good CBI course, we have to use current and authentic materials?

This question arose in all of the FSI sections that were experimenting with CBI (see Chapters 5, 8, and 10), and all seemed to be reaching the same conclusion: CBI and the use of a single textbook are mutually exclusive concepts. This same conclusion was reached at the Defense Language Institute. Corin (Chapter 4), describing a course for Serbian and Croatian in which students used authentic materials exclusively, concludes that a single integrated textbook is incompatible with effective CBI.

The Advanced Russian Course

As mentioned earlier, the ongoing development (and continued success) of the Russian Advanced Course during this time had a significant impact on the Basic Program. The advanced students and portions of their curriculum were constantly accessible to the Basic Program students and influenced them. The Advanced Course used an unusual model of instruction that compensated for lack of teacher expertise in esoteric subject-matter areas.

The Advanced Course functioned entirely at the ACTFL "Superior" level of proficiency, its purpose being to take students from ILR level 3 to level 4. Students in the Advanced Course interacted with Basic Program students and provided excellent models for them. Some of the Russian Section activities included joint participation by both the Basic Program and Advanced Course students. Most notable was the conference, during which the Advanced Course students conducted roundtables and debates, while Basic Program students made short individual presentations and acted as interpreters for guests. Students in the shorter specialty courses entertained with skits, rap, or music. In some cases, outstanding students who completed the Basic Program early were enrolled in the Advanced Course.

The Advanced Course presented students with the opportunity to completely "sculpt" the program to match their own interests, experience, and learning needs. Students selected the subject matter they wished to include in the syllabus and the length of time they wished to spend on each subject. For example, one class composed of many consular officers chose to spend over half the course on the topic of political dissidents. Other classes did not even include this topic. Because teachers could not be expected to be knowledgeable in all topic areas, students who were experts in the fields undertook to conduct research in Russian on the topics and lead the class discussions. Teachers facilitated students' work by providing authentic materials in addition to those that students were able to find in the Department of State Library and by assisting with the development of language skills needed to discuss the topic at an educated native-speaker level. In addition to participation in the conference and the term paper that each student wrote for the School of Area Studies, Advanced Course students had one more requirement to fulfill: a public lecture in Russian. Each advanced student selected a topic and presented an evening lecture at a gathering of local Russians. The lecture lasted thirty to forty minutes and was followed by a question-and-answer period in which views on the topic were exchanged. As with all other activities in the Advanced Course, the lecture used the Russian language as a medium of communication of complex ideas, not just as a linguistic system to be studied and analyzed. The class activities, including student research and student-led seminars, all led to the point where a student could stand alone in front of a Russian-speaking audience and lecture in Russian as an expert. The Advanced Course was highly successful in turning students into independent learners, capable of "flying on their own."

Evaluation and Conclusions

The CBI courses proved to be an asset to the Russian Section in a number of ways: 1) student response was favorable—the first time in many years; 2) student proficiency gains were evident; and 3) feedback from the American embassy in Moscow was positive. Unfortunately, the courses required levels of resources that made them difficult to maintain.

Student Response

On end-of-training questionnaires, Basic Program students routinely pointed to the CBI elements as the most effective aspects of their training. Comments from students who participated in field-testing of the CBI textbook generally focused on the confidence that they gained by discussing "adult-level content" in Russian from the very start. After completing the partially developed CBI textbook and returning to the standard textbook with supplemental materials, most students reported feeling a "loss of momentum" and a "change in intensity" of the program. On end-of-training questionnaires, many commented on their disappointment in having to return to a non-CBI textbook. Advanced Course students, who achieved parallel rapid increases in their language proficiency and confidence, became advocates of CBI. In fact, one student made a presentation on the course at a meeting of the Interagency Language Roundtable, and two other students made a promotional videotape, sharing the techniques used in the class and describing the impact of the CBI program on their learning.

Proficiency Gains

Results on the end-of-training proficiency tests were also positive. When CBI was introduced at the beginning of the FSI Russian program in 1984, the percentage of students who started at 0 and reached S-3/R-3 in a ten-month period rose from 52 percent (the previous five year average, as well as 1983 graduation level) to 83 percent in spring 1985. From 1985 to 1988 that percentage remained close to 90 percent. At higher levels of proficiency, the differences were even more pronounced. Prior to the addition of CBI elements to the program, only 18 percent of the students reached scores that exceeded level 3. After addition of the CBI elements, 42 percent of the students reached scores higher than a level 3. Of those students in the Basic Program who were placed in the CBI Advanced Course toward the end of their initial training, 100 percent reached at least S-3/R-3, 92 percent reached 3+ or higher, and 16 percent reached level 4 in a ten-month period of study. (Most had entered with no previous study of Russian.)

Even during the short period in which the new CBI textbook was used, there was a perceptible difference. Progress was rapid during the first ten weeks of the program and resulted in interim proficiency test scores of 1 or 1+ for most students, with more than half reaching 1+, a level equivalent to that typically achieved by fourth-year students in many college Russian programs and not reached with the traditional FSI Russian materials until much later in the course. When students returned to a program that was less intensive in its CBI structure, the rate of progress visibly slowed.

Realistically, some of the improvement could be accounted for by other changes in the curriculum, such as greater expectations placed on the students, immersion, greater flexibility in adapting classroom and homework activities to match learning styles, and the introduction of systematic use of Russian in a student-emigrant internship program. However, the students themselves most frequently attributed their increased confidence and proficiency to the CBI elements in the curriculum. The greatest gains in proficiency, as measured by interim tests, were made during the periods when students were receiving the greatest amounts of content-based instruction.

The conference appeared to be especially important to student language gains. In addition to very favorable student response, the conference gained renown both inside and outside the FSI. Invited guests came from the FSI, the Department of Defense, the U.S. Naval Academy, the Jewish Community Center, Russian emigrant groups, and local universities. Guests were impressed with the conference and student proficiency. A note from the director of the FSI called the conference "an imaginative and clearly very successful adjunct to everyday training," and went on to say, "I have heard nothing but rave reviews." A professor from a local university program, a native speaker of Russian, wrote, "I am impressed to see that someone is training students to this level of proficiency." More importantly, however, from the time preparation for the conference began (about two weeks before the event itself) to the final proficiency tests of students (about two weeks after the conference), most students made measurable linguistic progress. From 1985 to 1987 interim proficiency tests were given at the outset of the conference preparation. During that time period more than half of all students made a half-point proficiency gain in the short period of time surrounding the conference. On a qualitative basis, both teachers and students commented frequently on the way in which students' language skills developed into an effective communication tool that students used with comfort.

Even better results were obtained in the all-CBI Russian Advanced Course, one of the most successful courses ever implemented at the FSI. During the period that this course was taught, no student who entered the Advanced Course with the prerequisite level 3 in reading and speaking and who attended the full six-month course failed to reach at least a level 4 in both skills upon exit; some reached level 4+ in one or both skills.

American Embassy Feedback

Feedback from the embassy was very supportive. Students who completed the CBI-supplemented program found that they were comfortable in doing their daily work in Russian. They maintained contact with the FSI Russian Section, something that had not been done routinely, and assisted in providing materials for the subject-matter supplements for future students. The relationship with the Ambassador and the Post Language Officer improved. Where there had been criticism, there was now emerging support. Over time, supportive materials and interactions became routinely bidirectional. The Consul General in Leningrad, who had completed the first Russian Advanced Course, wrote that he would have been devastated following his first meeting with the Executive Council of Leningrad (the equivalent of our city council) had he not been exposed to comparative political behaviors as part of the Advanced Course. As a result of his studies, he knew how to react to the slow beginning of the meeting, and he knew when he had accomplished his aims. Instead of feeling devastated at the conclusion of the meeting, he was ecstatic. He went on to win the confidence of the Executive Council, to conduct all business in Russian, and to be a very effective consul general.

Difficulties in Maintenance

Although the results from the CBI courses between 1984 and 1988 were very encouraging, lack of resources and a change in administration with an accompanying wane in administrative support prevented their completion and consolidation. As a result, some elements of Stage One (text supplementation) were eliminated, and implementation of Stage Two (text preparation) was halted. Remaining today from Stage One are the use of cultural materials, the use of authentic reading materials (although the books and other textual materials themselves have become outdated and have been replaced), and the LSP modules (which have continued to receive administrative support and expansion). These materials and activities still give the FSI Russian Basic Program of the 1990s a CBI flavor.

Analysis of our text preparation efforts provides some insights into the problems inherent in a comprehensive CBI text at early stages. While the desire to move beyond textbook supplementation to something more broad-based was legitimate, forcing CBI into a textbook format was not practical. Had foresight the acuity of hindsight, a more appropriate approach of "textbook supplantation" would have been taken—with subject matter textbooks from Russia. Having learned this important lesson at the FSI, I was able to experiment with this approach in a Defense Language Institute (DLI) Czech course in the 1990s. The Czech Department at the DLI used task-based instruction and authentic materials exclusively for the first half of the course (Maly 1993). The latter half of the course was fully content-based, using student-elected subjects, such as physics, mathematics, grammar, and folklore. Teachers imported textbooks on these subjects from Czech high schools, or in the case of grammar and folklore, from elementary schools. Students reported that the course was "fun" and that they "could not help but learn." They considered themselves advantaged over their peers in the more traditional Czech course because they learned more with less effort (Duri 1992). Results showed that while typically 40 to 50 percent of graduating Czech students in the traditional course reached the exit goal of Reading-2, Listening- 2, and Speaking-1+, all of the students in the Czech CBI course reached levels of at least Reading-2, Listening- 2, and Speaking-2, and 60 percent reached a level 3 in one or more of the skill levels (Maly 1993). A Ukrainian "conversion course" (see Corin, Chapter 4, for an explanation of conversion courses) produced even more impressive results: 88 percent of students reached a level 3 in all skills after four months of half-time study (Leaver and Thompson 1993). In both cases, the "textbook issue" was resolved by using truly "authentic textbooks" rather than a single foreign language textbook.

In sum, the very nature of content-based instruction, whether for beginning or advanced learners, requires going beyond any single textbook and using many and varied authentic materials in a variety of content domains. The major conclusion I have reached concerning alternatives to a fixed textbook and syllabus design is that the best "content-based text" would not be a bound text with prescribed lessons but one which provides teachers with models and general methodological guidelines that could be adapted to any kind of content-based curriculum—not unlike the format of this book.

Betty Lou Leaver, President of the American Global Studies Institute in Salinas, California since 1993, served as Dean of the School of Central European Languages and Dean of the School of Slavic Languages at the Defense Language Institute from 1989-1993. From 1983 to 1989 she was Russian Language Training Supervisor at the Foreign Service Institute. Address: AGSI, 2 Rex Circle, Salinas, CA 93906. (E-mail: leaver@agsi.org, leaver@glasnet.ru)

List of Appendixes

Appendix A: *Mark Smith's Diary*

Appendix A is an excerpt (Lesson 15) from *Mark Smith's Diary*. In the original *Mark Smith's Diary*, the lesson is in Russian. It is translated here for readers' convenience.

Appendix B: Special Seminars

Appendix B includes sample lessons from the general services seminar, accompanied by a description of how these lessons were implemented.

Appendix C: *Area Studies Handbook*

Appendix C is a page from Lesson 1 of the *Area Studies Handbook* (and later, Lesson 1 of the CBI textbook) in which students learn geographic terms, first by locating American cities and terrain features, then by using the geographic terms to learn the location of Russian cities and terrain features.

Appendix A
Mark Smith's Diary

Lesson 15

Lessons from *Mark Smith's Diary* (which were actually Mark Smith's written records of conversations he had with his Russian friend, Nikolai) in some cases were accompanied by multiple-choice questions or quizzes. Other times the lessons were reenacted in the classroom. For example, in the lesson on popular literature, Boris Shekhtman and Natalia Lord, the two FSI instructors who authored the diary, would gather all staff and students into one room, with the Russian teachers sitting on one side of the room and the American students on the other. They would ask two questions: "Who are the greatest Russians?" and "Who are the greatest Americans?" Russians inevitably listed writers, such as Tolstoy and Pushkin, but not scientists or political leaders. Americans listed scientists, such as Einstein, and political leaders, such as Washington and Lincoln, but not writers.

The partial diary entry below comes from Lesson 15, "Foreign Relations," used about the thirtieth week of the course. This particular entry is entirely in Russian and translated here. Teachers used this entry in a wide variety of ways—discussion, as source material for a debate, enactment of a talk show, interviews of teachers or emigrants not associated with FSI, or a myriad of other activities limited only by teacher and student imagination.

Mark: Nikolai, if we take international political relations between the two countries, can we assume that some of their views of each other are the result of, so to speak, perceptual differences?

Nikolai: In principle, I don't know whether these differences can be called perceptual — but there is no doubt of their existence. I would more readily call them different approaches to the solution of foreign policy problems. In the first place, I would suggest that, if the Soviets in their foreign policy defend only the interests of the government-party apparatus, then the Americans often find it necessary to reflect the desires of groups whose interests do not coincide with the interests of the government. Take, for example, the problem of grain. American presidents have attempted more than once to halt delivery of grain to the Soviet Union, in order to punish it for aggressive policies. However, under the pressure of farmers interested in those deliveries, all American presidents, as if on command, have moved away from their positions and resumed the sale of grain to the U.S.S.R.

In this connection, it is appropriate to emphasize the fact that Soviet foreign policy is least of all susceptible to various types of humanitarian or moral influence. While young Americans were dying in Vietnam, lists of their names were published in the U.S. Their parents were interviewed, protest demonstrations were organized, petitions were signed, and virtually everything was done by American supporters of peace to end the war. Who knows how many Soviets have died in Afghanistan, but who has heard even one word of protest or seen even one mother sobbing over the grave of her son?

In addition, from my point of view, it wouldn't be bad to point out the effect of differences in the personalities of leaders on foreign policy. In the U.S., foreign policy is less coherent and stable because its leaders change often. In the U.S.S.R., individuals remain leaders for many years. How many Secretaries of State have come and gone in the U.S. in recent years, while Gromyko has been Minister of Foreign Affairs for more than 30 years? In addition, the individuals conducting foreign policy in the U.S. have more freedom of action. In my opinion, this is very important, since Americans are inclined to evaluate the actions of Soviet leaders from their perception of the role of personality in government. In this way, Americans thought that if a new General Secretary came to power, Soviet policy might change fundamentally. In reality, the General Secretary can do only that which is demanded of him by the totalitarian system.

Appendix B

Special Seminars
General Services Seminar

Example 1: The following excerpt is a sample of lessons that students complete in the middle stage of the seminar. Prior to doing this kind of lesson, students have worked with authentic documents, learning the basic vocabulary needed for filling them out accurately. Emphasis in the general services special seminar is on developing accuracy of expression. General services officers need to be precise in order to be effective officers. In the lessons, students enact role plays. The "problem" is reported to them by someone playing the role of a Russian employee. "What to say" provides them with some basic expressions to use in doing the role play. These expressions are instructions that could be given to Russian workers. Students are, of course, at liberty to elaborate and to use whatever else they know about repairs, living quarters, and the Russian language. These phrases are examples given to students of possible dialogue and are translated from the original Russian.

PROBLEMS	WHAT TO SAY
The freezer is not freezing.	Check out and, if needed, repair the freezer.
A pipe burst.	Mend the pipe.
	Replace the pipe.
The door does not shut properly.	Fix the door.
The shelf broke.	Repair the shelf.
	Put in a new shelf.
The refrigerator is not keeping produce cold.	Check the thermostat.
	Check the motor.
The refrigerator does not work.	Check the motor.
	Install a new motor.

Example 2: The following dialogue, from the third stage of the general services special seminar, has to do with fueling planes. Other topics include banquets, facilities rental (quarters, sports facilities, etc.), facilities maintenance, sales of personal merchandise, and excursions.

In general, the teaching techniques used with this seminar include role play, traditional reading for accuracy of information, and grammatical exercises. The scenarios are content-based in that the subject matter is general services content, and the situations and documents are authentic. The topics, tasks, and skills developed reflect the needs of this group of students. The dialogues are presented in two modalities, oral and written, to account for learning style differences among the students.

This lesson, including instructions on implementing the lesson, is entirely in Russian. A conversation between an American General Services Officer (A) and a Russian official (B) serves as a model dialogue and is translated here. The language may seem harsh. In post-USSR Russia, it would probably be inappropriate; however, in the Cold War days, when this seminar was first implemented, the language was typical. Relationships between general services officers and the Russians they worked with were often not very cordial. Students need to understand when they were being treated with lack of cordiality and how to respond accordingly.

Note: The purpose of question 4 in the exercise which follows the dialogue is to develop a feel for Russian syntax, which is much freer than English syntax. In general Russian word order is highly flexible. Here the student is asked to change subject-verb-object word order into a variety of other possibilities. The teacher would then explain the subtleties in meaning associated with the various word orders.

Refueling of an American Plane in Leningrad
    A. Did you already check out the cargo?
    B. Yes. I can say that almost everything is in order. The only thing unclear is this beat-up container.
    A. They've already called from the Consulate and given permission to open the container, in order to show you that these are instruments.
    B. That's another matter!
    A. And what about the fuel line, which is leaking?
    B. Our mechanic and flight engineer are changing the filter in the air pump right now. As soon as they finish that, they will attend to the fuel line.

A. How much time is that going to take?

B. I think, ten to fifteen minutes. Well, on second thought, maybe twenty. No more.

A. And after that you'll give an "OK" for take-off.

B. Right away. I do know that your military attaché has a meeting arranged for today at General Headquarters.

A. Okay, so now you understand why I am concerned about this delay. At first, some kind of problem with the engine, then this container thing . . .

B. Mr. Johnson, this is not our fault. Your engine was made in America. And the container . . . Well, you must agree that I cannot allow the flight of a foreign aircraft with an unknown apparatus over territory where our important military-industrial complex is located. You know that very well.

A. Your specialists will confirm that there are only measuring devices there.

B. What kind, for example?

A. Well, Geiger counters and some other such stuff.

B. What? Once again you want permission to go to the Chernobyl atomic energy station?

A. Ivan Stepanovich, after all, the medium range nuclear weapon agreement has already been signed. Our delegation will inspect the launch pads, silos, and depots.

B. Yes, but not the warehouses! There's no radiation in the places where you will be.

A. Well, just in case. You have the saying, "God takes care of those who take care of themselves."

B. OK. You've convinced me. Look, the dispatcher is calling us. Your plane is ready. Bon voyage! If you see Peters in Moscow, say "Hello." He and I serviced many special flights and there never were any problems.

A. I will definitely pass on your greetings. Good-bye.

Exercises based on the dialogue: (Instructions to students)

1. Listen to the dialogue.
2. Read the dialogue.
3. Answer the questions:
   a. Who went to Moscow?
   b. Why was the plane detained?
   c. Where is the meeting for the military attaché to take place?

        d.   How does the American explain the purpose of the military attaché's trip?

4.   Put the subject into various positions in the sentence.
    a.   You already checked the cargo.
    b.   Our mechanic and flight engineer are changing the filter.
    c.   I know that your military attaché has a meeting scheduled for today at General Headquarters.
    d.   You know that well.

5.   Explain the meaning of the following expressions:
[Here there are ten expressions in Russian which have cultural implications or odd grammatical features.]

6.   Find the expressions from exercise 5 in the dialogue. Use them in new situations.

7.   Imagine that you are Mr. Johnson and that your teacher is Ivan Stepanovich. You are the general services officer accompanying the airplane carrying the military attaché. Create a dialogue/role play based on this scenario.

8.   Retell the story in the dialogue in the first person (you are Mr. Johnson, and you are talking about what happened to you).

9.   Retell the story in the dialogue in the third person (you are telling about what happened to Mr. Johnson).

10. Write a report to your boss about the refueling incident in Leningrad.

Appendix C

Lesson 1: Geography of the USSR

This lesson is only one example of how teachers can implement a beginning geography lesson. The chart below (fig. C.1) is an example of the Lesson 1 geography activities from the *Area Studies Handbook* and subsequent CBI textbook. To help students acquire map terms, teachers show a map of North America and use the directions of North, South, East, and West to discuss where familiar cities and states are located. Students use the chart below as a worksheet to list cities that they know in each of these locations. After writing this information down, they share it with the teacher, in dyads, or with the larger group. Once students acquire the location terms and the expressions associated with them, they learn the locations of important Russian cities through a variety of means: map study, reading, teacher-provided information, and dialogue in which two teachers discuss the topic in front of the students, while the students "eavesdrop." Once again, students use this simple chart (in Russian, of course) to fill in the information.

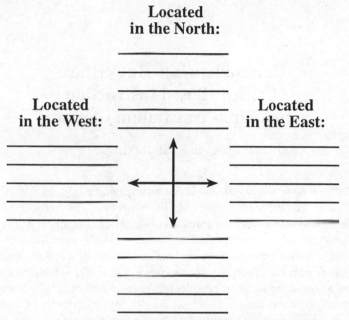

**Located
in the North:**

**Located
in the West:**

**Located
in the East:**

**Located
in the South:**

Fig. C.1. Geographical Chart

3

Caterpillars into Butterflies: Content-Based Instruction in a First-Year Italian Course

Steven R. Sternfeld

Editors' Note: Steven Sternfeld presents a unique approach to his first-year Italian class at the University of Utah. His course, part of the University's "Immersion/Multiliteracy" Program, uses CBI as one component in an eclectic curriculum model. The pedagogical philosophy of the Immersion/Multiliteracy program, at once interdisciplinary, collaborative, and reflexive, aims at transforming the classroom into a community of learners in which learning is defined as engaging in "intellectually challenging and culturally broadening activities." As contrasted to Leaver in the previous chapter and Corin in the following chapter, whose programs emphasize oral proficiency, Sternfeld uses CBI to focus on foreign language literacy skills. His use of literature for beginning students provides an innovative model for stimulating students' critical thinking skills and enhancing their cross-cultural knowledge, even as they learn a new language. He tells us how his course, initially offered as an alternative to the skills-based approach in the regular foreign language program, evolved into a hybrid "language and literacy course." Realizing the inappropriateness of any single text to achieve this dual goal, Sternfeld designed an imaginative series of "modules," based on, of all things . . . well, you'll read for yourself. General references for this chapter are located in the bibliography at the end of this volume.

The University of Utah's Immersion/Multiliteracy Program

Frank Smith (1988) has proposed a model/metaphor for first and second language and literacy development based on the notion of joining a club. According to Smith, when an infant joins the "spoken-language club," more experienced members demonstrate the many ways in which spoken language is used and how club members talk. They also:

... help infants to say what they are trying to say and to understand what they are trying to understand. Everything other club members do is an opportunity for learning, which is usually vicarious, provided the beginner identifies with the other members of the club (in Smith 1995,18).

Later the same child may join the "literacy club," where more experienced members accept children as "apprentices," who in time become "practitioners." Again, senior members are expected to demonstrate all the advantages of group membership to newcomers and facilitate their participation in all club activities. Smith also observes that second language acquisition, and in particular adult second language acquisition, is marked by "paradoxical contrasts," in that it can be "effortlessly easy or impossibly difficult."

The difference is not a matter of how motivated you are or how hard you work . . . It is a question of how easily you are able to join a community of people who speak the second language—*how ready you are to identify with them* and how open they are to accepting you [emphasis mine] (in Smith 1995, 23).

The University of Utah's Immersion/Multiliteracy (IM/ML) Program can be seen as an attempt to enhance the effectiveness of second language instruction by increasing students' readiness to identify with speakers of a given target language, as well as with the target language culture and the target language itself. The designation "Immersion/Multiliteracy" is intended to reflect both the methodology and the goal of the program. The methodology is based on the Canadian Immersion Model and, as such, is a content-based instructional (CBI) approach to second language instruction. The program's objective is the development of multiliteracy, defined as "the pursuit of intellectually challenging and culturally broadening activities in more than one language" (Sternfeld 1989, 342).

The content of IM/ML courses has varied from language to language, a function of the availability and comprehensibility of materials. Each year-long course has had a broad, albeit unitary, theme. For example, the first-year German IM/ML course adopted a three-volume world history text intended for students in German high schools. The first-year French IM/ML course focused on French history, using a series of five history books in French, including an elementary school level textbook published in 1914 and a high school level textbook published in 1939. The first-year Spanish IM/ML course, on the other hand, explored Hispanic culture in Latin

America and the United States, using as one of its primary "texts," five daily issues a week of *La Opinión*, a Spanish-language newspaper published in Los Angeles.

From its inception, the IM/ML Program was seen as an alternative to the skills-oriented courses offered by the Department of Languages and Literature. After the first year-long pilot section was offered in Spanish in 1985-86, students who chose to sign up for a course in the IM/ML Program were informed of the special nature and goals of the course. This included the fact that IM/ML courses did not articulate with other first-year sections of the same language, making it advisable for students who would not continue in the IM/ML Program for the full three quarters of the first-year course to transfer to the skills-based program.

While the IM/ML Program was designed to attract a wide range of students, we were particularly anxious to enroll those students whose primary or exclusive motivation for taking a foreign language was fulfilling the five-quarter B.A. foreign language graduation requirement and whose personal and/or professional goals did not include (spoken) fluency in another language. For such students, the IM/ML Program's "intellectually challenging and culturally broadening activities" were seen as providing the most persuasive demonstration of the "advantages of group membership" and, consequently, were held to be the key to encouraging and facilitating students joining the "Multiliteracy Club."

A "Hybrid" Course

An "Italian Language and Literacy Club"

I have described the rationale and development of the IM/ML Program extensively elsewhere (Sternfeld 1988, 1989, 1991, 1992). In this chapter I will focus on a specific first-year Italian IM/ML course that I developed in response to a problem posed by the very limited size of the Italian program at our university. As previously mentioned, the IM/ML Program was initially proposed as an alternative track alongside the traditional skills-based program offered by the Department of Languages and Literature. Each year a single section of an IM/ML course in French, Spanish, and German was offered in addition to multiple sections of the skills-based program. This allowed for a significant degree of self-selection, in that students who were most interested in focusing on conversational proficiency would tend to choose the skills-oriented sections.

Enrollment in my first-year Italian IM/ML course reflected the eclectic mix of students found in most of our department's first-year courses. Students ranged from those who were primarily concerned with fulfilling their foreign language graduation requirement to those who were preparing for summer travel to Italy and/or participation in our summer study abroad program in Siena. While the latter were often quite willing to engage in the "intellectually challenging and culturally broadening" activities of IM/ML Program, they were also very anxious to learn the specific vocabulary, grammatical structures, and background knowledge they associated with traveling and studying in Italy.

In an effort then to meet the needs of a more diverse student population, I set about designing a new first-year Italian course that offered more of the immediate skills-oriented instruction that so many students were seeking while maintaining, to the extent possible, the integrity of the IM/ML Program and its commitment to promoting multiliteracy through the pursuit of "intellectually challenging and culturally broadening" activities in Italian. What emerged is what I might call a "hybrid" course that mixes skills-based and content-based instruction, or, to borrow from Smith, one that invites students to join the "Italian Language and Literacy Club."

Course Description

The hybrid, first-year Italian program was taught as a three-quarter, fifteen-credit course during the 1995-96 academic year. Class was held five days a week for fifty-minute periods. I met with the class Monday through Thursday, while assistants worked with students on Fridays. Of more than forty students enrolled in Fall Quarter, approximately twenty-five remained for the full three quarters, a rate of attrition comparable to that of other first-year language courses in the Department of Languages and Literature.

The course can be conceived of as comprising two major components: the original IM/ML, or content-based, track and the skills-based track. Since it is the content-based track that is the focus here, I will provide only the briefest description of the skills-based track.

The Skills-Based Track

The skills-based track was built around two principal elements: an introductory Italian language textbook and a portfolio of student biographies. *Buongiorno Italia* (Cremona 1987) is an introductory-level text produced by the BBC as part of a home study television and radio series and includes audio- and videocassettes. I chose this text because I felt it would allow students to do much of their language study per se outside of class on their own, thereby leaving as much class time as possible available for content-based instruction. Organized along situational and functional/notional lines, the text is well suited to the needs of students planning a trip to Italy inasmuch as it contains an abundance of dialogues, all of which were recorded on location in Italy. Within each chapter grammar explanations are kept to a minimum, with an appendix providing a summary of all the basic grammatical concepts presented in the book. All exercises are placed at the end of the chapter and are easily corrected by students themselves with the aid of the answer key provided in a second appendix. Finally, twenty short, graded readings on various aspects of Italian culture and civilization are included.

The building of a portfolio of student biographies lasted the entire year. The process began the first quarter with students taking notes while I interviewed individual students one at a time in front of the class. Later these interviews became more interactive as students were encouraged to pose their own questions to the interviewee. By the second quarter, a portion of class time was set aside for students to sit in pairs to carry out one-on-one interviews. Students were also encouraged to use e-mail to exchange biographical information. Finally, students were required to make several five- to ten-minute oral presentations during the second and third quarters in which they were to provide the class with additional information about their lives. The information gathered was turned in at the end of the year in the form of a final "portfolio" of student biographies.

The Content-Based Track

When contemplating the adoption of *Buongiorno Italia* as a self-study text to be worked on primarily outside of class, I debated whether it would be reasonable to expect first-year students to handle that text in addition to the extensive daily reading assignments in *Storie della storia d'Italia* (Peccianti 1994), the Italian history text which had been the core of the Italian IM/ML course. A reduction in the number of reading assignments or the outright elimination of the text would have a strong impact on the design of the hybrid course. Indeed, not only had *Storie della storia d'Italia* provided a unitary content focus for the Italian IM/ML course, but the bulk of in-class, content-based instruction had revolved around introducing and going over the extensive daily reading assignments.

In the end, a number of factors dealing with instructional design, demands on student time, not to mention the total cost of the textbooks themselves, led me to accept the challenge of designing a CBI component for the hybrid course that did not use a content-based Italian language text such as *Storie della storia d'Italia*. Fortunately, the decision to abandon a unitary, content-based textbook approach to the development of a CBI component led to the development of three CBI "modules" that I consider valuable additions to my own repertoire of CBI activities. And move now to the design and implementation of these three CBI modules.

CBI Module I: Aphorisms, Proverbs, and Popular Sayings
Caterpillars into Butterflies

A popular Italian version of "T-shirt-as-text/art," often sold in bookstores, displays quotes from the works of some of the world's best-known writers and thinkers. Several years ago I received as a gift one such T-shirt with a quote from Lao-Tse:

> Quella che il bruco chiama fine del mondo, il resto del mondo chiama farfalla.
> What the caterpillar calls the end of the world, the rest of the world calls butterfly.

This quote was particularly apt for students in the IM/ML Program. Indeed, after being immersed in a CBI lesson for what seems like an eternity—although in actuality slightly less than an hour—many students are indeed convinced that the end of the world is imminent. I took to wearing my Lao-Tse T-shirt on the first day of my Italian IM/ML classes, integrating the quote into my opening lecture, which had always included an initial introduction to the nature and goals of the IM/ML Program itself. The quote considerably facilitated explaining the notion of learning a second language as potentially transformational in nature. The caterpillar into butterfly image, like those of the phoenix rising from its ashes and of Shiva, the god who destroys and creates, can help explain to students the notion that if they seek one day to become full-fledged members of the "Italian Language and Literary Club," they too may find themselves undergoing a sort of symbolic rebirth.

In a subsequent visit to Italy, I came upon a series of books containing aphorisms from writers such as Gandhi and Confucius. The brevity, the deceptive simplicity, and, perhaps most importantly, the often powerful imagery of many of these aphorisms led me to consider putting together an entire series of quotes that I could use as points of departure for discussions about the Italian IM/ML course. Indeed, given the unusual nature and goals of the IM/ML Program, reflection on the learning process has always been an integral part of instruction. Through English-language readings, process journals and in-class discussions, students are encouraged to explore how they and their classmates are responding to the IM/ML Program and how they might all become more effective learners.

While I have always seen the reading/journal writing component as critical to student success in the program, it is not always well received by students themselves for at least two reasons. First, reflection of this sort is for many students both new and uncomfortable, inasmuch as they may begin to recognize for the first time the extent to which they themselves create obstacles to their own learning. Second, since the bulk of this reflection (i.e., all of the readings, most of the journals and in-class discussions) is carried out in English, students may become impatient with the process, seeing reflection as time taken away from the task at hand, namely learning the target language. It is not by any means easy to convince students that these self-reflections are a wise investment, one that can do much to make their task seem, in the words of Smith, less "impossibly difficult," while perhaps not necessarily ensuring that their acquisition of a second language become "effortlessly easy." Thus, while carrying out a part of the reflection in Italian would not necessarily simplify or facilitate the process itself, it did have the potential of making the reflection component more attractive to students by integrating it into the content-based portion of the class.

Implementation

During the year-long course students were presented with more than fifty aphorisms, proverbs, and popular sayings (APPSs). In the end I used a variety of material, including aphorisms, proverbs, popular sayings, idiomatic expressions, poetry, and even song lyrics. Though the majority of these were chosen in order to facilitate the reflection component of the course, I did end up broadening the selection criteria to include material that, while perhaps not pertinent to the reflection component, nevertheless provided stimulating and challenging content.

Only on very rare occasions did I present more than one selection during a given class period. The presentation began with an explanation in Italian of its literal meaning. Any and all strategies—paraphrase, gestures, drawings, impromptu staging—were used to communicate the basic meaning of the selection. Only in exceptional cases did I resort to translation. When I felt that students had a fairly clear understanding of the APPS, I proceeded to interpret the selection in terms of its relevance to the nature and goals of the course as well as to the experiences that students were having in the program. While early in the year these presentations took the form of listening comprehension activities, later, when students' speaking skills were more developed, APPSs could be introduced in a more interactive nature by eliciting from the students themselves possible explanations and interpretations of the text.

Sample Texts

The following are samples of APPSs presented to students during the first year. I have included the Italian version as well as an English translation to give the reader a sense of how often even the most profound ideas can be surprisingly comprehensible to speakers of English with little or no prior exposure to Italian. For each APPS, I have written a brief commentary in which I suggest some of the possible ways in which a selection can be exploited as part of the reflection component in this particular course, although it is clear that these same selections are relevant to a wide range of learning contexts.

Since the CBI modules do not follow any linguistic syllabus, students are often perplexed as to how such a "disorganized" presentation of language can promote language learning. Here a somewhat facetious quotation is appropriate:

Ci sono imprese in cui l'accurato disordine è il metodo giusto.
There are endeavors in which careful disorder is the right method.

The fact that the IM/ML Program continues to evolve can lead the wary student to conclude that it is "experimental" in the sense of "untested" or "unproven." Hence, the appropriateness of this quote from Gandhi:

La vita non è altro che una serie incessante di esperimenti.
Life is nothing but an endless series of experiments.

This same quotation can be directed to students who are hesitant to make mistakes and need to be persuaded that language acquisition requires a heavy dose of "trial and error" learning. Thus, the relevance of the popular saying:
Sbagliando s'impara.
We learn by making mistakes.
The disappointment students experience as a result of the widening gap between comprehension and production is one that needs to be dealt with on an ongoing basis. Several selections touch on the notion that language and literacy skills, for both first and second languages, develop over long periods of time. Indeed, as the saying goes:
Nessuno nasce maestro.
No one is born a master.
Patience and perseverance do pay off, however:
Chi va piano, va sano; chi va sano, va lontano.
He who goes slowly stays healthy; he who stays healthy goes far.

A good deal of classroom time is spent in small group work. Collaborative learning, peer teaching, peer evaluation, etc., are integral to the course, though clearly not to the liking of all students. On the benefits of peer teaching, I was able to provide two very similar quotes, written some 2,000 years apart by the ancient Roman Seneca and the modern Frenchman Joseph Joubert:

Chi insegna impara.

He who teaches, learns.

Insegnare è imparare due volte.

To teach is to learn twice.

In facilitating group work, it is important to recognize the tendency for individual group members to see the other members of the group as the ones who are creating obstacles to effective collaboration. Hence George Bernard Shaw's "Irregular Verb Conjugation" as a reminder of how egocentric our perceptions can be:

Io sono risoluto.　　I am resolved.

Tu sei ostinato.　　You are obstinate.

Egli è uno stupido testardo.　He is a stubborn fool.

Instead of focusing on how they might get others in their group to "get their act together," students are encouraged to look within themselves to identify those values, attitudes, and behaviors that might pose a problem for productive group work. In the words of Confucius:

Combattere i propri difetti e non quelli degli altri, non è riformare e correggere il male?

To struggle with one's own defects and not those of others, is this not to change and correct what is wrong?

And since it is inevitable that in small group work students will err in attempting to help one another, it is important to remember that

Umana cosa è errare, divina cosa è perdonare.

To err is human, to forgive, divine.

CBI Module II: Folk Tales

Lost in the Woods

For the past half a dozen years, I have taught a course on community-building for our Liberal Education Program. One of the texts for the course, M. Scott Peck's *The Different Drum: Community Making and Peace* (1987), contains the following cautionary tale, which I have entitled "Lost in the Woods":

A rabbi was lost in the woods. For three months he searched and searched but could not find his way out. Then one day he came upon a group from his congregation who had also become lost in the woods.

"Oh, Rabbi, how happy we are to have found you," they shouted. "Now you can lead us out of the woods."

"I'm sorry, I cannot do that," replied the rabbi, "for you see, I am just as lost as you are. What I can do, because I have had more experience at being lost than you, is show you a thousand ways that do not lead out of the woods. With this poor help, working with one another, perhaps we will find our way out of the woods together."

It is a story I tell my Liberal Education students in the first days of class to warn them of the peril of assuming that I alone will lead them through the course. Although my tale is often perceived at best as a disclaimer, at worst as a total abdication of professional responsibilities, my intent is to invite students to take an active role in shaping the course and, in so doing, better manage the outcome of their learning.

The brevity, the deceptive simplicity, and the powerful imagery of this tale convinced me that it would make excellent material for a language class. I first used it in the form of a strip story in a college level ESL course and discovered that it lent itself quite readily to an impromptu staging, with students taking on the roles of rabbi, congregation, and, of course, the forest trees.

Just as my introduction to Lao-Tse's aphorism had led to my "discovery" of Italian collections of aphorisms, so did my familiarity with "Lost in the Woods" lead to my "discovery" of *Mazel Tov: 178 favolette yiddish*, an Italian translation of *Yiddish Folktales* edited by Beatrice Silverman Weinreich. A citation from Silverman Weinreich's book, taken from a turn-of-the-century publication on popular Jewish culture, helps explain why so many of these stories lend themselves so well to instruction:

> For fathers, recounting fables was not simply a pleasure, it was a duty . . . To teach while entertaining. To educate children by recounting fables. "You must tell stories" was God's commandment (translated from Weinreich 1992, 151).

I recognized that a careful selection of stories could be used to carry out more of the reflection process in Italian, thereby achieving even greater integration of the process component into the content of my Italian course.

My criteria for selection were similar to those for APPSs. I first looked for stories whose themes could be related to the nature and goals of the course and to the experiences of the students themselves. Since I was convinced that the brevity of the APPSs contributed significantly to their effectiveness, I preferred very short tales. Finally, I was especially interested in stories that lent themselves to impromptu staging with no special props.

Implementation

I introduced about a dozen stories during the year-long course. As with the APPS, I expanded the selection criteria to include tales that, while not closely related to the themes we were dealing with in the reflection component of the course, were nonetheless stimulating and challenging in content.

Tales were presented in a variety of fashions. In the case of short tales that I could easily memorize, I recited them in one session as would a traditional storyteller, using gestures and intonation to heighten the dramatic effect. For longer tales, which were introduced over a period of three or four days, I might first read a part of the tale before having students act out that segment. On subsequent days I might repeat the same section, this time without stage directions, leaving it up to the students, from memory and/or their understanding of the text itself, to recreate the scene. Finally, as with the APPSs, telling of the tale would be followed by an interpretation that connected the theme to the reflection component of the course.

Sample Texts

Following are synoptic English-language versions of tales from *Mazel Tov,* along with brief comments on how each tale could be related to the reflection component of the course.

La verità nuda e la parabola splendente
(The Naked Truth and the Resplendent Parable)

As with many of the "teaching" stories that I found in *Mazel Tov*, this story begins with a short introduction that explains the origin of the tale. One reb (wiseman) asks another why no one shows up in synagogue when he reads from the Torah, but the synagogue is packed if he tells just one parable. The friend replies that he will be glad to answer his question—with a parable, of course.

> One day Truth comes down to earth "as naked as the day she was
> born." Shunned by one and all, she is found wandering in despair
> by sumptuously dressed Parable. To Truth's lament that she is
> shunned because of her age, Parable responds that she too is old,

but that the older she gets, the more people love her. She tells Truth that people would love her too if only she were willing to dress up a bit since people like things to be "disguised" and "embellished." Parable offers to dress Truth in clothing as beautiful as her own; Truth willingly puts them on. From that day on the two walk hand in hand and are loved by all the people.

While it is easy enough to interpret this story as a lesson in how to get people to "swallow the truth" (cf. the saying "a little sugar makes the pill go down"), I find the relevance to my course goes much deeper. Pascal's quotation on miracles and truth comes to mind here:

I miracoli e la verità sono entrambi necessari, perché occorre convincere l'uomo tutt'intero: corpo e anima. Miracles and truth are both necessary, because one must convince man in his entirety: body and soul.

In Pascal's aphorism, miracles are not a "disguise" or "embellishment" of the truth, they are truth's complement. Indeed, miracle and truth together are presented as the proverbial "whole that is greater than the sum of its parts." This is the interpretation that I choose to give "Naked Truth and the Resplendent Parable," proposing that the complementarity of truth and parable (or truth and miracle) parallels that of language and content. Just as "sumptuous clothing" will ensure that people are better prepared to hear the truth and, by extension, to understand it, to learn from it and to integrate it into their lives, so can rich and varied content, i.e., content that challenges and stimulates the learner on as many levels as possible, ensure that students are more receptive to the target language and, by extension, more motivated to understand it, to learn it, and to integrate it into their lives.

Far entrare la luce (Let in the Light)

"Let in the Light" is presented as a tale told by Reb of Apt to explain to a colleague why he chooses not to keep an eye on his disciples in order to ensure that they "follow his precepts and pray devotedly":

Three men, two intelligent and one a simpleton, are locked up in a pitch black cell. One of the two bright men works hard to teach the simpleton the most basic tasks—how to dress himself, how to hold a fork, while his cell mate does nothing. One day the industrious one asks his cell mate why he won't lift a finger to help teach the simpleton. The latter replies that in this darkness the other will never succeed in teaching the simpleton a thing. He, on the other hand, is trying to figure out how to make a hole in the cell wall in order to let in the light. When he succeeds, the simpleton will be able to learn whatever he needs to on his own.

I have found this story particularly useful for explaining the design of the course and the concept of joining the "Italian Language and Literacy Club." I see the industrious cell mate as the teacher who works hard to teach the fundamentals of a second language to students who in some critical way are (as yet) unprepared for the task. This lack of preparedness may come from one or more sources, including:

- A lack or loss of familiarity with classroom-based learning in general;
- A weak or nonexistent formal understanding of the structure of language;
- Vague and/or conflicting notions about the nature of (adult) second language acquisition;
- Unsuccessful or no previous second language learning experience, either one of which may lead to a high level of "foreign language anxiety"; and
- Little or no personal or professional interest in the culture, its people, or the language itself.

As an instructional designer and classroom teacher, I argue that I can be more effective if I focus my attention on "letting in the light," i.e., demonstrating the full range of activities available to members of the "Multiliteracy Club." As the light will enable the simpleton to learn whatever he needs to learn, so should the sight of "all the advantages of group membership" render less "impossibly difficult" the task of classroom-based second language learning.

CBI Module III: Luigi Barzini's *The Italians/Gli italiani*

An English/Italian Text as Content

As previously noted, *Buongiorno Italia* replaced an Italian-language history text that had been the backbone of the Italian IM/ML course. It was in an attempt to compensate for the loss of this source of substantive CBI material that I had turned to the use of folk tales as well as aphorisms, proverbs, and popular sayings. I was confident that this new material would in fact fulfill the goal of the IM/ML Program to engage students in "intellectually challenging" activities in a second language. Nevertheless, these activities did very little to broaden students' awareness and understanding of Italian culture and civilization, an equally important objective of the Italian history text.

Once again what seemed initially to seriously compromise the integrity of the content-based component of the course led to the development of a third and novel CBI module. Building on my experience with using English-language readings to stimulate students' reflection on language learning process, I adopted as one of our texts *The Italians*, written in the 1960s by Italian journalist Luigi Barzini. I found the book appealing for several reasons. First, Barzini, who lived for many years in the United States and attended the Columbia School of Journalism, wrote the book in English for an American audience for whom he wished to provide a panoramic sketch of the Italian people, their country, and their culture. Thus, the book had the advantage of being the work of an "insider" who was intimately familiar with the "outsiders" who were his primary audience. Second, Barzini makes no attempt to be comprehensive, choosing instead a number of themes and notable figures around which he develops this portrait of his fellow countrymen. The result is a book that in some ways resembles a centuries-old family album: one that provides the reader with a unique opportunity to learn at least one family member's version of the history of the *"la famiglia Italiani."* Finally, there exists an Italian translation of the book, an indispensable factor given the use to which I planned to put the text.

Implementation

Two very different types of activities were associated with this CBI module: one that focused primarily on subject-matter learning and another which was more properly a form of content-mediated instruction aimed at developing extensive reading skills. The first type, introduced in the first quarter and continued throughout the entire year, saw students using *The Italians* as English-language background reading for lectures/discussions which I prepared using *Gli italiani*. The second type, begun during the second quarter, consisted of exercises intended to develop students' extensive reading skills using photocopies of selected pages of *Gli italiani*.

Subject-Matter Learning Activities

Throughout the year-long course, students would be assigned specific chapters from the text in preparation for a discussion in class. As was the case with the earliest APPS presentations, these discussions were essentially lectures in which paraphrase, gestures, drawing, and impromptu staging were used to ensure student comprehension. As students' speaking skills developed, the lectures became far more interactive as I elicited information from the students about the assigned chapter.

The actual content of the lectures/discussions varied considerably throughout the year, a function both of the content and structure of a given chapter and of students' expanding comprehension and production skills. In the earliest discussions, I planned the content of my lectures to mirror as faithfully as possible the content of the text. These lectures tended to take one of two forms: either a comprehensive, albeit superficial, summary of a chapter or a rather detailed retelling of a short, but evocative, excerpt from the chapter. For example, in a chapter in which Barzini discusses what he calls the four "evil spirits" that plague Italy, i.e., poverty, ignorance, injustice, and fear, my lecture consisted of a brief review of each of the "evil spirits." On the other hand, in chapters built around (in)famous Italians, e.g., Cagliostro, Casanova, Cola di Rienzo, Mussolini, I would often choose to retell an incident which was likely to strike students as bizarre or outrageous. In this way, those students who had already read the chapter would find that their memory of the incident considerably aided their comprehension while those students who had not read the chapter would find the subject matter so stimulating that they might make the effort to follow the story despite their lack of preparation. Such lectures also lent themselves to the impromptu staging that was so successful with the folk tales.

Later in the year, a given discussion could move in any number of directions. As we advanced in the text, I was able to make references and connections to earlier chapters. I began to use information presented in a given chapter to open up discussion on related topics, including drawing parallels between the events and people portrayed in the text with similar events and people in American history.

Whenever possible, I sought to connect the text to the lives of my students, and in particular to the shared experience of the Italian course. For example, in a chapter entitled "The Fatal Charm," Barzini attempts to explain why "all roads lead to Rome," i.e., why "visitors," peaceful and otherwise, have been coming to Italy for centuries. Here then is the ideal moment to talk in simple but powerful terms about all the different "Italies" there are and about which "Italy" might hold the greatest attraction for the students. Who was interested in the Italy of Giotto and Simone Martini or of Michelangelo and Leonardo? The Italy of Chianti and parmigiano or of pasta al pesto and lasagne al forno? The Italy of the Pope and the Vatican or of St. Francis and Assisi? The Italy of the Pantheon and the Colosseum, or of Pompeii and Herculaneum? The Italy of Capri and Portofino or of Venice and Siena? The Italy of Dante and Petrarca or of Marco Polo and

Casanova? While such questions are appropriate to any Italian course, they can take on added significance in a discussion of a text that places American college students of Italian in the context of a millenary phenomenon.

Content-Mediated Skills Development Activities

The reading selections in *Buongiorno Italia* provided students with only limited opportunity to develop reading skills. The readings, when compared to the content-based materials traditionally used in the IM/ML courses, are characterized by extreme brevity, limited vocabulary and structures, and simplicity of the topics. Hence, my Italian students were missing an opportunity to develop the extensive readings skills that facilitate students' access to the kinds of written texts that can make membership in the "Multiliteracy Club" more attractive. Indeed, part of encouraging and facilitating IM/ML students' membership in the "Multiliteracy Club" is teaching them that with extensive background knowledge and effective reading strategies, they can use their nascent second language skills to read highly challenging and stimulating texts that also develop their language skills. It was in an effort then to develop students' extensive reading skills that I created a series of exercises based on selected passages from *Gli italiani*, Barzini's own translation of his book.

Every one or two weeks I would photocopy several pages of the Italian version of the text which students had already been assigned to read in English. In class students would be divided into groups of three, with each group receiving only one photocopy to underscore that this was a collaborative exercise. Using their knowledge of Italian as well as their familiarity with the text in English, each group was asked to translate out loud a given passage. Again, the goal here was not to learn the content itself but to learn how to do this type of reading, i.e., how to integrate prior knowledge, linguistic competence, and reading strategies so as to maximize the comprehensibility of a given text. New groups were formed each time the exercise was carried out to better allow students to observe how and with what success others approached this particular reading task.

After the groups had had sufficient time to discuss, among themselves and in English, their various suggestions for an accurate translation, the class as a whole would listen to individual groups read their proposed translations. I would then open a discussion about the reading/translation itself. For example, I often began by asking to what extent individual group members were already familiar with the text and in what ways this prior knowledge may have affected the translation process. I would ask students to compare how different members of the group handled words and phrases which no one in the group immediately understood, e.g., did someone immediately open a dictionary or did someone suggest that they skip over the word/phrase for the time being and only come back later, if necessary?

Evaluation

Building Community Inside and Outside the Classroom

In attempting a first evaluation of the three CBI modules described in this article, it is important to remember the context in which they were developed. The hybrid first-year Italian course sought to maintain the IM/ML Program's use of content-based instruction as a tool to encourage membership in the so-called "Multiliteracy Club" while at the same time providing skills-based instruction to meet the expectations of students planning to travel and/or study in Italy. Hence the notion of creating a sort of a combined "Italian Language and Literacy Club" which would encourage students to identify with the Italian-spcaking community, its culture, and its language.

In identifying these contributions, it is useful here to distinguish between, on the one hand, the Italian-speaking community that already exists outside and independent of the classroom and, on the other, the Italian-speaking community which develops inside the language classroom itself. The former represents the community which monolingual English-speaking students must ultimately identify with and participate in if they are to become truly multilingual and multiliterate. At the same time, it is identification with the Italian-speaking community as it emerges in the classroom that will propel many students to aspire to membership in the "greater" Italian-speaking community, i.e., the "Italian Language and Literacy Club," that exists beyond the four walls of their classroom. For this reason, I believe it is important to recognize the contributions that the three CBI modules can make to the community-building process both inside and outside the language classroom.

Folks Tales and APPSs

The holistic and interdisciplinary nature of the folk tales and APPS modules clearly extended the range of benefits associated with the "Italian Language and Literacy Club" beyond those demonstrated in the textbook-based, unitary-theme approach to traditional IM/ML courses. The folk tales and APPSs expanded the range of literary forms students were exposed to and opened cultural and philosophical horizons that reached from Eastern Europe to the Far East. The physicality of the impromptu staging combined with an emotionally charged and spiritually infused content made the folk tales and APPSs significant contributions to building the nascent Italian-speaking community in the classroom.

At the same time, the wider range of themes increased the likelihood of students being able to make connections between content they had been exposed to in Italian and their own lives. Since the messages associated with the folk tales and APPSs are, in a sense, universal, their applicability was limitless; indeed, students pointed out to me on more than one occasion that a particular folk tale or APPS came to mind when coming face to face with a problem outside of the Italian class.

Several of the APPSs became the equivalent of popular refrains or inside jokes that groups of students would recite spontaneously when prompted by a particular event or remark. For example, when in the course of a discussion it became clear that we were dealing with someone who was resistant to the notion of reflection as an integral part of study, it was not uncommon for a group of students to recite Confucius on this theme. In this sense, both the APPSs and the folk tales helped shape the "language and culture" of our emergent classroom Italian-speaking community. The APPSs and titles, themes and characters of the folk tales became the classroom equivalent of the "prefabricated routines" so often used by language learners in the early stages of linguistic development. Thus, for example, a student could give voice to her frustration by reciting "ogni inizio è difficile" ("getting started is the hardest part"). Another student who recounted to the class an episode involving a speed violation might be reminded by others "chi va sano, va piano" ("to go slowly is to stay healthy"). Or someone who hesitated to speak in class out of fear of making a mistake would be reassured by others with a choral repetition of "sbagliando s'impara" ("we learn from making mistakes").

Just as a native speaker can be caught off guard when a second language learner unexpectedly produces an appropriate and highly idiomatic expression, so too was I surprised initially when students would spontaneously quote one of the APPSs at a particularly opportune moment. To appreciate the impact of such moments, it is important to keep in mind that students were expected to memorize the APPSs, in part to work on spelling and pronunciation. Consequently, students' speech would make a quantum leap in complexity, accuracy, and fluency whenever they used one of these APPSs, creating occasions in which, for a moment, students recreated **inside** the classroom an aura of the "greater" Italian-speaking community **outside** the classroom to which they were drawing closer.

Finally, the use of APPSs and folk tales helped teach the lesson that students can make their way up through the ranks of the "Italian Language and Literacy Club" by engaging in *any* language-mediated activity in Italian, be it studying Yiddish folk tales, surfing the Internet, or learning how to ski. The last two are by no means hypothetical examples since our third- and fourth-year Italian instructor regularly offers courses on the Internet in Italian and last winter Italian became the fourth language in which students can take skiing classes. (French, Spanish, and German skiing classes have been offered for four years now.)

The Italians/Gli italiani

Each version of Barzini's book made a distinct contribution. The English-language version replaced the Italian-language history text in terms of providing both intellectually challenging and culturally broadening material. Those students who seriously studied the English-language version got both a wider and deeper view of Italian culture than otherwise obtainable from the Italian-language culture readings in *Buongiorno Italia*. Thus, to the extent that *The Italians* offers a rich and nuanced portrait of Italy and the Italians, a text of this sort can constitute an additional enticement for certain students to join the "Italian Language and Literacy Club."

The Italian version, on the other hand, provided a means of showing students how they could continue to develop their Italian-language skills in the future. A lesson students had ample opportunity to learn over and over again during the year was that their ability to understand the Italian lectures and the text was strongly conditioned by their familiarity with the English-language version. For some students, this lesson led to the realization that they could pursue their study of the Italian language by choosing to read texts whose content they were already quite familiar with. One art history major, for example, realized that she could continue to study Italian on her own by reading Italian texts in her area of specialization, Italian Renaissance art. Another student, who was already an avid reader of Primo Levi's poetry in English , got Italian versions of the same poems. Another student went on to read Italian translations of English-language novels they had already read, such as *The Hobbit*. For those students who at the end of the first year were doing independent, content-based reading in Italian, *Gli italiani* was a means of discovering the "power of reading" (Krashen 1993) and, as such, an important stepping stone towards greater involvement in the "Italian Language and Literacy Club."

Conclusion

These three CBI modules have proven to be a highly effective means of introducing content-based instruction into a first-year Italian class. Of particular interest to foreign language teachers is the potential such modules provide to make beginning language classes more intellectually challenging and culturally broadening. Indeed, while most would agree that proficiency in a second language is a valuable tool for general education, the acquisition of that proficiency, especially in the early stages, is often portrayed as lacking in intellectual integrity. By enabling students to engage in the interpretation and application of complex ideas, these modules can help develop students' critical thinking skills. This "intellectualization" of the beginning foreign language classroom helps us foreign language teachers refute the claim that what we do in basic language instruction is essentially preparatory or remedial in nature.

Of course, the intellectualization of beginning language instruction does not benefit the students alone. For those of us who dedicate a considerable amount of time to teaching first- and second-year language courses, an infusion of intellectually challenging texts and activities promotes our own on-going education. I have found the CBI materials I work with—the fables, the APPSs and *Gli italiani*—to be both personally and professionally enriching. Moreover, I am often enlightened by my students' interpretations and applications of the texts. For example, I once presented students with the following Yiddish proverb:

Chi giace a terra non può cadere.
He. who lies on the ground cannot fall down.

I related this proverb to our English saying, "Nothing ventured, nothing gained," with the image of the man lying on the ground representing an extreme case of risk avoidance. Thus, the proverb was intended to be an exhortation to my students to "get off their duff." Much to my surprise, a good number of students understood the man lying on the ground as someone who had already hit "rock bottom" and could fall no further. On those days when a particular classroom activity or homework assignment had left some students feeling as if they were "back to square one," the image of a man now "resting" on the ground was a source of comfort or even a morale booster, as was clear in one student's reflection that, like the man lying on the ground, she too could only go in one direction now—up!

These student-generated interpretations bring me to my concluding observation. While these CBI modules can provide rich intellectual stimulation, they can also exacerbate students' frustration that their ability to speak or write Italian cannot keep up with their ability to understand it. I have written elsewhere (Sternfeld 1985, 1987) that CBI instruction in a beginning language classroom can further widen the gap that naturally develops between students' productive and receptive skills. This widening gap often leads students to conclude that, at best, they are falling behind and, at worst, failing miserably. Students who in a matter of weeks can understand and interpret quotes in Italian from the likes of Gandhi, Proust, Confucius, and Aristotle are confounded by their inability to put together even a relatively simple, grammatically correct utterance in Italian. These students need constant reassurance that it is normal for comprehension to progress more rapidly than production and that progress in all modalities will vary considerably from learner to learner. Thus, while the CBI modules described in this chapter are intended to generate greater interest in membership in the "Language and Literacy Club," there is the risk that fast learners become "early joiners" who can make membership appear inaccessible to slower learners in the class. For this reason, the final proverb that follows is one of the most important I present to the class, a stern reminder of the importance of both perseverance and humility in creating a "Language and Literacy Club" that welcomes **all** students:

> *Tieni sempre in tasca due fogliettini che tirerai fuori a seconda delle esigenze. Sull'uno scrivi <<Il mondo fu creato per me>> e sull'altro <<Non sono altro che cenere e polvere>>.* Always carry two pieces of paper in your pocket to be taken out as needed. On the one write, "For my sake was the world created," and on the other, "I am nothing but ashes and dust."

～◇～

Steven R. Sternfeld is Associate Professor at the University of Utah with a joint appointment in Linguistics and the Department of Languages and Literature. He has taught ESL, French, Spanish, and Italian at the PreK-8 and college levels. His research centers on critical pedagogy and the role of multilingualism, multiliteracy, and multiculturalism in contemporary American society. His interest in CBI grows out of a commitment to curricular innovation as a means of bringing greater integrity and integration to undergraduate education. Address: Linguistics Program, LNCO 2300, University of Utah, Salt Lake City, UT 84112; (E-mail: steven.sternfeld@m.cc.utah.edu)

List of Sources for the Italian Course

Barzini, Luigi. 1964. *The Italians*. New York: Atheneum.

Barzini, Luigi. 1965. *Gli italiani*. Milan, Italy: Arnaldo Mondadori Editore.

Cremona, Joseph. 1987. *Buongiorno Italia*. Saint Paul, MN: EMC Publishing.

Peccianti, M. Cristina. 1994. *Storie della storia d'Italia*. Turin, Italy: Petrini.

Peck, M. Scott. 1987. *The Different Drum: Community Making in Peace*. New York: Simon & Schuster.

Weinreich, Beatrice Silverman, ed. 1992. *Mazel Tov: 178 favolette yiddish*. Milan, Italy: Arnoldo Mondadori.

4

A Course to Convert Czech Proficiency to Proficiency in Serbian and Croatian

Andrew Corin

Editors' Note: Andrew Corin demonstrates how a CBI approach, using task-based techniques and four-handed teaching, can be used to "convert" the proficiency skills of students in one foreign language to an equivalent proficiency in a related foreign language. In this case, Czech is converted to Serbo-Croatian. Programs aimed at accelerated "conversion" from one foreign language to another are not entirely new. They have been employed upon occasion and individual student need at the Foreign Service Institute and the Defense Language Institute for decades. Results obtained by Corin point to the possibility of dramatically reducing classroom hours needed for acquisition of a second or third foreign language when those languages are closely related and programs take into consideration students' linguistic schemata and learning styles. Corin's conversion course is a model of collaboration among a team of language teachers who often use a "four-handed teaching" approach to great advantage. He discusses with insight and clarity many of the core issues that surround CBI in adult education—the use of the first language, text preparation, teacher competencies, student learning styles, and testing for proficiency. General references for this chapter are located in the bibliography at the end of this volume.

Setting

The Defense Language Institute (DLI) in Monterey, California, is one of the largest foreign language education institutions in the world. It provides year-round intensive language training in nearly sixty languages to approximately three thousand United States military personnel. Since 1995 the DLI has been open to enrollment by civilian students on a space available basis. Military students are tested for language aptitude prior to entering the DLI, and their placement in specific languages generally corresponds to their aptitude scores. Not all students will use the language they study in their follow-on assignment; hence, the motivation level is mixed.

Programs of study at the DLI are highly intensive. Students are in class for up to seven hours per day, five days a week, for periods ranging from six months (for languages such as French and Spanish) to sixty-three weeks (for languages such as Korean and Arabic). Classes are relatively small, with no more than ten students per class. Language instructors range from educated native speakers (ILR-5) to native speakers of English who possess at least a "superior" (ILR-3) level of proficiency in the language they teach.

In 1993 the DLI began to conduct intensive courses in Serbian and Croatian.[1] This is a report on one such course conducted over the twelve weeks of June, July, and August 1993. Because of its innovative, indeed experimental, character and the far-reaching implications of some of the lessons which can be drawn from it, this account should be of interest to teachers of many foreign languages. The severe time pressure under which we operated prohibited systematic data gathering on student performance controlled against background, learning style, and instructional technique. These observations must therefore be phrased in the form of impressions requiring both formulation and testing or as hypotheses requiring further experimentation.

The timeframe for basic courses of study at the DLI is one year. The institute's ongoing program in Serbo-Croatian had been discontinued several years prior to this course, with the result that the supply of fully trained Serbian/Croatian linguists in the United States armed forces ceased to be replenished. When it became likely that American units would be deployed in former Yugoslav republics, the military found itself faced with the need to train students in Serbian/Croatian at an accelerated pace. The effective length of the course on which I am reporting was ten weeks, as proficiency testing began in the eleventh week. Despite this limitation, our goal was to develop proficiency sufficient for students to utilize the language in carrying out real-world tasks under demanding and often dangerous conditions. Specific proficiency goals were set at Reading-1+, Listening-1+, and Speaking-1 (using the ILR system).

Students

Our students were forty U.S. Army enlisted personnel. All had previously completed the DLI basic course in Czech. During the course we discovered that their aptitude for language learning varied considerably, as did their learning styles and motivation for learning the language.

Instructors

From the moment when it was informed of the imminent arrival of the forty students, the DLI had two weeks to organize all aspects of the course. The goal was to divide the students into four sections of ten each, with two instructors assigned to each section. Since the DLI's ongoing Serbo-Croatian program had been disbanded several years earlier, an entire team of native-speaker instructors, drawn from a variety of ethnic and dialect backgrounds, had to be hired and prepared to meet this challenge. The entire team was not yet assembled on the first day of classes, but we ultimately built up to a team of seven instructors and a coordinator/course developer (the author of this chapter) who taught in the classroom in addition to his coordinating and course development roles. Aside from the coordinator, only two of the instructors had language-teaching experience, while a third had general pedagogical training.

Course Preparation and Instructor Development

A key to the project's success was a one-week seminar in the foundations of language-teaching methodology, language proficiency, and the task-based and content-based approaches to instruction. The several instructors who joined the course after it began had to be given a much reduced version of the seminar. No instructors taught classes before they had received at least some methodological orientation. The price paid for this seminar was that actual course preparation began on the Friday immediately preceding the Monday on which our students arrived. As a result, when we first met our students, we had little more than a general outline for the course and the first day's materials. On the one hand, the task-based and content-based instructional concepts were our most important resource—in fact, our sole means to achieve the goals which the Army had set in the allotted time. On the other hand, the coordinator had sufficient experience to be able to work up introductory materials in the three available days. Throughout the course we underwent a constant process of adjusting our daily schedule and activities, as well as a daily process of materials development to which the instructors contributed more and more as their expertise developed. After a month of instruction, a second one-day seminar was held in order to fine-tune techniques and correct deficiencies.

Other contributors to this volume have also faced the need to train novice language teachers for participation in content-based instructional programs, and in general have devised similar responses to this need. Note in particular the comments of Klee and Tedick in Chapter 7 of this volume.

Materials

Virtually none of the usual study materials were available for this course. The students had no textbooks. Older versions of the Army's *Basic Course in Serbo-Croatian* were available, as was a test version of a newer Foreign Service Institute text, but these were judged to be unsuitable: the content of the Army materials was quite outdated, and both texts imposed a traditional classroom-type approach based on successive lessons to be studied over an extended period of time. With little more than two months in which to prepare our students to perform actual military tasks using standard Serbian and Croatian, such restrictive materials simply could not be used. No reference grammar was available to students. Small pocket dictionaries became available only in the second half of the course. We did have a very limited number of newspapers and magazines from Serbia and Montenegro on current subscription at the DLI library, as well as that library's small and woefully outdated but, nevertheless, useful reference and monograph collection. We also had access to daily SCOLA broadcasts of television news from Zagreb and Belgrade, the capitals of Croatia and Serbia, respectively. (See Appendix A for details concerning SCOLA.) Aside from these, the only materials available came from the instructors' and coordinator's personal collections. Our largest stroke of luck was that one other Serbian and Croatian course based on similar principles (though consisting of a combination of Russian conversion students and semi-native speakers) was already underway under the coordination of Dr. Michael Vezilich. Dr. Vezilich was able to brief the coordinator of our course on the content areas which would normally be covered in a DLI course, and graciously made available materials, including newspaper articles and excerpts from books and magazines, which he and his instructors were developing. Without his assistance and collaboration the course could not have achieved as much as it did.

Methods and Strategies

The obvious disproportion between the goals of the course and our resources (including the mere ten weeks allotted to the course) dictated strategies and specific methods. Since our students had studied another Slavic language and there was obviously no time for a thorough introduction to the grammar,[2] the general strategies chosen were *conversion* and *immersion*. The classroom methods chosen were *task-based* and *content-based* instruction. Content-based instruction is a standard component of DLI courses; however, a heavy emphasis on task-based instruction is not.

Task-based instruction is to be understood in the sense of Krahnke (1987, 57-63). It utilizes activities which learners might have to perform for noninstructional purposes as opportunities for language learning (this is a slight adaptation of the wording in Krahnke). In task-based instruction, language, per se, is not taught, but is learned as needed for the completion of the task. According to Krahnke, the strategy behind this approach involves an attempt to compel students to apply higher order thinking skills to a combination of new and old information.

By *conversion* I mean that students already had set in their minds a grammar and vocabulary in most respects congruent with that of the target language. Rather than teaching students the target grammar and vocabulary, we immediately exposed them to normal native usage, set them to work on communicative tasks, and began the course with content-based instruction, assuming that, over time, they would, literally, convert their Czech proficiency into Serbian/Croatian proficiency. It must be pointed out that our assumptions concerning students' proficiency in Czech (at or near level 3 in all skills) were not in all cases borne out. Though we did not have access to our students' Czech proficiency scores, we learned through conversation with students that some were either poorly motivated or had, for some other reason, not performed well in the DLI Czech language course.

By *immersion* I mean use of only the target language in all activities from the outset of the course. Compelling students to formulate and test hypotheses about effective communication in Serbian/Croatian, with success gauged by reactions to actual attempts at communication, was considered imperative as the quickest and most effective means for discovering and mastering Czech-Serbian/Croatian correspondences. We assumed students' proficiency in all normal linguistic skills in Czech, and their ability to begin immediately the process of substituting Serbian/Croatian items for Czech, and to make adjustments where the lexical and grammatical systems of the two languages were not congruent.

The overall communicative strategy was envisioned as a spiral-type recycling through sequences of ever more complex skills (e.g., the active skills of naming, description, narration, and, to the extent possible, argumentation) at ever higher levels. In working with any given topic, we would begin our activities with the most simple (e.g., naming), and work gradually toward more complex tasks. The specific choice of tasks would vary from one topic to the next, but they would always be ordered so as to reflect this progression in level of complexity. Repeating the series of ever more complex tasks over and over in connection with various topics created a cyclic process in which successive cycles were performed at ever higher levels of proficiency, thus creating the upward spiral. Over time, as students increased their proficiency in the types of tasks at each step in the series, the specific tasks assigned would become more demanding; that is to say, a descriptive task assigned toward the end of the course would be more demanding than a descriptive task assigned three weeks earlier, which would itself be more demanding than one assigned near the beginning of the course. Conversely, where a task assigned late in the course was not intrinsically more demanding than one assigned several weeks earlier, we would nevertheless demand and expect a higher level of performance.

Due to the overall inexperience of the teaching team and experimental nature of the conversion method itself, this general plan could not be consistently followed, especially in the earlier portions of the course. When it was, however, it proved strikingly successful. (The advantages of spiraled instructional sequences are also discussed by other contributors to this volume, for example Ryding and Stowasser in Chapter 5, Vines in Chapter 6, and Stryker in Chapter 8.)

The primary classroom methods—task-based and content-based instruction—are related and in many cases overlap. They share the assumption that language learning is most effective when higher cognitive processes are brought into play and the target language is used to analyze and interact with the real world. (For a recent discussion of some of the theoretical underpinnings of this assumption and practical motivations for it, see Williams et al. 1994). For proper implementation both methods require an awareness of language-teaching methodology beyond what would be expected of a novice teacher. It was in this respect that we faced our greatest challenge: due to teacher inexperience in the beginning, the task-based/content-based approach was not applied in a consistent and skillful manner, but by the end of the course, most instructors were developing an ability to apply the methods productively.

Content Areas

DLI courses typically involve instruction in the geography, history, economics, politics, and culture associated with the target language, as well as in military affairs. We spent a seemingly disproportionate amount of time on geography (three of the ten weeks); however, this was deemed appropriate since it is crucial for effective functioning abroad, and can be understood and discussed at a relatively low proficiency level. All instruction was supported by—indeed based on—authentic materials ranging from tourist guidebooks and maps to articles from the daily and periodic press, articles from reference works and technical journals (e.g., on military science), railway timetables, and, of course, SCOLA (see Appendix A). In short, we utilized whatever was available. In only a few instances did we utilize contrived "pedagogical" materials. Each team of instructors was free to develop its own approach to classroom application of content area materials, though under the directive to remain within the task-based framework to the greatest extent possible.

Daily Schedule

At the beginning we devoted two hours each day to our current content area (geography, history, etc.) and one or two hours each to the popular press and conversation (bearing in mind that "conversation" classes were often based on articles from the press), with one hour for SCOLA, for a total of six organized hours of instruction. As was the case with content area materials, each team of instructors was free to develop its own lesson plans. A seventh hour (usually that immediately following lunch) was designated a "processing" hour for individual study with an instructor available to answer questions or lead whatever discussions might arise spontaneously. The processing hour was the sole period in which English was allowed, though the use of Serbian/Croatian was encouraged.

Teaming and Rotation of Instructors

Instructors were teamed in pairs to reflect, to the extent possible, a variety of dialects, ethnic backgrounds, and teaching styles. At two- or three-week intervals, teams of instructors were rotated to a different group of students, so as to broaden exposure. Whenever possible, "four-handed" teaching was encouraged, and when the two instructors complemented each other, the results justified the additional expense in time and energy. (Note the similar conclusions of Stryker in Chapter 8.) Given the emphasis on task-based instruction, students spent considerable time working in small groups. In such instances, having two roving problem solvers often made the difference between the small groups receiving adequate facilitation or inadequate facilitation in completing their tasks. Also, instructors with varying expertise (content vs. language, one dialect vs. another, one generation vs. another, training or experience in one profession vs. another) could complement each other when both were simultaneously present in the classroom. The participation of more than one instructor was especially valuable in projects involving role playing (e.g., car search and first aid activities), in which observation of students engaged in disparate activities was crucial and a single instructor could not attend to all students simultaneously. In analyzing SCOLA news broadcasts, the interaction of differing expertise and experience in commenting on the content, tone and language of reports and their accompanying film clips added an engaging intellectual aspect to what could otherwise be a rather dry exercise. Among the most useful four-handed techniques involved allowing pairs of instructors to interact with each other in situational role playing so as to provide living examples of extemporaneous conversation which could then become the focus of classroom discussion or emulation. It was unfortunate only that four-handed techniques could not be applied consistently. Instructors were expected to teach several hours each day, but none could teach every hour because of the need for lesson planning and materials preparation. Had more time been available for preliminary course preparation, and had a more experienced team of instructors been available (or at least had there been more time for instructor training), the number of class sessions with two instructors could have been increased. For an elaboration of the approach to four-handed teaching utilized in our course, see Goroshko and Slutsky (1993); also note the comments of Stryker in Chapter 8 in this volume.

Projects

The incongruity between our classroom setting and the real-life tasks which students might soon have to perform quickly became apparent. The problem seemed especially acute because we had reason to believe that some of these students would be deployed without having an opportunity for advanced specialized study. In order to meet the need to perform in specific real-life situations to benefit general language acquisition, and as the epitome of the task-based approach, we introduced a system of projects or activities based on real-world premises. We began in the second week with an exercise in which students prepared, using whatever maps, slides, tourist guides, and instructors' personal knowledge we could muster, a plan for a unit to deploy to Mostar, the historical, political, and economic center of Hercegovina, and occupy it as part of a UN or NATO peacekeeping force. This was essentially a level 0+ to level 2 task for all skills, but had enough facets to generate genuine interest. Moreover, as was already clear at that time (and as events have since borne out), this was an undertaking which NATO or UN military forces seemed very likely to have to actually carry out. Motivation among the students was therefore high.

Tasks included identifying the least dangerous roads from the Dalmatian ports to the city of Mostar capable of supporting heavy military vehicles (such as sixty-ton tanks) and the routes which those roads followed, locating major strategic objects such as approaches to the city, main thoroughfares, bridges and other crucial infrastructure (the Neretva River runs through the center of Mostar), major political and social institutions in the town, basic demographics, and deployment of forces (including numbers and types of forces required, locations of roadblocks, etc.). The students were assigned to small groups, each of which sought information in one thematic area, prepared a concise document, and then briefed the larger group.

A pattern which emerged in this exercise and which we made considerable use of later was a reliance on the students' professional training. As trained military personnel, some students already knew the types of information which were required, others knew the best way to organize activity in small groups, while yet others knew how to organize and conduct a briefing. Thus, while the team of instructors gave the initial impetus and guidelines for the exercise, it was to a certain extent "self-propelled."

By the middle of the course, we had made group and individual projects a regular activity, with at least one hour devoted to them each day. We actively solicited suggestions and detailed plans for projects from students and utilized projects as a way to allow students, to the greatest possible extent, to self-design the course to meet their specific needs. Some of the more successful were preparations for and execution of a road block and car search exercise in which students manned the road block and instructors (as well as a few unsuspecting passers-by) played the role of drivers with various contrived and genuine circumstances (see Appendix B); first aid and medical evacuation exercises in which some students played the role of wounded or injured personnel, others the personnel attempting to aid them, and yet others hospital dispatchers (Appendix C); and interrogation (Appendix D). In short, as the course progressed, we approached ever closer the concept of preparing for and performing regular army training exercises in the target language, to the extent that this could be done given our daily schedule and logistics, and in an environment without security clearances. Other cultural projects such as cooking were also carried out.

An important pedagogical corollary of the emphasis on projects with real-life premises is that the classroom became less the locus of language study and more a *training facility* for language-learning exercises in which we prepared students to carry out certain activities and later debriefed them on the outcomes and carried out problem solving and further training preparatory to trying the activities again. Though the extent to which this shift actually took place during this single ten-week course was limited, we did achieve the experience necessary to carry it out more consistently in a future course.

The concept of projects elaborated here is closely related to that of "bridges" (between the classroom and the real world) described by Stevick (1996) and mentioned by Chadran and Esarey in Chapter 10) of this volume. Of course, bridges to the real world can take many forms. A unique example can be found in the reflective component (based on aphorisms, proverbs, and popular sayings) of Sternfeld's Italian course (Chapter 3 of this volume), which treats the real-world problems encountered by a community of students struggling to attain membership in the "Italian Language and Literacy Club."

Student Scores

Oral proficiency ratings at the eleventh-week testing were:

2 students:	3
1 student:	2+
11 students:	2
17 students:	1+
9 students:	1

Reading scores on the Defense Language Proficiency Test (DLPT) were:

1 student:	2+
5 students:	2
18 students:	1+
16 students:	1

Listening scores on the DLPT were:

1 student:	2+
1 student:	2
10 students:	1+
21 students:	1
7 students:	0+

These scores were based on the ILR scale. Oral proficiency scores were based on an interview with no fewer than two testers. The overall outcomes were quite encouraging. None of the forty students failed to meet the program goal of speaking level 1. The two students receiving a score of 3 were retested by different testers in order to validate this unexpectedly high result. Their second interviews also resulted in scores of 3. Reading and listening scores appeared to be encouraging as well (program goals had been set at 1+); however, these scores cannot be considered to reflect students' actual proficiency levels, as this was the first large-scale application of the DLPT Version II test for Serbo-Croatian. For security reasons, neither instructors nor administrators in the Czech to Serbian/Croatian conversion course had access to either the test itself or the data on which it was calibrated. The experience of one educated native-speaker instructor who took a nonclassified preparatory version of the test and received inappropriately low scores led us to suspect that realistic scores might have been somewhat higher.

Lessons Learned

The outcomes in terms of proficiency ratings should be viewed against the limitations which we faced in preparing and conducting the course, as well as our lack of information concerning students' proficiency in Czech at the outset of the course. One cannot escape the conclusion that with adequate time for course and materials preparation, and instructor development, and especially taking into consideration the lessons of this first attempt at a large-scale conversion course, a significantly higher and perhaps more consistent outcome could be achieved in the same ten-week period using the same general methodological principles. It is this prospect, as well as the fact that in such an intensive environment we were able to observe effects of various instructional strategies that would have escaped notice in a more leisurely course, which endows the lessons of this course with special interest. It must especially be noted that, based on our experience, the optimal outcome in a conversion course would result from a radical break with certain time-honored principles of instruction in Slavic (and, to be sure, most other languages). Among these are the central role of a textbook and the use of a classroom as the primary locus of instruction.

The Conversion Principle

The most general conclusion would be that the conversion approach works. However, it seems reasonable to hypothesize that in a relatively short conversion course of the type which we conducted, potential outcomes are inevitably limited by proficiency in the previous (already-known) language. In short, students do not enter the course as equals; therefore, the base-line goal for any student should be successful conversion to the same level of proficiency which exists or existed in the previous language. We were wrong to assume that all of our students had a fully functional Czech grammar, and we were unrealistic in setting our goals absolutely at Reading and Listening-1+, and Speaking-1.

The conversion approach forced us to deal with students' learning styles in a novel manner. The "traditional" textbook course is based on study of grammatical structure through exercises and vocabulary-building through memorization, with an admixture of communicative activity. Analytical learners flourish in such an environment (at least in terms of their perceptions of successful learning), while global learners are subject to frustration and the perception of an inordinately difficult task. The conversion/immersion approach dictates an opposite orientation. This is the optimal environment for a global learner. Analytical learners feel frustrated by the demand to communicate using structures which they do not completely control. A great deal of frustration would have been avoided in our course had reference grammars and good dictionaries been available from the start, at least for those who could benefit from their use. A certain admixture of analytical study, instituted especially in the second half of the course, did prove beneficial for some students. Toward the end of the course, in response to demand, we instituted classes in translation of sophisticated journalistic prose articles into English. Not only did this result in an immediate lessening of tensions, but it also yielded for some students a rapid improvement in their ability to accurately assess the information contained in such articles.

Another striking observation is that use of computerized grammatical exercises of the noncontextualized or marginally contextualized variety resulted in rapid and noticeable increases in accuracy on the part of some students (though, unfortunately, not measurable in our circumstances). The obvious hypothesis would be that it is the analytical learners who benefited from these exercises. It also became clear that an admixture of explicit grammatical discussion is useful, though we reached no conclusions as to the most effective means of doing this without sacrificing the conversion/immersion principle. (Note the similar conclusions reached by Stryker in Chapter 8 of this volume.) The overall lesson for dealing with varying learning styles would be that while insisting on task- and content-based organization of the course, it is necessary to employ a sufficient admixture of analytic-type activities to meet the needs of this type of student, and to avoid simply reversing the type of prejudice which has existed in "traditional" analytic-type courses. (Of course, consideration for learning styles in course design goes far beyond the "global" vs. "analytical" distinction employed here. For example, on the relation between learning style, on the one hand, and personality type and in-coming proficiency level, on the other, see Stryker's comments in Chapter 8 and note the articulated model of learner types incorporated into the FSI Indonesian course by Chadran and Esarey in Chapter 10.)

A further serious implication of the success or potential of the conversion approach concerns graduate-level courses in a second Slavic language. (Analogous considerations certainly apply to graduate programs in other languages.) Since the conversion approach promises more rapid development of proficiency in students with the necessary background, it should be strongly favored in graduate-level language programs. The benefit to the students is obvious, while institutions may save money by attaining a satisfactory outcome from fewer terms of instruction. The negative effect of instituting conversion as the principle for teaching second Slavic (Romance, Germanic, etc.) languages would be that it would eliminate the enrollment of true beginners. Such enrollments, especially those of what are currently referred to as "heritage learners," play a major role in justifying the expense of courses in so-called minor languages.

The Task-Based Approach

The basic motivation for this approach is well-known: by involving so-called higher level cognitive skills in language learning, we achieve a more permanent, less ephemeral learning, especially where it is possible to generate genuine interest in a task. In our experience, the combination of content- and task-based instruction did indeed have this effect (i.e., of stimulating genuine interest in course material). It should be borne in mind that not all tasks which generated interest were necessarily connected to content-based instruction. For example, a unit on using personal ads from a magazine, culminating in compilation by each student of a personal ad (seeking companionship) and an attempt by the group to determine which student had authored each ad, generated a most animated response and effective, innovative language use from most students.

Implications of the task-based approach go far beyond its application in a conversion course or in a content-based curriculum, and can be linked to the preconditions for successful communicative activity in any elementary course. Specifically, as a precondition for communicative activity, it is necessary to get the skeleton of the grammar (i.e., the major structures necessary for simple sentence formation) introduced as quickly as possible. In the conversion environment this is not an issue, since we assume control of a linguistic system related and congruent to that of the target language. However, for a nonconversion elementary course, rapid introduction of the skeleton of the grammar must be made a major principle of course organization. An approach which, for example, introduces the case system of a Slavic language gradually across the entire first year makes a task-based approach with its associated benefits impossible at the elementary level, or at least introduces artificial limitations which will unnecessarily handicap any effort at communicative activity. In a language like Serbian/ Croatian, a "first pass" through the case system must be completed early in the first term.

Textbooks

It is time to recognize that the primary resource for language teaching is the instructor, not the textbook. An integrated course textbook, after all, is fundamentally a record of how some instructor has organized his or her course. To support its claim to universal applicability for some large class of learners (e.g., high school students, second-year college students), it may indeed contain supplementary exercises or activities from which instructors are expected to choose. Such a textbook may provide a valuable reference, but when employed by another instructor as a course syllabus, it inevitably robs the course of spontaneity and the instructor of the opportunity to tailor the course to needs of a particular group of students and to harness his or her own talents and inclinations. This is true even if the textbook being used is itself based on authentic materials. The testing results from our course suggest that not only can one do without an integrated course text, but if (hopefully current) authentic materials are available and are skillfully utilized, the gain in flexibility and spontaneity, augmented by the increased possibility of generating genuine interest in the content of course materials, can make possible a rate of proficiency growth beyond that which is usual in a textbook-based course.

Incompatibility of content-based instruction with a textbook-based course design is noted explicitly also by Leaver (Chapter 2). Our own solution to the question of basic instructional materials is in fact very similar to the "texts" described by Klahn for her Spanish course at Columbia University (Chapter 9).

Implications of a reorientation away from textbooks as a basis for course organization are, to be sure, far-reaching, though they are really no more than corollaries of what is already known about the components of effective language teaching. One of the most important of these concerns is the time devoted to daily lesson planning. Any experienced instructor can "wing" a class, but it is a challenging and time-consuming process to build into a daily plan: 1) an appropriate curve of complexity, 2) oscillation in pacing (fast-slow-fast), 3) preparation of students for each task and, most importantly, 4) definition of the goals for each class and appropriate activities to meet those goals. In a non-textbook-based course even more time must be spent on materials and class preparation, though the payback is significant. (Chadran and Esarey, for example, note that more than 250 hours were necessary for the development of the original four content-based modules for their FSI course in Indonesian.) One obvious inference to be drawn from this is that language is best taught by someone who can devote his or her full energy to that job (i.e., not professors). Though it is obvious and unavoidable, this conclusion entails certain unpleasant consequences for higher educational institutions, as well as potentially dire consequences for some small academic disciplines. Most directly, dependence on dedicated language instructors (lecturers) for language instruction requires additional hiring. By the same token, however, being "freed" from the burden of language instruction leaves researchers in some small scholarly disciplines, who had traditionally depended on language instruction to justify their presence on campus and thus "pay" for their research, without an economic raison d'être. A case in point is the field of Slavic linguistics, which finds itself at the present time being squeezed by a variety of factors, one of the most important of these being the rise of applied linguistics.

At the same time, there is a tension between, on the one hand, the conclusion that language instruction should be left to dedicated language instructors and, on the other hand, the need for instructors, at least at the higher educational level, who possess a specialized knowledge of the structure of the language. It is (in the Slavic field, but very likely in others as well) professors with a linguistic specialization who establish the model of the syntax, morphology, sound system, and orthography of a language which will be adopted and referred to by instructors at all levels. There is therefore a need for interaction, somewhere in the institutionalized framework of instruction in a given language, between specialists in structure and specialists in instruction. This need can best be met in a university department containing both types of expertise.

In the absence of a textbook, which contains someone else's articulation of the grammar, an instructor is left to his or her own background in deciding how to structure the course and schedule the introduction and discussion of structural (grammatical) topics. Clearly, then, a move away from textbooks as a basis for course organization entails a dual need—on the one hand, a necessity that training in language pedagogy include a strong component in the structure of the target language, and on the other hand, a requirement for reference grammars designed to meet the needs of instructors and students in a non-textbook-based course.

Thus, all other things being equal (though of course they never are), the ideal language instructor is one for whom this (as opposed to scholarly research) is a full-time occupation, who is trained in language-teaching methodology, and has a solid grounding in the structure of the language (e.g., for Slavic languages an M.A. in Russian or Slavic linguistics). The worst outcome of language teaching can be predicted for an instructor who lacks any of these characteristics. Small colleges and small university departments will feel uncomfortable with this point of view because of their need to maintain staffing in the traditional literary specializations, but it is no more than a restatement of what is otherwise known about effective language teaching, given new impetus here by the opportunity to put into effect principles of course organization that promise to yield a superior ratio of outcome to time of study. There is, after all, nothing new in emphasizing the benefits (to a language curriculum!) of having language instructors concentrate their full energies on that occupation.

Nevertheless, in the absence of textbooks, we require, especially in order to meet the needs of analytical learners, reference grammars structured so as to correspond to their intended use. A project to identify the attributes of a useful reference grammar and to produce such grammars for languages in which they currently do not exist, would allow instructors to devote a maximum of energy to course organization, materials development, and daily lesson planning, and a maximum of classroom time to communicative activities.

The Classroom as the Locus of Instruction

Virtually every language course is conducted in a classroom. Excursions are apt to be exceptional or indeed rare, except in study abroad courses. One might argue that outside the target culture this is unavoidable. Our experience at the DLI suggests another approach (the following remarks are foreshadowed, in a more tentative way, by Krahnke 1987, 57-63). Over the course of the ten weeks, our attitude gradually shifted from one of using the classroom as the locus of training toward one of using it as a "home base" where we prepare for training exercises which simulate real life. Of course, some analytical activities, such as analysis of newspaper articles and news broadcasts, must inevitably remain linked to a classroom environment, and did so in our course. In fact, in the final analysis only a small proportion of student time was spent out of the classroom and even a majority of projects were carried out in a converted classroom. Nevertheless, to the extent that our *attitude* changed from one of conducting a classroom course to one of conducting a program of practical training for which we do some classroom training, not only did morale and interest in language acquisition increase, but students did indeed rapidly develop the ability to deal with real or simulated situations out of proportion to what could be expected of first-year students regardless of previous experience with a related language. For example, in both the car search and first aid exercise (see Appendixes B and C), students successfully carried out simulated military tasks in an environment in which complex perceptual and information gaps were built in.

This result is not unexpected. First, military personnel typically use a classroom only when necessary to prepare for training, actual training exercises being conducted in as realistic a setting as possible. It should not be surprising, therefore, that our students felt confined when restricted to a classroom chair and felt relieved when they were able to perform in a more realistic setting.

Second, learning to coordinate linguistic performance, on the one hand, with physical activity, evaluation of situations, and decision making, on the other, allowed students to work their way through part of the "language shock" which is usually encountered upon first contact with the target culture. For example, in the car search exercise, it was relatively easy to learn necessary phrases in the classroom. However, students also needed to know that attention to language and grammar would be only one consideration in facing a potentially life-threatening environment when they actually put these phrases to use in the field. Moreover, linguistic performance had to be coordinated with other physical activities, such as walking, aiming a rifle, etc. In such a situation one got a much more realistic (and, I might add, modest) assessment of the degree of language acquisition which had taken place in classroom training prior to the field exercise. Understandably, linguistic tasks that could be successfully performed in the field exercise were far more likely to be retained, given both the greater degree of mastery which such performance indicated, and also the fact that the linguistic knowledge became interconnected with a far broader range of associations.

Third, the project-based approach, entailing an abandonment of the idea that language learning is primarily a classroom activity, represents no more than a distillation of the task-based approach. The same considerations which would lead us to predict an increased rate of acquisition using task-based instruction would lead us to predict a maximal rate of acquisition using a project-based approach. As already noted, the classroom, with its blackboards, overhead projectors, and assorted other accouterments, remains an invaluable tool. All I am suggesting is that it is time to reevaluate its function in the language training process.

The general lesson to be drawn from this discussion is that the most effective language learning is that which uses the classroom not as the primary locus of language learning activities, but rather as a laboratory and training facility for proficiency-building exercises to be carried out in "real-world" contexts in which linguistic and nonlinguistic performance must interact. An anecdote from the course may help to understand the benefits of this approach. One month into the course a student was in the coordinator's office when the telephone rang. Since the coordinator was not present, the student answered the telephone and took a short message for him. The person leaving the message was the coordinator's sister-in-law calling from Belgrade. Since she had expected to address the coordinator in Serbo-Croatian, the conversation was conducted in that language. What is most striking is not the fact that the student was able to master a linguistic task of this level following only four weeks of study, nor that the coordinator's sister-in-law assumed within the confines of this short conversation that she was addressing a native speaker of Serbo-Croatian, it is rather that the student reacted with no apparent surprise and no hesitation.

Testing

Though DLI courses usually include regular quizzing and testing, in our context this was impossible and indeed undesirable. It was precluded both by the severe time constraint for reaching our goals (ten weeks of instruction before the beginning of proficiency testing), and because no two sections of students (they were divided into four sections of ten students each) were exposed to exactly the same material. The goal of the course was to *build* proficiency through continual *reinforcement* of proficiency, using materials which, to the greatest extent possible, would be of intrinsic interest to our students. We had few goals which could be stated in terms of specific knowledge. We were aware, of course, that oral proficiency interviewers would have expectations concerning, say, certain sets of vocabulary items which represent a "litmus test" for "graduation" from level 0 to 0+ and 1, and we made certain that no student failed to pass some threshold on account of a minor gap in vocabulary. Otherwise, we were oriented throughout toward the building of *skills*. During the eighth week of instruction we conducted mock DLPT testing in order to gauge progress and identify weaknesses while there was still time to correct them. During the two weeks between mock testing and real testing, we did make several changes in order to ensure optimal outcomes. For example, we separated out for special assistance two students who were still at the 0 level of oral proficiency. We also increased the quantity of situational role playing and analytical exercises, such as analysis of the syntax of complex journalistic prose (among the most difficult styles in most Slavic languages) and instituted a program in which, each afternoon, students could choose from a variety of courses those which they felt best met their individual needs.

It is safe to conclude that a task-based and content-based conversion course requires new models for evaluating performance, but these remain to be devised and explored. (As was the case with our conclusions concerning the role of the classroom in the instructional process, this issue is noted already in Krahnke 1987, 62.)

Though there has been considerable discussion of testing in a content-based instructional environment (most notably in the contributions to the present volume), the suggested models or techniques are not necessarily appropriate to a task-based methodology. While a content-based evaluation could, in principle, take the form of a traditional pen-and-paper test of the essay or fill-in variety (though of course this need not be the case), in task-based testing such an approach would be excluded. Task-based testing would optimally be administered by testers with training similar to, but nevertheless distinct from, that of oral proficiency interviewers. These testers could be expected to observe both the performance (process) of activities and the products derived from them, probably with less interaction than is the case in an oral proficiency interview. The question of task-based testing must first be addressed on its own terms, and the answer to it then reconciled with the demands of a content-based curriculum.

Given the obvious difficulty of quantifying proficiency or proficiency gain within the context of most academic (secondary school or college-university) courses, even such fundamental questions as the basis of grading in such courses remain open. Whether grades in a task-based/content-based course should reflect (a) skills in carrying out certain tasks and (b) knowledge of the content area, or whether some measure of specific linguistic knowledge and effort should provide the basis of a course grade, inevitably depends on our ability to relate these skills and this knowledge, respectively, to a scale of language proficiency.

Admittedly, this problem does not arise in institutions such as the DLI and the FSI, where the performance of a homogeneous group of learners can be related to the demands of their specific jobs. In adapting content-based and task-based methodology to the academic environment, however, it takes on crucial importance. Given the type of materials which are most likely to be used in such a course, we should especially note Sternfeld's admonition (Chapter 3) that "Traditional notions of success and failure become problematic in a course where students are continually exposed to both language and content that they cannot, nor are they expected to, fully understand, let alone in any sense master." In fact, it is far from obvious that a course grade on the A-F scale has any relevance in a proficiency-based language course. In addressing these issues, it should be borne in mind that it is, ultimately, proficiency—the ability of students to perform a range of tasks and the degree of their facility in performing them—which is the final measure of a student's or a course's success.

Endnotes

1. Throughout this chapter I refer eclectically to Serbian and Croatian, Serbian/Croatian, and Serbo-Croatian. As early as 1974 most Croats had begun to refer to the "Croatian literary language," while in Serbia since 1991 the term "Serbian literary language" has been current. At least until 1991 most instructors and researchers outside Yugoslavia referred to a

unified Serbo-Croatian (or Croato-Serbian) literary language. Today, the DLI refers to these languages as Serbian and Croatian. The two standard languages or varieties are at the present time diverging, especially at the lexical level, though for all intents and purposes mutual intelligibility remains, as does virtually identical phonology (though the standard prosody, based on a Hercegovinian model, is especially difficult to maintain in Croatian cultural centers) and overlap in a majority of morphological, syntactic, and orthographic features. Still, the degree of syntactic divergence between the two standards has yet to be fully explored.

2. Given the confusion which exists in the pedagogical literature concerning use of the term "grammar" (for a survey of the problem see Garrett 1986), let me emphasize that in this chapter I use the term to refer to the system of patterns which any proficient speaker of a language can be said to have mastered. I do not use the term to refer to explicit statements of the nature of these patterns or to judgments concerning the "acceptable" vs. "substandard" status of this or that form. The only exception to this rule will be in mention of "reference grammars," which are concise statements of the main patterns which must be mastered by students, presented in a non-syllabus-type format.

⸻

Andrew Corin has taught practical, structural, and linguistic courses in Russian and Serbo-Croatian at the University of California, Los Angeles, the University of Southern California, and the Defense Language Institute. By training he is a specialist in Slavic linguistics, the South Slavic languages, and the cultural history of the South Slavs, and has published and lectured widely in all of these areas. He holds a diploma from Belgrade University and an M.A. and Ph.D. from UCLA. Formerly a coordinator of the Czech-to-Croatian-and-Serbian program at the Defense Language Institute, he is currently a Lecturer in the Department of Slavic Languages and Literatures at UCLA. Address: 1937 Loyola Court, Claremont, CA 91711 (E-mail: corin@humnet.ucla.edu; corin@ucla.edu; ARKcorin@aol.com)

List of Appendixes

Appendix A:

Information concerning the programs transmitted by Satellite Communications for Learning (SCOLA)

Appendix B:

A description of the seven activities that comprised the Car Search Exercise

Appendix C:

A description of the First Aid and Medical Evacuation Exercise

Appendix D:

A description of the Interrogation Exercise

Note: Acknowledgment of the students who played crucial roles in the design of the exercises in Appendixes B, C, and D above is omitted for security considerations.

Appendix A
Satellite Communications for Learning (SCOLA)

The following information is reproduced from SCOLA's home page (Summer, 1997). Further information, including current programming schedules, can be found on the World Wide Web at: http://www.scola.org/

SCOLA (Satellite Communications for Learning) is a nonprofit educational consortium that receives and retransmits television programming in their original languages from more than 40 different countries. These programs are transmitted via satellite to schools, colleges, universities, government and military installations, cable TV systems, independent TV stations, businesses, and private individuals throughout North America and much of the Northern Western Hemisphere. SCOLA operates two 24-hour satellite channels with more in the planning stages.

Channel 1: News programs from approximately thirty-five different countries in their national or regional languages.

Channel 2: Variety, entertainment, and the arts from approximately ten different countries (changes occur monthly as we get rights to more varied programming).

Channel 3: China Channel offers programming from the People's Republic of China (Mainland China). The programming is in Mandarin for the most part. Programs deal with Education, News, Documentaries, Literature, Travel, Poetry, and Leisure Time. Programming subject to change without notice.

Channel 4 (future): Courses and classes in many disciplines produced by each country or participating colleges/universities (French Philosophy, Russian Physics, Chinese Confucianism, Japanese Math, etc.).

Channel 5 (future): Classes in the speaking of less commonly taught languages (Chinese, Swahili, Czech, Lakota Indian, Arabic, etc.).

Channels 4 and 5 will be followed by live electronic study halls allowing for interactive teaching and learning.

Reception is via satellite system (dish and receiver) or through your local cable system if they're affiliated or through a local over-the-air broadcaster who is affiliated. SCOLA is C-Band Digital using the Wegener DVR-95 or DVR-96 compression system (MPEG I).

SCOLA can be contacted at:

E-Mail:	scola@creighton.edu
Phone:	(712) 566-2202
Fax:	(712) 566-2502
Address:	PO Box 619, McClelland, IA 51548-0619

Appendix B
Car Search Exercise

Module A. Activity Overview

A search is usually performed by at least two persons. Once the vehicle has come to a halt, two soldiers stand in front of it. They ask the person(s) in the vehicle to get out. The occupants are directed to open the trunk and hood, and then to stand approximately ten to fifteen meters behind the vehicle with their backs to the checkpoint. The inspectors approach the front of the vehicle. One inspects high and goes clockwise, one inspects low and goes counterclockwise. When the inspectors reach the doors, they stand in front of them as they open them. This is done so that if there is an explosion the door will shield the inspector.

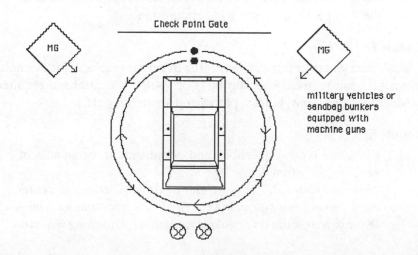

Check Point Gate

MG

MG

military vehicles or
sandbag bunkers
equipped with
machine guns

If a bomb or suspicious material is found, the inspectors do not attempt to remove it or even to touch it. E.O.D. (expert ordnance disposal) is called. The vehicle's driver and passengers are then arrested.

The activity must be conducted in a large open area out of doors, such as a parking lot. In each exercise four students perform. Two play the role of inspectors, and two the role of armed guards. Guards carrying rifles may replace the machine guns. The remaining students should gather around at a safe distance and observe the performance critically.

Remaining modules are developed by small groups of students with the advice of their instructors (Modules B, C, D), or as a group activity of the entire class (Modules E, F, G).

Module B

Contrive stories and roles for native-speaker occupants of automobiles, including identification, destination, reason for travel, etc. Produce I.D., drivers' licenses, passports. List weapons, propaganda, and other contraband which vehicle occupants may be carrying (these will be produced or gathered in Module D).

Module C

1.) Contrive situations for searches, including location, time of day, political and military situation in the vicinity, and role of the American forces. Provide a map.
2.) Contrive instructions for inspectors: materials to be considered contraband; point at which a search is to be considered complete, including possible outcomes (e.g., allowing the vehicle to pass and under what circumstances, turning a vehicle back and under what circumstances, arresting one or more of the occupants and under what circumstances).

Module D

List, then gather or produce remaining materials required, for example: automobile, native-speaker occupant(s) of vehicles, contraband required by Module B (weapons, bombs, propaganda materials, etc.).

Module E

1.) Elaborate typical questions and commands to occupants of vehicles, for example:
May I see your I.D.? Do you have a passport, driver's license, etc.? Where are you going? Where are you coming from? What is your business at your destination? How long will you

be there? Whom can we contact to verify your I.D./destination/
business? Is this your car/vehicle? If not, whose is it? Do you
have any weapons? What type of bomb is this? Where did you
get these materials? You are not allowed to enter here. You
must turn around. Put your hands on your head! Spread your
legs! Lie on the ground!

2.) Bear in mind that it is not enough to be able to pose questions and state commands. You must be able to understand replies! It will require practice to become familiar with typical responses, and it is therefore necessary to include an elaboration of such typical or expected responses to questions or commands.

Module F

Elaborate necessary grammatical structures, for example:

1.) Commands: *Lie down! Turn around! Give ...! Put ...!*
2.) Modal expressions, such as: *You should/must/can/may go. Don't go!*
3.) Yes-no questions
4.) Accusative case (direct object, object of prepositions indicating the end point of motion)

Module G

Elaborate cultural schemata, for example:

1.) An interview may begin with *Dobar dan* (Good day) or salutation appropriate for the time of day.
2.) When in doubt, use the *Vi* (formal address) form to address unknown people. This will be by far the most common case. Inappropriate use of *Vi* forms may seem comical to a native speaker, but inappropriate use of *Ti* (informal address) forms in a potentially adversarial situation may appear to a native speaker as an attempt at posturing or intimidation and can lead to unnecessary tension.
3.) *Molim, Molim Vas, Molim te* (Please)
   Hvala (Thank you)
   Molim (You're welcome)

It is appropriate to use *Molim Vas* in making requests of vehicle occupants, especially since this allows you the option of repeating a command without this nicety if necessary. Native speakers are less likely to thank people for carrying out a request, however. If you thank people with *Hvala* for exiting their vehicle or carrying out some other command, this may be perceived as artificial and insincere.

Appendix C
First Aid and Medical Evacuation Exercise

I. Activity overview

The members of a military unit come across a wounded or ill person. They attempt to direct the person to aid. The goal is to find the most appropriate and efficient means to get the person to medical help (walking unassisted, walking with assistance, carried on a stretcher, or in an ambulance or helicopter). In order to do so, they must determine: a) whether the injury is life-threatening; b) whether time is of the essence in getting the person to help; and c) whether the person can walk unassisted and how far.

The activity consists of three roles:

A. **Sick or injured person(s).** The task of this person or these persons is to respond to questions concerning the nature of the injury (illness) and how it occurred, allergies to drugs or medicine which the rescuers may be able to dispense on the spot, and whether (s)he can walk.

B. **Rescuer.** This person performs three tasks: 1) attempts to determine the nature of the injury or illness and its cause, and whether the injured/ill person can walk; 2) calls to request an ambulance or helicopter if necessary, and must explain the nature of the injury or illness to the dispatcher (to simplify the exercise, we will assume that the rescuer is in direct contact with the hospital dispatcher), and understand the dispatcher's response; 3) explains to the injured/ill person(s) how they will reach the hospital (whether a helicopter or ambulance will be sent, whether the person will have to walk there alone, or whether they will be carried there on a stretcher).

C. **Hospital dispatcher**. This person must determine whether help can be sent and what kind (ambulance or helicopter). (S)he will take into consideration availability of transport, seriousness of the injury or illness, and any other pertinent information which is provided (e.g., expected influx of a large number of seriously injured persons, necessitating that transportation be reserved for the most critical cases).

II. Organization of the activity (to be conducted by the class)

A. Set a time limit for each exercise (ten minutes?)

B. Compile information that must be available to injured/ill persons:

1. Identification (name, unit)
2. Any pertinent medical information (allergies to drugs which rescuers might dispense on the spot)
3. Symptoms or the nature of the injury/illness and the manner in which the injury was incurred

C. Compile information that must be available to rescuers:
1. Map showing the present location and that of the hospital or aid station
2. Orders showing whether the rescuer's unit is stationary or in movement and whether the movement is urgent
3. Whether the rescuer has any medicine or medical equipment readily available

D. Compile information that must be available to dispatchers:
1. Total number of ambulances and helicopters, perhaps also drivers and pilots available
2. Current disposition of ambulances and helicopters (how many are currently in use or available for use)

E. Prepare as wide as possible a variety of situation cards for injured persons, rescuers, and dispatchers.

F. Randomize the order of each set of situation cards.

G. Prepare the setting for the exercise. Optimally, the exercise should be conducted out of doors with a radio connection between rescuer and dispatcher. It may be conducted indoors with the injured/ill person(s) and rescuer in one room, and the dispatcher in a separate room with a telephone connection to the rescuer. The most expedient (and noisy!) setting is with all students in a single room with various teams, each consisting of injured/ill person(s), a rescuer, and a dispatcher, occupying various corners of the room.

III. Linguistic preparation

Much of this will be accomplished during the process of organizing the activity. Review names of body parts, verbs relating to illness and injury, as well as transportation and movement. Explore phraseology likely to be required during the activity.

IV. Practice

Practice is conducted as a group, allowing for maximal feedback and brainstorming concerning ways to circumvent difficulties.

V. Perform the activity

This is done with randomized distribution of situation cards.

VI. Follow-up

Debrief students concerning performance and explore solutions to problems that occurred.

VII. Repeat the activity

The activity is repeated as many times as possible with students shifting to different roles and different situations.

VIII. Additional material

A *Supplementary First Aid Guide: Serbo-Croatian* has been compiled by a team of students and is available for distribution.

Appendix D
Interrogation Exercise

The purpose of this activity is to prepare students to conduct interrogations in Serbo-Croatian. It was planned and performed by a limited number of students who were trained as interrogators. It consists of four stages:

1. Questions from a standard tactical order of battle interrogator notebook are translated into both major standard varieties of Serbo-Croatian. This is done in conjunction with a native-speaker instructor, preferably one with military experience.

2. Situations are contrived, including location, units, their missions, and environment (human and natural). Interrogators and subjects of interrogation are given access to relevant aspects of the situation.

3. Personalities, attitudes, situations, and stories are contrived for subjects of interrogation.

4. Students interrogate the subject (a native-speaker instructor adopting the subject's personality, attitudes, etc.), and attempt to extract and transcribe from the responses information which is crucial in the light of the contrived situation. Students are not allowed to conduct interrogations in a situation which they have contrived, or to interrogate a subject whose personality, etc., they have contrived.

Part Three

CBI at
Intermediate Levels
of Proficiency

5

Text Development for Content-Based Instruction in Arabic

Karin Ryding and Barbara Stowasser

Editors' Note: Ryding and Stowasser and their colleagues at the Foreign Service Institute had success with a multi-teacher, interdisciplinary approach for beginning students of Arabic. In this model, a portion of the intensive language training was designed to provide "integration" between the area studies program and the language studies program. The Arabic language teacher attended the weekly English-language area studies lectures, then designed follow-up language lessons based on the content of those lectures. This approach, similar to the "adjunct model" discussed in Chapter 1, is highly collaborative in that it requires that two teachers, one a language teacher and one a content teacher, coordinate separate classes so that the content is aligned and the two courses complement each other. This technique is reminiscent of the "preview-review" bilingual education model in which students are given a preview in their native language of a subsequent lesson in their second language. The authors highlight a number of special problems involved in teaching Arabic to English speakers: 1) the "opaqueness" of the language, 2) the difficulty of learning a new script system, 3) the diglossic nature of Arabic, and 4) some negative stereotypes to be overcome. To deal with these challenges, especially those relating to affect, the program incorporated two methods conducive to lowering students' "affective filters"—Community Language Learning (CLL), and the Natural Approach. General references for this chapter are located in the bibliography at the end of this volume.

Arabic Teaching Today

Arabic language teaching has been handicapped by a lack of methodologically up-to-date materials and by negative attitudes of potential learners about the level of difficulty of the language. A number of students are intimidated by the seeming impenetrability of the script and by what appears to be an exotic sound system. Moreover, many American students have negative images about Arabs and about Islam. Even well-traveled students who consider themselves open-minded about culture and behavior patterns often reveal that they have absorbed some very negative stereotypes about Arabic culture, values, and behavior.

In this respect, there is as much to unlearn about Arab culture and language as there is to learn. Unless negative affective barriers are broken through on both sides of the language/area equation, very little learning occurs.[1]

This Project

Several years ago, we collaborated on a project at the Foreign Service Institute (FSI) that was innovative for Arabic teaching and that was highly successful. We prepared a series of Arabic texts dealing with specific regional content material that reflected what FSI students were studying in English in their Arab area studies courses. Thus, they were to be exposed to content material that was already somewhat familiar, but in the target language (TL). This is in line with Krashen's Input Hypothesis, which functions effectively when learners are able to contextualize incoming TL information through extralinguistic knowledge. As John Oller states, "The IH (Input Hypothesis) succeeds because the acquirer does not rely only on TL input. TL input which would otherwise be incomprehensible becomes comprehensible because of the scaffolding provided by contextual sources of information" (1988, 171).

The problem we faced, however, was two- or even three-fold. For many English-speaking learners, foreign language input (both written and spoken) is partially comprehensible because of recognizable cognate lexical and/or morphological items, at least for Indo-European languages. For Arabic, and for other non-Indo-European languages, the opaqueness of the language can be impenetrable even at nonbeginning levels. Moreover, for reading purposes, the use of a totally different script, read in a different direction, from right to left, imposes another dimension of cognitive complexity.

Yet, we felt that the validity of the Input Hypothesis would hold true for Arabic as well, if we could structure learning experiences that would: 1) reduce negative affect and anxiety, 2) draw upon the real-world knowledge of the students, 3) allow access to as many cognate or borrowed words as possible, at least in the initial stages, and 4) overcome the barrier of Arabic script.

These principles ultimately lead to the issue of "authenticity" of TL materials and their role in the learning experience. Although both of us know and appreciate the pedagogical value of authentic Arabic texts as models of genuinely Arab thought and expression, we did not believe it necessarily followed that we had to be limited, for the reasons listed above, to texts written for native speakers of Arabic, especially in the early stages of the course. Without a transitional stage for nonnative speakers of Arabic, we would not be able to take advantage of the power of comprehensible input; without that stage the learning would be considerably slower, more frustrating, more alienating, and more superficial. That is, the shallowness of comprehension of authentic texts at the elementary level does not prepare the learner for deeper learning at subsequent stages. Since we had both been trained to a great extent in the "authentic text" tradition, we knew its effects, both positive and negative, and we were willing to experiment with a new approach.

The task was divided into two stages. Although we collaborated throughout the project, Stowasser was essentially responsible for stage one (text development) and Ryding for stage two (pedagogical procedures).

Stage One

Program Background and Design

FSI trains Foreign Service Officers, military officers, and other foreign affairs personnel who have been assigned to posts abroad. That training includes intensive, full-time language instruction as well as a weekly seminar on regional topics related to the country of assignment. Language training is the responsibility of the School of Language Studies (SLS), whereas the regional seminars are run by the School of Area Studies (SAS).

In 1982 FSI officially adopted an educational policy of "language/area integration" in the belief that this would enhance the ability of Foreign Service Officers to discuss regional issues in the TL of the country to which they were assigned. Ability to deal competently with this content area had long been a tacit pedagogical goal for students who reached the ILR level 3 or higher in speaking and reading, and discussion exercises dealing explicitly with regional issues were often built into language classes near the end of training. The "integration" approach, however, was based additionally on the idea that area studies topics would hold the attention of the students and would involve them in more meaningful applications of language. Since this was a new aspect of language/area training, the procedure for implementing integration activities was not initially spelled out. At first, language studies teachers sat in on the Area Studies lectures, took some notes, and provided follow-up discussions in the TL later in the day or the week. That system did not work very well: in the first place, the follow-up was usually presented in a loosely structured "free conversation" format, and in the second place, it was still considered ineffective and inappropriate at lower levels of proficiency.

Arabic Text Development

In 1984, therefore, FSI decided to commission the writing of area studies texts in Arabic for use in the language program. Specifically, these texts were to reflect the area studies curriculum of the Arabian Peninsula and the Fertile Crescent seminars, the main area studies sections for FSI students who study Arabic and go to the Arab world.[2]

First, it was necessary to get a very clear idea of the topics typically addressed in these area seminars. The main blueprint for this was provided by past syllabi which reflected an "ideal matrix" of nine course segments for the FSI academic year.

The next step was to obtain a list of relevant themes and subthemes addressed by area studies lecturers in order to design a detailed master plan of integration topics. With the help of Peter Bechtold, Near East/North Africa Area Studies Director, Stowasser obtained a number of lecturers' texts (in English) as well as "critical" technical vocabulary items for each course segment (again, in English).

In addition to scouting out the area studies syllabus content, it was necessary to calibrate the texts with the methodology, lesson plans, and teaching materials used in FSI's Arabic language training program, as well as to take into account student levels of language skills, which would be approximately 0 in week one and 2, 2+ or 3 in week forty-four.

On a very large, week-by-week flow chart, Stowasser collected and collated the language training and area studies data, the result looking something like a cross between a train schedule and a store inventory. This visual aid was of immense help in the actual writing of the materials.

The flow chart had five columns for the listing of: 1) timeframe (month/days) of course segment in area studies syllabus, 2) area studies course segment topics, subtopics, and key vocabulary items, 3) timeframe (month/days) of course segments ("lessons") in language studies syllabus, 4) language studies lesson topics, key vocabulary items, and grammar points, and 5) integration materials "blueprint," for the planning of texts that would provide area studies themes in the target language and also include vocabulary items and grammatical features previously introduced in language studies. For example, Area Studies course segment IV, "Domestic Economic Development," chronologically coincided with language studies lessons on "Shopping and bargaining in the *suuq* (market), bargaining at the grocer's, buying foodstuffs, and shopping by phone." In addition to a large number of vocabulary items pertinent to shopping and bargaining, these language studies lessons also introduced collective and unit nouns, active and passive participles, and some important syntactic structures such as "because of," and "in order that."

The four Arabic Integration Materials texts on economic themes were then written, or edited, to include as many of the language studies-introduced items and grammatical features as possible. Not by design but expediency and availability of pertinent materials, one-half of the four Integration texts ("Agriculture and Industry in Egypt," and "The Gulf Cooperation Council") were based on a number of articles published in American and British newspapers. The other two texts ("Industrial Development in Saudi Arabia" and "OPEC and OAPEC") were based on economic analysis items that appeared in Arabic-language economic journals. These "original" texts were then abridged; in some cases, sentence structure was simplified and, wherever possible, familiar vocabulary and syntactic structures were substituted for unfamiliar ones. This "down-editing" without sacrificing the meaning, correctness of data, or idiomatic flow of the texts was more doable than anticipated.

The final step was to research the subject matter fully, in Arabic and in other languages, focusing on topics involving U.S. foreign policy issues, inasmuch as these texts were to be used to train official representatives of the U.S. government. In some cases, the ultimate versions of the texts were based on Arabic materials that were modified to make them effective sources of input. In most cases, however, it proved more practical to compose new texts that more precisely reflected area program topics. Furthermore, we decided that the texts should strike a balance between case studies and more general approaches to the region as a whole.

An important principle of text presentation and organization was the recycling of topics, or "spiraling," i.e., providing a short text in the initial stages followed by a more extensive and complex one near the end. The complete list of topics is included in the appendix.

Stage Two
General Theory and Design of Arabic Training

It is important to point out that the content-based texts were to be integrated into an ongoing, intensive, proficiency-based language training program which already included a substantial amount of regional information in the target language.

One issue relevant to Arabic training is the problem of diglossia. That is, spoken Arabic and written Arabic are related, but they are not the same. In order to be communicatively competent, therefore, students must learn two types of language: a spoken form of Arabic as well as what is usually termed "Modern Standard Arabic," the written language. This is a major reason why Arabic materials development is so complex. How does one compose a text in a language that is spoken but not written, or discuss a written text in a language that is not normally used for conversation?

Therefore, in addition to the affective factors mentioned earlier in discussing student attitudes towards Arabic, students are faced with the fact that they must become proficient in essentially two languages rather than one. This is often a surprise, if not a shock, to the learner.

Dealing with Affect

Accordingly, students embark upon Arabic training with many reservations, not to mention resistance. The most important thing to accomplish, especially during the initial stages of training, is to reduce or eliminate the negative affect.

In most approaches to language teaching, affect is not openly dealt with, and may even be ignored. If, however, the learner feels threatened in any way by exposure to this new realm of knowledge and behavior, it is most likely that he or she will encounter resistance to assimilating and learning the language.[3]

For the past twenty years, Ryding has been involved with Community Language Learning (CLL) and has been implementing the approach in language classes as well as in materials development.[4] CLL, developed by Father Charles A. Curran of Loyola University in Chicago, was the first approach to tackle the issue of learner security head on and to make it a cornerstone of the teaching philosophy.[5] It applies particularly well to Arabic because of the number of potentially negative affective factors facing American learners.

As can be seen from the types of activities, another major influence on the structuring of text-based Arabic tasks was the Natural Approach.[6] In particular, the concepts of comprehensible input and the development of receptive skills prior to requiring production were seen as very helpful for Arabic.[7]

Design Principles

The design and methodology of the course is not only important, but critical, to subsequent success, and there were four principles that informed the overall design of Arabic training.[8] First, the curriculum is task- and proficiency-based, centered on communicative functions and situations. Second, a great deal of comprehensible input is deliberately structured into the activities. Third, a comprehension stage, or preproduction stage, is designed for the first three weeks of the course, when students are not required to produce any Arabic but can absorb and react to a great deal of information *in* Arabic.[9] Fourth, no transcription is used—only Arabic script, even for texts and exercises in spoken Arabic.[10]

Initial Stage

During the first three to four weeks of the course, students are allowed time to adjust to the features of Arabic script through exposure to Arabic texts which are heavily weighted with cognate or borrowed words—words of high frequency and transparent meaning, such as names of people and places. They are confronted with many variations on Arabic reading tasks and listening tasks, but not *required* to produce Arabic right away. By exposing learners to a heavy dose of information with which they are already familiar, and by allowing them time to absorb it rather than require that they immediately reproduce and manipulate it, the stress of reading from right to left, of discriminating a letter in as many as four different shapes within a word, and of associating sound with a new script is cushioned.

Strikingly, the first few weeks became so easy and comfortable for learners that many took the initiative to engage in speaking without being required to do so. This confirmed the theory that informed our design of the materials and meant that we gave students a means of access to Arabic that opened the door welcomingly.

The content of the lessons of the first three to four weeks is of two sorts: geographical and political. By describing the geography of the Arab world early on, we kill two birds (so to speak) with one stone: we refresh the memory of those who might not remember the locations and relationships of the various countries of the Middle East and Africa, and we give them plenty of occasion to identify the names of places written in Arabic. By discussing the names of the leaders of the various Arab countries, students are able to compare authentic pronunciation and spelling with what they already know. They hear texts read and reread so that they begin to assimilate correct forms of pronunciation, and, as an incidental but nontrivial grammatical goal, they develop a sense of sentence structure in Arabic.[11]

Area and Culture Texts

It is only after the students have gone through this initial stage that they are exposed to the area studies materials in Arabic. By that time they are used to hearing and seeing a lot of Arabic that is above their heads and are accustomed to using selective comprehension techniques to cope with it. By that time they also have acquired rudimentary writing skills in Arabic. Although writing in Arabic is generally not a skill that they will need in their professions, written exercises are included throughout the course as pedagogical tasks which reinforce the learners' reading and speaking capabilities.

At approximately the fifth week into the course, students split their language study time into three different tracks: 1) practicing functional speaking and listening skills based on tasks and situations, 2) practicing reading "newspaper Arabic," and 3) dealing with area studies texts in Arabic.

The major pedagogical problems in using these texts about Arab culture and society are that they are in Modern Standard Arabic (the written language), and much of the content is still beyond the grasp of the student. A series of tasks was therefore designed for each text. The main point of these activities was *not* for students to be able to translate the texts, but for them to be able to: 1) acquire some basic vocabulary, 2) practice listening for specific bits of information, and 3) guess meaning from context.

These have been identified as communicative skills that FSI students will need at their posts, and they are also skills that any learner can use in order to deal with language above his or her proficiency level.

Stages of Activity

The text-based activities are divided into stages. In the first stage, students are exposed to five sentences culled from a narrative matrix. These are "core" sentences that contain salient facts from the text. They are presented to the learners in writing with translation.

These sentences are then exploited by the teacher as a source for pronunciation and structure drills and rehearsed extensively in class to prepare for eventual memorization. Students may ask questions on structure or vocabulary, but the aim of the class exercise is to get them used to comprehending sentence-length utterances as well as to have them grasp certain basic cultural facts. The assignment for the students is to copy all the sentences by hand and to memorize at least three out of the five for recitation a day or two later. Although the copying exercise may seem elementary, the issue here is that they are trying to handwrite in a completely new way, and the motor memory that results from writing in the new script reinforces their command of both the visual and the verbal input.

During the next class period, usually a day or two following the first, students are expected to recite their memorized sentences. While this obviously reflects audiolingual practice, it serves more purposes for Arabic learners in this phase, since in addition to giving them a toehold in the foreign language, it prepares them for listening to and at least partially comprehending a narrative matrix in which these concepts are embedded.

Students are first allowed to hear the entire narrative on audiotape. Since they are already familiar with the topic, getting the general idea isn't beyond them. The second step is for them to listen specifically for their memorized sentences. This allows them to focus on familiar specifics and not to get distracted by what they *don't* know.

The students are then provided with a list of approximately ten "listening items," key words or phrases from the text, and asked to listen specifically for them. These items are not glossed, and students are encouraged to guess their meaning from context, confirming or correcting their guesses with their teacher. The teacher winds up the exercise by reviewing the "listening list" and providing cultural and/or linguistic explanations of its items.

The last thing the learners do at this stage is copy the tape for future reference. Usually they also want to see the written text at this point, and it is provided for them. The printed text itself, as well as the recording, can serve as a way of measuring their comprehension level in later months, when they can recycle it using different types of exercises and grasp considerably more of the content.

Conclusion

The materials developed for the integration of area studies and language studies were highly successful components of the Arabic program. The students progressed through the taped and written area studies materials at the pace of two or three hours a week. It did not occupy much of their class time, but enough to give them a sense of having covered the material in the TL, and to get their feet wet in listening to narratives such as they might hear on radio or television, or in lectures and speeches.

The classroom activity traditionally associated with texts on the target culture—discussion and questions—has been explicitly avoided. This is for two reasons: 1) the students' level of spoken language skills is nowhere near high enough to do this, and 2) the language of discussion, spoken Arabic, would be different from the language of the text, Modern Standard Arabic. Although they do not have total control of the text, the students have at least tackled a basic cultural topic in the TL and practiced several skills: listening comprehension, guessing meaning from context, reading, handwriting, and pronunciation. They have also acquired, at least in terms of recognition, some new and culturally significant vocabulary. This does not overtax their limited skill repertoire, and it lays the groundwork for building more advanced skills. Most importantly, what they have already covered in their area studies seminars in English has now been given a contextual linguistic reality.

One of the benefits of developing and using these cultural texts was that they lent themselves to be used at multiple levels of proficiency. In the beginning phase of training they were used to develop certain basic listening and receptive skills, and at later phases those same materials were used for more sophisticated tasks incorporating more ambitious cultural and communicative goals.[12]

Endnotes

1. See Ryding, 1994, for further discussion of this point.
2. There is also an area studies seminar on North Africa, but most of the students headed for North African posts are assigned to French language study.
3. See for example, Curran 1976 and 1978; Rardin and Tranel 1988; Samimy 1989. Recent articles on language learner anxiety include Aida 1994 (for Japanese) and Ganschow and Sparks 1996 (among high school women).
4. See Ryding 1994.
5. See Ibid.; also, see Campbell and Ortiz 1987; Stevick 1980, 1990, and 1996.
6. Krashen and Terrell 1983. See also Long and Porter 1985.
7. For a summary of listening comprehension research see Rubin 1994.
8. In developing these lessons, the Arabic section had the invaluable advice and counsel of Earl Stevick, who deserves much of the credit for developing this approach.
9. Nagel and Sanders 1986, 21: "A solid foundation in listening comprehension appears to lay the foundation for language learning so successfully that speaking, writing and reading skills are acquired relatively quickly in its wake." See also Morley 1985, 31; Rubin 1994.
10. It is not common practice in the Arab world for the spoken language to be written.
11. These elements are incorporated in Ryding's basic Arabic textbook: *Formal Spoken Arabic: Basic Course* (1990).
12. An earlier version of this paper was presented at the Northeast Conference on Language Teaching.

Karin Ryding is Associate Professor of Arabic and Dean of Interdisciplinary Programs at Georgetown University. From 1980 to 1986, she was Arabic Language Training Supervisor at the Foreign Service Institute. Address: College Dean's Office, Box 571058, Georgetown University, Washington, D.C. 20057. (E-mail: rydingk@guvax.acc.georgetown.edu)

Barbara Stowasser is Professor of Arabic and Director of the Center for Contemporary Arab Studies at Georgetown University. From 1978 to 1989 she was Area Studies Chairperson for Greece and Turkey at the Foreign Service Institute. Address: Center for Contemporary Arab Studies, Georgetown University, Washington, D.C. 20057.

Appendix

This appendix contains a complete list of area studies topics covered during the academic FSI year in Arabic as an integral part of the language training program. Although it pertains specifically to the Middle East, the overall approach and organization of topics could reasonably serve as models for other regions of the world as well.

Segment I: Introduction to the Region (Four weeks)

This is covered in the FSI Arabic textbook. It is devoted to geography and identity of key political figures.

Segment II: The Cultural System (Four weeks)

1. The Prophet Muhammad and the Rise and Spread of Islam
2. a. The First *suura* (verse) of the Holy Qur'an
   b. The Five Pillars of Islam
3. The Orthodox Caliphs and the Rise of the Shi'a
4. Religious Traditions and Social Customs

Segment III. Current Social Issues (Five weeks)

1. Women's Issues in the Arab World
2. Urbanization and Labor Migration in the Arab World
3. Education in the Arab World
4. The Media in the Arab World

Segment IV: Domestic Economic Development (Five weeks)

1. Agriculture and Industry in Egypt
2. Industrial Development in Saudi Arabia
3. The Gulf Cooperation Council
4. International Economic Relations: OPEC and OAPEC
5. Special Session: A Poem by Nizar Qabbani as sung by 'Abd Al-Halim Hafez

Segment V: Current International Issues (Five weeks)

1. Arab-American Relations
2. a. Arabism and Arab Unity
   b. A Short Selection from Sati' Al-Husri's *Arabism First*
3. The Arab-Israeli Problem
4. The War between Iraq and Iran
5. The Lebanese Civil War

Segment VI: Historical Legacies (Five weeks)

1. Introduction to Arab History
2. The History of Egypt (Case Study)
3. The History of Iraq (Case Study)
4. Arab Nationalism: a Statement by Sati' al-Husri
5. From the Islamic Renaissance to Twentieth Century Western Technology

Segment VII: Political Systems (Four weeks)

1. Fact Sheet on Egypt
2. Fact Sheet on Iraq
3. The Military in Politics
   a. A General Overview
   b. The Sudan (Case Study)
4. A Biographical Study of the Life of King Hussein of Jordan

Segment VIII: Regional and International Political Economics (Two weeks)

1. The Organization of Arab Petroleum Exporting Countries (OAPEC): Conference on Cooperation between OAPEC and Japan (Case Study)
2. Historical Dimensions of U.S.- Arab Economic Relations

Segment IX: Inter-Arab Issues, Foreign Policy Issues (Six weeks)

1. The Iran-Iraq War (extended text)
2. The Gulf Cooperation Council (extended text)
3. Basics of U.S. Policy in the Middle East
4. Saudi-U.S. Relations
5. U.S. Policy towards Terrorism
6. Atomic Energy: Hopes and Fears

6

Content-Based Instruction In French For Journalism Students At Ohio University

Lois Vines

Editors' Note: Lois Vines describes a successful program in French for journalism and telecommunication majors at Ohio University that was designed to encourage students to continue their foreign language studies beyond the beginning level. Vines uses her own experience as a case study in meeting the special challenges of switching to a content-based approach: 1) "retraining" language or literature teachers in a new content field; 2) acquiring appropriate materials; 3) identifying helpful organizations; 4) participating in workshops and conferences; 5) linking up with colleagues in the new content area; and 6) researching in the new content area. Vines' program is not a single course but a series of six courses, three at intermediate level and three at advanced level. The two-year program emphasizes all four skills: listening, speaking, reading, and writing. The continuing success of this model, which has been in place since the mid-1980s, demonstrates the viability of CBI in a university foreign language setting. The participants have written enthusiastic reviews, and the enrollment in upper division French classes has increased significantly. Professor Vines makes clear that, although a fulfilling experience, this project has been no easy undertaking. For the benefit of teachers of French, Vines' appendixes provide a comprehensive list of books, periodicals, audio-visual materials, and organizations offering pedagogical support for the Francophone media, as well as a model syllabus for a module on French-language television. General references for this chapter are located in the bibliography at the end of this volume.

Introduction

A two-year sequence of content-based courses designed to meet the interests of journalism and telecommunication majors studying French became part of the curriculum in the Department of Modern Languages at Ohio University in 1984. The previous year, an examination of enrollment data at the second-year level indicated that students from the College of

Communication were dropping their foreign language studies after taking one quarter at the intermediate level. Upon further investigation we learned that the School of Journalism required only one course beyond the beginning level to fulfill the school's foreign language requirement, thus explaining, in part, the sudden enrollment reduction. That was the bad news. The good news was that we discovered that journalism students have the option of taking thirty-six quarter hours in one foreign language to meet their requirement for a concentration outside the professional courses in journalism. As one might say in the business world, "We identified a potential market and decided to design a product to meet the need." Our goal was to create content-based courses in French and Spanish that would teach these languages through the use of print and broadcast media, thus attracting journalism and telecommunication students who would continue their foreign language studies at the intermediate and advanced levels.

Although we were convinced that our plans to initiate content-based instruction had excellent potential for success, good ideas also require financial support. In collaboration with the School of Journalism, our department applied for funding to the U.S. Department of Education's Undergraduate International Studies and Foreign Language Program. We were able to make a strong case for internationalizing the undergraduate curriculum in a significant way by creating special sequences of courses in French and Spanish for journalism and telecommunication majors. We received a $42,000 grant the first year and a renewal the second year for a total of $84,000. The award covered release time for faculty members to develop new courses, materials and equipment, expenses and honoraria for international journalists visiting campus, a summer workshop to train additional faculty members to teach courses on the media, and travel to conferences. After the initial euphoria of receiving the grant began to subside, we faced the major task at hand: developing new courses for the two-year sequences.

Faculty and Materials

A major component in the implementation of content-based instruction is the faculty member's willingness to devote the time and effort required to attain a level of competence needed to teach the subject matter. Foreign language degree programs at the graduate level focus on literature and linguistics. When venturing beyond these areas, we enter new territory, whether it be the media, business, or international relations. Although foreign language teachers involved in content-based instruction do not claim to be experts in the second field, we must nonetheless engage in retraining, or recycling as some prefer to call it, in order to acquire the knowledge and special skills required to train students in the specific subject matter.

The ongoing education of the instructor of a content-based course often takes place in workshops and special conference sessions devoted to the subject matter. Two organizations have played an important role in providing training workshops in the French media. Marie Galanti, publisher of the *Le Journal Français* and Marie-José Leroy and Richard Nahmias at the Centre International d'Etudes Pédagogiques (CIEP) organized an eight-day workshop in Paris (July 1987) designed to train teachers in the use of the media to teach French. Sessions demonstrated various teaching techniques and increased the participants' knowledge of the French press through visits to several Paris newspapers. CIEP is willing to organize similar workshops on demand for eight to ten participants. My expenses at the Paris workshop were covered by an Ohio University Faculty Development Award, created to support the activities of professors engaged in innovative course development. Similar funding might be made available to faculty members at other universities.

Conference sessions on the use of the media in the classroom are becoming more frequent. Marie Galanti's sessions at American Council on the Teaching of Foreign Languages (ACTFL) and American Association of Teachers of French (AATF) conferences offer excellent opportunities to learn more about using newspapers in class. Ross Steele also gives presentations on the media at national and international conferences. Middlebury College and the Project for International Communication Studies (PICS) (see Appendix A for addresses) have sponsored workshops on using video and television in the classroom. Although content-based courses designed specifically to teach the Francophone media to journalism students are rare, incorporating print and broadcast media into existing courses is becoming more common. It is through workshops and conferences similar to those just mentioned that the instructor of content-based courses can learn more about the specific subject and how to teach it.

While many university professors read newspapers in the target language, most do not have an in-depth knowledge of the history of the media, the current conflicts, and the financial problems threatening the existence of certain publications. How does one go about retraining in the content field while at the same time carrying out the duties of a language and literature professor? I can address this question by drawing on my own experience during the past ten years. Retraining is a continuous process.

A reduced teaching load made possible by grant funds during the first year of our program helped provide the extra time I needed to identify and order books, newspapers and periodicals, and audio and video programs dealing with the French-language media (Appendix A). Through the use of these materials, I have been able to acquire the background knowledge needed to teach content-based courses and set up files that keep the information current. For example, in the past decade the French media have experienced more changes than during the previous fifty years. The only way to remain up-to-date is to keep files of articles gathered from the press. These materials contribute to my own knowledge of the field, and I use them in class in place of a textbook.

In addition to educating oneself in a new field, the instructor of a content-based course must also explore pedagogical techniques for teaching the specific subject matter. Using the media to teach French has been the focus of books and articles by Berwald (1986), Steele (1993), Ruprecht (1981), and others (see Appendix A). Adapting their approaches to the needs of my courses and coming up with new techniques of my own have resulted in a stimulating, creative teaching experience.

When I embarked on the project of creating content courses on the media, I recalled that my colleagues at other universities who teach French for business majors are in touch with the Paris Chamber of Commerce, which provides materials and workshops in the field of French business. I needed to identify a similar group that linked the study of French and the media. My search resulted in the discovery of four organizations that provide pedagogical support dealing with the Francophone media (see Appendix A for addresses). France Presse publishes *Le Journal Français*, an excellent newspaper at a reasonable price, and a booklet entitled *Using French Language Newspapers in the Classroom,* which provides vocabulary dealing with the press and specific ideas on how to use a newspaper as a pedagogical tool.

Using the media to teach French is the primary mission of the Departement Presse at the Centre International d'Etudes Pédagogiques located in Paris. This French government organization publishes *Le Journal des Journaux*, a bulletin that lists current articles from the French press categorized by subject matter. A subscriber to the publication can order photocopies of specific articles at the cost of one *franc* per page (about 18 cents). For schools that cannot afford subscriptions to a variety of French newspapers and magazines, this service provides an economical source for up-to-date material from the press.

Also located in Paris is an important journalism school, the Centre de formation et de perfectionnement des journalistes (CFPJ), which trains students for various careers in the French media. Although the primary goal of the school is to graduate professional media personnel, members of the staff have also taken on a pedagogical mission designed to introduce adolescents to the media through books written at a level comprehensible to French students ages twelve and above. For our adult students learning French as a second language, the level is appropriate for understanding a complex subject matter (see Appendix A for titles of these books).

Since content-based instruction normally involves a field of specialization outside the formal education of the foreign language instructor, close ties with teachers in the content area are important and, in my own case, have been very fruitful. While working on the federal grant proposal with colleagues in the School of Journalism, we discovered a number of interests in common. Prestigious internships with AP and ABC in Paris are awarded each year to Ohio University journalism students who are outstanding in their major and proficient in French. My colleagues in journalism include my evaluation of language skills in their selection process. I work closely with Anne Cooper-Chen, Professor of Journalism, on grant proposals that have resulted in campus visits by French-speaking journalists who participate in my content-based classes in French and in her Foreign Correspondence and International Communications courses. Professor Cooper-Chen and I sit in on each other's classes, share many of the same students, and exchange materials dealing with the media. By writing joint requests we have succeeded in convincing the university library to increase the number of French-language news periodicals and to purchase an expensive index to *Le Monde* (Appendix A). The current interest in interdisciplinary courses at the university favors the efforts of departments that link their disciplines in ways that are advantageous to students. Making journalism and telecommunications the content of foreign language courses serves as an excellent example of breaking through departmental boundaries.

At the university level, faculty members are encouraged to contribute to their disciplines through research and publication. Since content-based courses are relatively new to foreign language education in general, articles and books designed to improve our knowledge of the subject matter and its pedagogy contribute to the implementation of these special courses at other institutions. As these courses become more numerous, journals and conferences devoted to specific content areas could be created. The annual Conference on Language and Communication for World Business and the Professions, sponsored by Eastern Michigan University, has grown each year since its inception in 1982. As interest in content-based instruction increases, the possibility of a conference devoted entirely to teaching foreign languages through the media could become a reality.

At the moment, there are very few foreign language periodicals that publish articles on subjects other than literature and linguistics. In French, one finds occasional articles on content-based instruction in *The French Review*, *The Canadian Modern Language Revue*, and *Contemporary French Civilization* (i.e., see articles by Vines and Ruprecht). New journals dealing with specific content areas would accomplish three purposes: keep instructors up-to-date on recent developments in the field, offer ideas on teaching techniques specifically related to the content area, and provide more opportunities for faculty members involved in content-based instruction to publish their research.

Scope and Sequence of the Program

Training journalism students to function in French while acquiring a basic knowledge of the Francophone media cannot be accomplished in one course. We created six one-quarter courses taught in sequence, three at the intermediate level and three at the advanced conversation and composition level. Students are admitted to the content-based courses after having completed two years of French in high school or one year in college. These courses, which run parallel to the regular sequences of intermediate and advanced French courses, are identified in the schedule of classes as being reserved for journalism and communication majors. At the beginning of the second-year sequence, twenty to twenty-five students are enrolled in the media-content course. Our goal, which has been met so far, is to have at least fifteen of these students continue at the advanced-level sequence and complete all six courses. Students leave the sequence for a variety of reasons, such as scheduling conflicts, low grades, or interest in pursuing another area of concentration. Admission to the sequence at the beginning of winter or spring quarters is possible, if the student is willing to catch up on the content-based material. Because students have the option to leave or enter the special sequences throughout the year, it is necessary to use the same grammar book as the regular courses. With this exception, the materials used in the French media courses are related specifically to the content-based subject matter and are therefore different from those used in other courses at the same level.

The goal of the six-course sequence is to strengthen all four language skills—reading, writing, listening, and speaking. Four class meetings per week (fifty minutes each) are devoted to activities designed to perfect these skills.

Grammar Review

Students have indicated on course evaluations that they need the structured grammar review offered at each level throughout the sequences. In order to remain in tandem with other sections taught at the same level, specific chapters in a common grammar book must be covered. In addition, I include an intensive review of skills that journalists need right away, such as the ability to ask clear, concise questions. The review of question formation in French continues throughout the six-course sequence. Using the wrong verb tense, an incorrect interrogative adverb, or garbled syntax can completely demolish an important question. Students practice writing questions by preparing opinion polls on specific subjects, after having studied many examples in the press. I correct the questions and multiple-choice answers on each student's poll; they retype them and provide photocopies to pass out in one of my other French classes. The completed forms are returned to the pollster, who then summarizes the results in an oral report in class. Some of the polls are directly related to the media, such as questionnaires dealing with students' television-watching habits or their sources for knowing what is going on in the world (newspapers they read, etc.). The students enjoy this activity because it involves a practical application of points reviewed in the grammar book and elicits information that is of interest to them as journalism students. One student used information gathered from a questionnaire in French to prepare an article for his news writing class in journalism.

Another practical application of grammar review is the oral interview with an invited guest. Funding in the original grant plus subsequent awards have provided the means to invite Francophone media professionals to campus. Preparation for the in-class interview begins well in advance. After reading about the journalist's news organization, each student prepares ten written questions, which are submitted to me for correction. Accuracy, especially in the use of verb tenses, is essential. Students have particular difficulty with questions asking, "How long have you been . . . (working for *Le Monde,* living in Washington, etc.)?" Instead of using the present tense, students tend to substitute the compound past in French. In one of our early interviews, a student inadvertently used the compound past to ask the regional director of Agence France Presse how long he had been working for the wire service. Upon hearing the past tense, the guest laughed and remarked facetiously in English, "I hope I am still working there, unless they fired me after I left the office yesterday." He then repeated the question correctly in French using the present tense and gave a serious answer. Although it was an embarrassing moment for the student, the point was well made. As students prepare questions for a live interview, they have the opportunity to apply what they have learned in the grammar book. They become all the more aware that grammar is not just a set of abstract rules but rather the key to accurate communication.

Professional courses in journalism such as news writing and editing place a great deal of emphasis on accuracy and attention to detail. In order to be admitted to the School of Journalism, students are required to pass a rigorous English proficiency exam, which includes grammatical analyses of sentences. Thus, in my view, journalism majors possess an understanding of how their own language works to a higher degree than most students. They are already convinced that grammar is an integral part of written and oral expression.

My goal in the content-based courses is to make grammar come alive by constantly going from textbook to reality, which in this particular case is the print and broadcast media. Some examples of the activities for teaching such grammar points as question formation, verb tenses, passive voice, pronouns, adjectives, conjunctions, and the like are described below.

Questionnaires and live interviews as just described constantly review the use of the interrogative. In addition, students examine interviews in print, listen to interviews on video, and study questionnaires to observe the use of the three ways to ask a question in French, by using *est-ce que*, by inversion, or by intonation. This activity was inspired by a student's question several years ago, "Which way is most common among native speakers of French?" The answer is, "That depends on the situation." Students find examples of interviews and questionnaires published in the written press, then they watch several interviews on video in the language laboratory. Each student prepares his or her own observations, which become the basis for a class discussion to see if we can come to a conclusion on interrogative formation in French. The research project also reinforces their own skills in asking questions, one of the most important attributes of a good journalist.

A review of verb tenses in most grammar books is spread throughout ten to fifteen chapters with the passive voice often relegated to an appendix. During the first two or three weeks of the media-based courses, students must learn to recognize six tenses in the indicative mood (present, compound past, imperfect, pluperfect, future, and future perfect), the present and past conditional, and the present and past subjunctive. They also learn to recognize the journalistic use of the conditional, which in French is used to indicate that something *allegedly* or *supposedly* took place. As I read the press, I collect examples of this particular use of the conditional so that students can observe the context and message the journalist wishes to convey.

The passive voice is frequently found in the French press, although most grammar books stress that a writer should avoid its use. Instead of going through the mechanics of converting the passive voice to active, the type of exercise found in many grammar books, it is more important for students reading the press to recognize the passive voice in news articles, observe its use, and understand why it is used. One assignment is for the students to scan French newspapers for verbs in the passive voice. When we pool these examples in class, students observe that many are found in articles dealing with terrorism and violence. Through this study of verb use, we came to the conclusion that we are indeed a society that is "acted upon."

While reviewing pronouns, adjectives, conjunctions, and other points of grammar, students go beyond book exercises to learn how one can communicate more accurately and on a more sophisticated level through correct usage of the language. Using the press as both the medium and the message increases the students' interest in applying what had earlier seemed to be abstract notions called "grammar."

Media Content

The content-based material has a double focus: the media itself and what is being reported by the media. Since the early 1980s there have been so many dramatic changes in the French media that the media have often been the subject of their own reporting. The audiovisual reform act passed by parliament in 1982 permitted private ownership of radio and television stations for the first time. The ripple effect of this act has caused major repercussions that are often the subject of press reports. The creation of three new private TV networks and the sale of one owned by the government (TF1) have created a demand for advertising that is unprecedented in France. Since the print medium has always been privately owned, and thus dependent upon advertising as a major source of income, the creation of privately owned networks poses the threat of redistributing large portions of the advertising pie to television, which before 1982 allowed only a small number of commercials. The subject of the media itself is a fascinating one that provides many current topics of interest to students majoring in journalism and telecommunications.

In addition to learning about the media through the media, we also focus on a variety of current topics such as the environment (both the problems and the new political parties created to protect the earth's ecology), social problems (drug and alcohol abuse; racism and immigration), politics (the French presidential elections and the elections for the European parliament), medicine (AIDS, test-tube babies, the pill, and abortion), and technology (especially France's outstanding accomplishments in the transportation industry). The content of each course is both planned in advance and dictated by current events.

The pedagogical approach to each topic is similar. The first step is for the instructor to select articles that present the subject as clearly as possible. For example, I have used articles from *Le Journal Français, L'Express, Le Point, and Le Monde*, all dealing with the same topic. Students are given a work sheet that helps them organize notes for a discussion in class. Their first task is to read the article and make a list of the essential points. The next step is to make a vocabulary list of words that are basic for a discussion of the topic. This is a task that is most often accomplished by textbook authors. I find that students are able to do it quite well themselves and in the process acquire a valuable skill, learning new words in context rather than from a dictionary. Students then answer specific questions that I have prepared to guide our discussion, which also includes spontaneous opinions and questions. At the advanced level, each major topic has a video component that the students either watch or produce themselves.

Video assignments that students watch are carried out individually in the language laboratory and then discussed in class. Students sign up for a specific time to use the videocassette and VCR station so that multiple copies of the tape are not needed and last-minute confusion is avoided. Assignment sheets for the video viewing include various types of activities designed to focus student attention on both the detail and the broad issues under discussion. Through their reading assignments, students have learned much of the vocabulary and are familiar with the subject matter. Students have mentioned that this preparation in advance makes the video activity very enjoyable because they can understand most of the program.

In addition to watching videos, we also produce videos in class. Interviews with native speakers play an important role in the content-based courses because they help develop speaking and comprehension skills and place the responsibility for finding out information on the student (as opposed to a guest speaker giving a lecture with the students simply taking notes). The interviews follow five steps: 1) preparation of questions, including background reading; 2) practice of delivery (correct pronunciation, loudness of voice, looking the speaker in the eye, and not reading from notes); 3) the live interview recorded on videotape; 4) individual review of the video in the language laboratory; and 5) writing an article in French based on the interview. Guests have included French journalists working in Washington, Quebec media professionals, and Francophone graduate students on campus studying journalism and telecommunications. Every class member is required to ask questions, and the order is established in advance so that students do not interrupt each other or wave their hands in the air to be called upon by the speaker—a rather awkward format used at presidential press conferences. Students mention these interviews on course evaluations as being among the most valuable activities for improving all four language skills.

At the advanced level students not only ask questions on video, they also produce their own news programs. The class is divided into small groups of three or four students to create a fifteen-minute broadcast dealing with current events. They choose the format and title of the program, which I videotape at the professional broadcast studio in the School of Journalism. One group titled their program "La voix de la presse" (The Voice of the Press) and used a moderator/journalists format; another group called their production "Quinze minutes de controverse" (Fifteen Minutes of Controversy) and debated the issues of immigration and racism in France. Information and vocabulary for each presentation are gathered from the French press and then prepared as a paper so that I can correct errors before intensive oral practice begins. Adequate preparation requires a great deal of individual and group practice out of class so that the participants can look at the camera instead of reading from notes. Responding to the students' suggestion, we make a first recording on Monday, place the tape in the language lab for reviewing and self-evaluation, and record again on Friday. The students then indicate which tape they want me to view for a grade. The results have been excellent. I never cease to be impressed by the amount of effort the students are willing to make, and they are proud of the results.

Content material from the media is introduced into the six-course sequence from the very beginning of the first course at the intermediate level and continues throughout the advanced conversation and composition courses. At the intermediate level students are introduced to the subject and are given an overview of the print and electronic media; at the advanced level, the approach is more in-depth, with one whole quarter devoted entirely to television (see Appendix B).

Since many students entering the intermediate sequence from high school have had no experience in the language laboratory or have never heard French spoken except in classroom pattern drills, listening comprehension must be developed by starting with programs produced specifically for learning French, then gradually phasing in carefully selected broadcasts intended for native speakers. Two programs have been very effective in building listening comprehension at the intermediate level:

Aérodrame, an audio sequence of twenty-five episodes recounting the adventures of a young journalist pursuing a scoop, and *French in Action,* a fifty-two-episode video program that serves as an excellent review of vocabulary and grammar points. Each week the intermediate students individually in the language laboratory view an episode from each program (without using a transcript), prepare notes based on an activity sheet, and participate in an oral discussion in class. In addition to these two programs, which continue throughout the three-course intermediate sequence, clips from French television broadcasts are introduced so that when the students reach the advanced-level sequence, they are able to deal with videos coming from sources intended for native speakers. The TV broadcast clips used at the intermediate level are directly related to reading assignments in order for students to understand the vocabulary and content of the video. Some of the selections from the French Collection produced by PICS (Appendix A) include transcripts and can easily be coordinated with articles from the current press.

Reading skills at the intermediate level are developed through articles from various sources. At the local bookstore students purchase *Le Journal Français*, a monthly (formerly biweekly) paper that can be ordered according to the number of students in the class during the year. The convenience of having the same issue in the hands of all students facilitates interesting activities. Students learn the specific vocabulary dealing with a newspaper, become acquainted with its different sections, and learn to read and discuss various types of articles, from the *faits divers* (recounting the basic who, what, why, when, where, and how of accidents, crimes, and other events) to the editorial expressing an individual's opinion.

Also useful for developing the student's ability to understand the press is the book *L'Express: Aujourd'hui la France* by Steele and Pavis. It includes strategies specifically designed for reading newsmagazine articles and comes with audiocassettes of selected articles read by a native speaker of French. Once the students become familiar with a specific subject by reading the article and learning the vocabulary, it is much easier for them to understand the oral rendition of the same article. Students find this approach to listening comprehension very helpful.

Articles from French and Quebec news periodicals (Appendix A) are photocopied for use in class so that students read from a variety of sources. They also make use of the news periodicals available in the library to carry out individual assignments. For example, after discussing several *faits divers*, each student must find additional ones from other news sources to present to the class. Other assignments include researching articles on the same subject presented in newspapers representing different political points of view, such as *L'Humanité* and *Le Figaro*. The "hands-on" approach to learning about the media while improving reading skills motivates students more than simply following chapters in a textbook.

Evaluation and Conclusion

Formal testing of proficiency levels among students in the journalism sequence and the regular sequence remains a future goal of the program. Because of the relatively few students involved in the special sequence (about fifteen at the end of the six courses each year), evaluation comes in the form of student opinion expressed on evaluation forms, retention rates, increase in the number of students from the sequence going on to complete a major in French, and the success of students from the sequence who receive journalism internships in Paris and others who find jobs in the field of international communications. Students' written evaluations reveal a very positive attitude toward the media-based French courses and toward the relationship between the foreign language and their majors. One student wrote: "The course is excellent for journalism majors—it is relevant to what we are studying in other (journalism) courses." Similar comments are repeated each year, and the courses are consistently given the highest rating by 90 percent of the students enrolled.

One of the goals of creating the content-based courses was to increase student enrollment in French at the fourth-year level. The realization of this goal can best be seen in my senior-level French phonetics course, where the undergraduate enrollment over the past few years has jumped from eight to fifteen to twenty-eight with half the students identified as journalism or communication majors. After completing the six-course media sequence (twenty-four quarter hours), students take an additional twelve quarter hours to complete the thirty-six-hour area concentration required for their journalism major. Students also have the choice of taking eighteen hours in each of two areas, such as French and political science, an option many of them choose. In any case, the enrollment increases that we have experienced beyond the conversation and composition level are largely due to journalism and communication students who continue their studies at the fourth-year level.

The two students selected each year for internships in Paris and Brussels have all reported that their proficiency levels upon arrival were adequate to function on the job, and the knowledge of the French media acquired in class was a great benefit to them. One student remarked that her prior knowledge of the French press allowed her to ask intelligent questions.

When possible, I invite these interns to class after they return to share their experiences in order to inspire and encourage their peers on the long, tedious road to proficiency in a foreign language.

Content-based courses in the French media have been very successful in motivating students and giving them self-confidence in their comprehension and speaking abilities. Because of the training the students receive in their majors, they are particularly receptive to using television and video to increase their foreign language skills and knowledge of current events. In a world of instantaneous international communication, linking the studies of foreign languages and the media seems long overdue.

Lois Vines is Professor of French and Distinguished Professor of Humanities at Ohio University. Co-recipient of a U.S. Department of Education Grant to internationalize the undergraduate curriculum, she has taught a sequence of French courses for journalism majors and initiated a course in French for business. Address: Dept. of Modern Languages, Ohio University, Athens, OH 45701 (Email: lois.vines@ohiou.edu)

List of Appendixes

Appendix A: Sources for Material About Francophone Media

This appendix is divided into five parts: (1) background reading on the Francophone media; (2) books and articles on the media with a pedagogical focus: (3) Francophone news periodicals; (4) audio and video materials; and (5) organizations offering pedagogical support for the Francophone media.

Appendix B: Module for French-Language Television

This is the syllabus for a module in which students study French and French-Canadian television operations and programming.

Appendix A
Sources for Material about Francophone Media.

1. Background Reading on the Francophone Media

The following list is a selected bibliography of books and articles that provide background reading and reference works on the French-language media. This list does not include articles from the current press kept in up-date files too numerous to include here.

Albert, Pierre, and F. Terrou. 1988. *Histoire de la presse.* 5th ed. Paris: PUF.

———. 1988. *La Presse.* 8th ed. Paris: PUF.

Bellanger, C., ed. 1969-1976. *Histoire générale de la presse française.* 5 vols. Paris: PUF.

Berkowitz, Janice and Daniel Gross. 1981. "Change and Exchange: French Periodicals since 1968." *Contemporary French Civilization* 6: 237-253.

Bonvoisin, Samra-Martine, and Michèle Maignien. 1986. *La Presse féminine.* Paris: PUF.

Bourdon, Jérôme. 1994. *Haute Fidélité, pouvoir et télévision, 1935-1994.* Paris: Seuil.

Brusini, Hervé, and Francis James. 1982. *Voir la vérité: le journalisme de télévision.* Paris: PUF.

Charon, Jean-Marie. 1991. *La Presse en France, de 1945 à nos jours.* Paris: Seuil.

Chauvet, Philippe. 1986. *Le Câble, la télévision au pluriel.* Paris: Média et vie sociale.

Cortade, Jean-Emmanuel. 1993. *La Télévision française.* Paris: PUF.

Coulomb-Gully, Marlène. 1995. *Les Informations télévisées.* Paris: PUF.

Daniels, Douglas J. 1987. "Information, Image and Illusion: The *journal télévisé* in France, 1949-1985." *Contemporary French Civilization* 11: 1-25.

———. 1988. "*Publicité*, Politics and Public Service TV: Crisis at the Crossroads." *Contemporary French Civilization* 12: 36-63.

Delporte, Christian. 1995. *Histoire du journalisme et des journalistes en France.* Paris: PUF.

Eisendrath, Charles. 1979. "'Surplus Freedom' and the French Press." *Contemporary French Civilization* 3: 331-352.

——. 1980. "State Aid to the French Press: Can $500 Million Be Impartial?" *Contemporary French Civilization* 5: 1-21.

Freiberg, J. W. 1981. *The French Press: Class. State and Ideology*. New York: Praeger.

Fressoz, Roger. 1981. "La Liberté de la presse." *Contemporary French Civilization* 5: 289-298.

Gingras, Pierre-Philippe. 1985. *Le Devoir.* Montréal: Editions Libre Expression.

Guillama, Yves. 1988. *La Presse en France*. Paris: La Découverte.

Jeanneney, Jean-Noël. 1996. *Une Histoire des médias des origines à nos jours*. Paris: Seuil.

Jullian, Marcel. 1981. *La Télévision libre*. Paris: Gallimard.

Kuhn, Raymond. 1995. *The Media in France*. New York and London: Routledge.

Mathien, Michel. 1983. *La Presse quotidienne régionale*. 2nd. ed. Paris: PUF.

Mousseau, Jacques, and Christian Brochand. 1982. *Histoire de la télévision française*. Paris: Nathan.

Pinto, Louis. 1984. *L'Intelligence en action: Le Nouvel Observateur.* Paris: Métailié.

Sablier, Edouard. 1984. *La Création du 'Monde'*. Paris: Plon.

Thibau, Jacques. 1996. *Le Monde, 1944-1996: Histoire d'un journal dans l'histoire*. Paris: Plon.

Vines, Lois. 1988. *"Le Monde*: Survival of an Independent Press." *Contemporary French Civilization* 12: 64-73.

——. 1991. "Le Paysage audiovisuel français: Dramatic Changes and New Horizons." *The French Review* 64: 817-28.

Vines, Lois, and Alvi McWilliams. 1991. "The French Media 1980-1989: A Bibliographical Article." *Contemporary French Civilization* 15: 100-120.

Watts, Françoise. 1990. "Nouvelles Tendances dans la presse écrite."*Contemporary French Civilization*. 14: 11-20.

2. Books and Articles with a Pedagogical Focus

The following list includes textbooks that make use of the media to teach French and articles describing how to teach French through the media. Although the press articles presented in these works are out-of-date, the techniques and activities can be applied to current material.

Berwald, Jean-Pierre. 1986. *Au courant: Teaching French Vocabulary and Culture Using the Mass Media*. Washington, D.C.: Center for Applied Linguistics.

Lawrence, Katherine. 1987. "The French TV Commercial as a Pedagogical Tool in the Classroom." *The French Review* 60: 835-844.

Leroy, Marie-José, Richard Nahmias and Ross Steele. 1986. Vivre *au pays: Les Français dans leurs régions à travers la Presse.* Paris: Didier.

Monnerie, A. 1987. *Le Nouvel Observateur: en France aujourd'hui. Idées, Arts. Spectacles.* Paris: Clé international.

Ruprecht, Alvina. 1981. "Les médias dans la salle de classe: L'enseignement du français aux étudiants en journalisme." *Canadian Modern Language Review* 37: 320-328.

———. 1982. "L'article de presse: Pour une lecture en profondeur." *Canadian Modern Language Review 39* : 70-82.

Schorr, Natalie Gillingham. 1983. *En Revue: Le français par le journalisme.* Lexington, MA: D.C. Heath.

Steele, Ross, and José Pavis. 1993. *L'Express: Aujourd'hui la France.* Lincolnwood: National Textbook. Instructor's Manual. 1994. Audiocassettes.

3. Francophone News Periodicals

Current news periodicals available at the Ohio University Library include newspapers and magazines from France and Quebec. Selecting among the many periodicals available is a difficult task. Our choice is based on publications that have a wide readership and represent a broad spectrum of political views. We are attempting to acquire subscriptions to periodicals from Francophone African countries but have had difficulty obtaining these through subscription services.

Students have direct access to the newspapers and magazines in the reference room. Magazines are bound each year and kept in the stacks while newspapers are discarded after a couple of months. Upon request, the library will save the newspapers for use in class. The only French-language newspaper for which we have back issues on microfiche is *Le Monde.* There are two very helpful indexes to French periodicals, *Le Monde, index analytique* and *French Periodical Index,* both essential tools for research projects. Newspapers: *Le Canard enchaîné, Le Devoir* (Quebec daily published in Montréal), *Le Figaro, L'Humanité, Le Journal de Montréal, Le Journal Français, Libération,* and *Le Monde.* Magazines: *L'Express, Jeune Afrique, Le Figaro Magazine, Le Nouvel Observateur, Paris Match,* and *Le Point.*

4. Audio and Video Materials

Ideas on how to make effective use of video are found in Rick Altman's *The Video Connection. Integrating Video into Language Teaching.* Boston: Houghton Mifflin Co., 1989.

Audio:

Aérodrame St. Paul, MN: EMC Publishing, 1974. A twenty-five episode program dramatizing the adventures of a journalist in pursuit of a scoop.

Champs Elysées P.O. Box 148067, Nashville, TN 37215. A monthly news magazine on cassette with transcription and notes.

L'Express: Aujourd'hui la France. Set of three sixty-minute audiocassettes that go with book by Steele and Pavis (see above).

Video:

France Panorama. Lexington, MA: D.C. Heath, 1989. A video magazine produced in cooperation with French TV network Antenne 2.

France-TV Magazine. This French news and information series is available via satellite for a fee. For information contact Victor Aulestia, AC IV, Rm 214, University of Maryland Baltimore County, Baltimore, MD 21228.

France From Within. Prod. Bernard Petit. Boston, MA: Heinle & Heinle, 1986.

French in Action. Prod. Pierre Capretz. Yale UP, 1987.

PICS (Project for International Communication Studies). This consortium provides a good selection of French-language TV programs on videocassette along with pedagogical guides, transcripts, and videodiscs. For a catalog call 1-800-373-PICS; E-mail: pics@uiowa.edu or write to PICS, The University of Iowa, 270 International Center, Iowa City, IA 52242- 1802.

La Publicité en France. New York: Gessler Publishing Co., 1987.

97 Publicités télévisées. Lexington, MA: D.C. Heath, 1989. A student workbook, *Le français en réclame,* can be purchased to go with the video. A *Guide Pédaqoqique* is provided free with the purchase of the videocassette.

La Télé des Français. Middlebury, VT: Middlebury Language Schools, 1986. A selection of French TV shows and a pedagogical guide in French.

5. Organizations Providing Pedagogical Support for the Francophone Media

Centre de formation et deperfectionnement des journalistes (CFPJ), 33 rue du Louvre, 75002 Paris, France. CFPJ editions offer books on the media written for the nonspecialist: *La Radio* by Gérard Ponthieu; *La Télévision* by Edouard Guibert; *La presse audiovisuelle* by Caroline Mauriat; *Quotidiens régionaux. Les connaître, les utiliser à l'école* by Louis Guéry; and *La Presse écrite* by Jean-Luc Pouthier. Other books about the media and manuals for professional journalists are also available. A booklet describing the training program at CFPJ is an interesting document in itself, providing a description of the media curriculum offered by the school.

Departement Presse du Centre International d'Etudes Pédagogiques (CIEP), 1 rue Léon Journault, F-92311 Sevres Cedex, France. This government-sponsored, teacher-training institute offers workshops on request and publishes the monthly *Le Journal des Journaux*, a list of recent articles from the French press categorized by subject. Each issue also offers ideas on how to make use of the press in class. Subscribers can order photocopies of articles listed in the bulletin.

France Presse, 1051 Divisadero St., San Francisco, CA 94115. Publisher of the *Le Journal Français*. Phone: (415) 921-5100. E-mail: Fpress@hooked.net A teacher's guide is available: *Using French Language Newspapers in the Classroom* by Marie Galanti.

Appendix B
Module For French-Language Television

The purpose of this module is for students to participate in an in-depth view of French and Quebec television as part of their studies in the Francophone media taught entirely in French. This module is set up for a ten-week quarter with four classes meeting each week for fifty minutes. Approximately two and a half class meetings per week are devoted to this module. The remaining one and a half meetings per week are needed for grammar review, tests, and in-class interviews. All video viewing is done individually out of class in the language laboratory. Reading assignments are prepared on Monday for class discussion on Tuesday. Since the class does not meet on Wednesday, there is time to view the videos between Tuesday and class meeting on Thursday, when discussion based on the viewing is held. A wrap-up discussion of the readings and videos usually carries over to half the period on Friday.

Each weekly assignment deals with a specific topic related to television. Materials include two books, articles from news periodicals, videos, and live television relayed by satellite from Montréal. The two books, *La Télévision* and *La Presse audiovisuelle*, can be ordered from the Centre de formation et de perfectionnement des journalistes (see Appendix A, part 5). Reference to dates of periodicals are given in the module description. Brief references to video sources are given with complete information included in Appendix A, part 4. For each assignment, whether reading or video, students are given an activity sheet on which to prepare notes for oral discussion in class.

Week 1: Introduction to television vocabulary.

Each student is loaned the television schedule from *Nice Matin* (I purchased 20 issues for use in class). The activity sheet consists of questions using television vocabulary with the answers to be found in the broadcast schedule.

Historical perspective of television in France: *La Télévision* (henceforth abbreviated *LT*) pp. 38-41; La Presse *audiovisuelle* (abbreviated *LPA*), pp. 9-12.

Video: "24 chaines à New York" (from *Télé-Douzaine*, PICS). The program shows how the French view American television and wonders whether French TV will follow suit. The contents lead to an interesting comparison of French and American TV.

Week 2: Television news.

LT pp. 4-17, "Le journal télévisé." Description of how an evening news program is organized and carried out.

Video: "Le journal du soir" (La Télé des Français, Middlebury College). Also live broadcasts via satellite recorded on video in our lab.

Week 3: The role of the anchorperson in French TV.

LPA pp. 77-82, "Les journalistes de l'audiovisuel: Ils ne sont pas tous des supervedettes." *Paris Match* (2 mars 1989) "Interview avec Christine Ockrent." Other recent articles from the French press about well-known anchorpersons.

Video: Selections from PICS; newsprograms I have recorded in France and converted from SECAM to NTSC.

Week 4: Innovations in French programming, "Télématin and Téléachat."

LT pp. 24-27; LPA, pp. 35-40.
Video: "Télématin" (PICS)

Week 5: Financing French TV.

LT, 27-33; LPA; "Redevance télé: Pourquoi elle va augmenter." Le Point (15 août 1988) p. 24.
Video: "La Publicité en France" (Gessler Publishing Co.)

Week 6: Financing French TV.

LPA, pp. 53-57.
Video: "Publicités politiques" and "Grands Prix de la Publicités" (Télé-Douzaine, PICS).

Week 7: Invasion of American programs on French TV and its relationship to financing.

LT pp. 56-61; LPA, pp. 35-40 "Feuilletons américains, jeux et publicité." "Télévision: la loi des séries" L'Express (21 aout 1987) pp. 42-44.
Video: "Les Chiffres et les lettres" (La Télé des Français, Middlebury College). Comparison of French and American game shows.

Week 8: French television production, quantity, and quality.

Cable TV in France. LPA, pp. 59-63, "La France câblée." "Télé par câble: 20 milliards pour un fiasco" L'Express (28 octobre 1988) pp. 66-71.
Video: "Apostrophes." Could this program be a success in the U.S.? Audio assignment: "Interview avec Bernard Pivot" Champs-Elysees (février 1989), transcription p. 4-5.

Week 9: Live broadcasts from French-Canadian television.

Background on Quebec television presented in class. Preparation for TV viewing: "Le français parlé au Canada" (Toronto: Ontario Institute for Studies in Education, 1979) audiocassette and reading material. This program gives students an idea of the basic differences between French pronunciation in Canada and in France.

Video: During the whole week each student watches a program broadcast live from Montréal. We divide the broadcast day into segments so that all programs are covered by at least one student. On Friday, each student gives an oral report on the program he or she watched, indicating its content, format, and an evaluation of the program.

Week 10: Presentation of student-produced TV programs.

At the beginning of the quarter, the class is divided into groups of 3 to 4 students. The assignment is to produce a news broadcast or debate dealing with the French media. During the last week of class, these programs are presented to the class and recorded on video.

7

The Undergraduate Foreign Language Immersion Program in Spanish at the University of Minnesota

Carol A. Klee and Diane J. Tedick

Editors' Note: Klee and Tedick and their colleagues at the University of Minnesota have designed a content-based Foreign Language Immersion program (FLIP) for students with an Intermediate-High level of proficiency (approximately three years of college-level foreign language study). In this chapter they describe their successful pilot program in Spanish, which has since been expanded into French and German. This model is quite different from others seen so far in this volume. It is a "full immersion" academic program. Students choose blocks of courses depending on their interests and academic objectives. The authors describe the challenges in preparing and training instructors (mostly graduate students). They have done a particularly outstanding job of developing assessment instruments for their program. Their formidable "assessment battery" includes traditional academic testing, oral proficiency tests, cloze and reading comprehension tests, focus groups, diaries and student self-assessment. Appendixes provide statistical data and, for the benefit of Spanish teachers, a model syllabus of a FLIP Spanish course. Klee and Tedick address all the thorny issues involved in CBI in foreign language instruction in a college setting: student entrance requirements, curricular development and coordination, balance between content and language learning, teacher competencies, program assessment, cost effectiveness, and administrative support. General references for this chapter are located in the bibliography at the end of this volume.

Introduction

The Foreign Language Immersion Program (FLIP) at the University of Minnesota was launched in the spring of 1993 as an expansion of our Foreign Language Across the Curriculum program which dates from the mid-1980s (Klee and Metcalf 1994). The purpose of the program has been to provide an opportunity for undergraduate students to immerse themselves in a foreign language for one academic quarter, studying the culture, literature, history, and politics of the region in which the language is spoken. The initial FLIP, developed as a pilot program in 1993, was available only in Spanish, but in the fall of 1994 the Institute for International Studies in the College of Liberal Arts received funding from the National Endowment for the Humanities for a three-year project to expand FLIP opportunities to French and German (Metcalf and Tedick 1993). Currently, programs are offered in each of the three languages every spring.

In order to participate in FLIP, students need to have completed at least nine quarters of college-level language courses. Students who have only completed the minimum number of courses and/or are not at the Intermediate High level (or above) on the American Council on the Teaching of Foreign Languages (ACTFL) Oral Proficiency Interview (OPI) have found the program to be too rigorous and generally have had to drop one or more classes before the end of the quarter. Most students who have participated in Spanish FLIP to date are Spanish majors and most have spent some time abroad.

Once in the program, students are required to take three four-credit courses: two are in the social sciences and change from year to year, and one is a two-credit course on international news coverage. For the third four-credit class, students can choose from several options within the language departments. The first year the program was offered, in 1993, students could choose from three different blocks of courses: the first focused on Spain and Western Europe, the second focused on Latin America, and the third was called "Humanistic Studies of Hispanic Culture." We found that the vast majority of the students chose the Latin American block; consequently, in subsequent years the Spanish FLIP has focused on Latin American topics. The course choices are as follows (number of credit hours are shown in parentheses):

Block 1: Spain and Western Europe

1. Politics and Cultural Expression in Twentieth Century Spain (4)
2. Topics in International Relations: The Ibero-American Community (4)
3. Foreign Language News Coverage of International Events (2)
4. One Spanish Language or Literature Course (4):
    Advanced Communication Skills
    Reading Literary Texts
    Spanish Literature: Aspects of Prose and Fiction
    Topics in Spanish Peninsular Literature

Block 2: Latin America
1. Topics on Latin American History: 1900 to the Present (4)
2. Topics in International Relations: The Ibero-American Community (4)
3. Foreign Language News Coverage of International Events (2)
4. One Spanish Language or Literature Course (4):
   Advanced Communication Skills
   Reading Literary Texts
   Spanish-American Literature: Aspects of Drama
   Topics in Spanish American Literature
   Caribbean Literature

Students must successfully complete all four courses to remain in FLIP. If they drop one or more courses, they are not considered full FLIP participants. If students successfully complete FLIP, they receive one extra credit, and if they are not language majors, they may request a special designation on their transcripts that reads "Language Achievement in Spanish" (or French or German). FLIP courses count toward majors in both Spanish (or German or French) and International Relations.

Instructors for the three required FLIP courses have generally been advanced graduate students in the social sciences who are native or near-native speakers of the language of instruction. The first time the Spanish FLIP was offered they were given no workshop or seminar to prepare them to teach their subject matter to non-native-speaking students. This resulted in numerous problems. For example, the history instructor, a graduate student from Latin America who had taught history at a university in his native country, did not realize that he would need to make adjustments in his course for nonnative speakers of Spanish. The first day of class he assigned 150 pages of reading in Spanish for the next class period and had to deal with a near-revolt by FLIP students. During the past three years, instructors have participated in a three-day seminar to introduce them to sheltering techniques, syllabus preparation, text selection, and ways in which they can make their courses more student-centered. (See Appendix A for an outline of the seminar topics.)

At this training seminar, instructors are given a number of recommendations as they begin to design the syllabi for their FLIP courses. First, when selecting texts, instructors are asked to focus on primary documents (e.g., speeches, interviews, letters, homilies, newspaper articles, and government and military documents) rather than scholarly texts. In the Foreign Language Across the Curriculum program (formally in operation at the University of Minnesota since 1988), we discovered that students find primary documents to be more accessible and, providing they have background knowledge, easier to understand than theoretical texts. We also suggest that instructors limit the amount of reading required in Spanish to a maximum of forty pages per week. Even this amount of reading has proven to be overwhelming to students at the lower ranges of proficiency. In addition to the readings in Spanish, we suggest that instructors provide background readings in English to furnish the historical, social, and cultural context for the primary documents. (See Appendix B for a sample syllabus and required readings in English and Spanish.) We also strongly recommend that instructors provide reading guides that direct students to background readings in English or provide information on the context in which the document was written. The reading guides might also include questions to help students focus on important issues within the text itself as well as a post-reading section that structures the discussion session and places the reading in a larger social and historical context. (See Appendix C for a sample reading guide.)

There is also a need for a number of other instructional adjustments in FLIP courses. For example, in content courses offered in a second language, good organization is essential; instructors must provide students with a detailed outline of the course of study and also be sure that learners are aware of how each day's class will be structured (Migneron and Burger 1989). Frequent references should be made to the reading material. Following Migneron and Burger, we also suggest that instructors give students frequent feedback on their progress and that they require shorter but more numerous written assignments so that they can identify problems quickly and adjust their teaching if necessary. Because students' language skills vary, we recommend that instructors include a brief lecture on the topic of the day to provide a framework for students and then allow opportunities for structured discussion in both large and small groups. We have found that shyer students are more willing to talk in small groups than in whole-group sessions, and this provides an opportunity for them to participate more actively in the class. While most of these recommendations can be viewed simply as good pedagogy, whether a class is given in English or a second language, we have found that many of these ideas are new to FLIP instructors. In spite of the three-day workshop, some instructors have preferred not to make adaptations. One, for example, believed that sheltering techniques would compromise the content of his course. Another became frustrated when he told students to form groups and "discuss the readings" without specifying a task to accomplish and found that students were unable to engage in fruitful discussions.

The Third-Year Spanish FLIP Courses (1994)

In 1994 the topics of the three social science courses were identical to those taught in the Latin American block in 1993. The course on Twentieth Century Latin American History was taught by a Ph.D. student in the Department of History who was from Puerto Rico. The course provided students with an overview of the most important political, social, and economic processes that have shaped Latin America in this century. It began with an introduction to the formation of the region's economies, the exploitation of the region, and the first nationalistic movements at the beginning of the century. Attention then turned to an examination of the history of individual Latin American nations, followed by a brief analysis of the role of Latin America today.

The instructor's teaching style was very teacher-centered. The class period normally included a lengthy lecture on the topic of the day. Near the end of the class period students were asked if they had any questions and the instructor attempted to engage the full group in discussion. When students were given the opportunity to interact in small groups, the instructor remained behind his desk and did not circulate or appear responsive to potential questions. During class observations, the observer, who was a graduate Research Assistant, expressed concern that much of the lecture was over the students' heads but that the instructor did not seem to be aware of this fact. He never sought feedback from the students until the end of class and then only the most advanced students were able to articulate questions. This instructor expressed concerns that sheltering techniques (e.g., the reduction of the amount of reading in Spanish, the development of reading guides, adjustments in the pacing of lectures, requests of frequent feedback from students) would water down the content of the course and chose not to follow the recommendations that had been made to him in the workshop. In addition, he did not engage students in active learning techniques (e.g., the use of small groups, cooperative learning). Many students expressed concerns about his course and we scheduled a second seminar for instructors midway through the quarter to discuss students' (and our) concerns based on our observations, but he chose not to make any modifications in the way the course content was "delivered." (See comments by Frances, one of the students in this course, below.)

The course on the Ibero-American Community was taught by a Ph.D. student in the Department of Political Science who was from the United States but had extensive experience in Latin America. The course explored the idea of a community formed by Spain, Portugal, and the Latin American countries, with links derived from economic, political, and cultural ties. It began with a historical overview of the notion of "Ibero-America" and moved on to examine the nature of the diplomatic relations between the countries that form this community. By the end of the term, students were expected to explain the economic, cultural, and social bases that might make the existence of an Ibero-American community possible. Students were evaluated based on three short exams (60 percent), an oral presentation (10 percent), a final exam (20 percent), and class participation (10 percent).

The instructor of this course began each class with a very brief overview of the day's topic and then had students break into groups to work through the reading and discussion (i.e., post-reading) questions on their reading guides. During the last fifteen minutes of the class, the groups came together and addressed the major issues that had arisen during their discussions. Students were actively involved during the class and the instructor circulated among groups to answer questions or ask for clarification of the points that students were discussing. The one concern expressed by students, especially those with lower levels of proficiency, was that there was not enough lecturing done in this class. Some students felt that they needed the instructor to provide an overview of the topic and present background knowledge (in addition to the background readings in English) so that the readings would be more comprehensible. They were unsure of their own ability (and perhaps of their classmates' ability) to understand and clarify the important issues in the readings. They felt that they would benefit from a more structured class and a balance of lecture and small-group discussion. Because the majority of the students in the course were Spanish majors rather than social science majors, they lacked background knowledge on the topics of the class and found it difficult to discuss them without more guidance from the instructor.

The "Foreign Language News Coverage of International Events" course was taught by a Ph.D. journalism student from Central America. The course was designed to familiarize students with the Latin American press, journalistic practices, media materials, and general studies related to media coverage of international events. The general objectives of the course were to introduce some theoretical approaches to the study of Latin American news media, to acquaint the learners with a broad range of Spanish language sources of information, and to familiarize them with journalistic and mass media material useful for interdisciplinary work. Students were asked to read Spanish language newspapers from Latin America and compare their coverage of events to that of a U.S. newspaper or any other foreign newspaper in English. Students were evaluated based on class participation (15 percent), a mid-quarter exam (25 percent), a term paper (40 percent), and an oral presentation (20 percent).

The weekly meetings consisted of two parts. During the first part, the class discussed, in both large and small groups, the general theoretical and topical readings assigned each week. The topics included comparative media studies and press criticisms, the press in Latin America, international/ transnational communication, international news agencies and foreign correspondents, and journalism practices: ideology of professionalism and objective reporting, journalistic ethics, development news and alternative communication, new technologies, and international relations. The second part of the class was designed to focus on specific events and how they are covered in the press. The instructor used a wide variety of techniques in teaching this class—lectures, small- and large-group discussions, student presentations, invited speakers, and videos of newscasts. She seemed to strike an excellent balance and was able to maintain the interest and enthusiasm of students with very different learning styles and levels of proficiency in Spanish.

In addition to the three required courses, students selected one course from the offerings in the Department of Spanish and Portuguese related to advanced language study or Latin American literature. Although courses from the Department of Spanish and Portuguese were included in the FLIP curriculum, only a handful of FLIP students enrolled in each class because of the relatively large number of courses available to choose from. As a result, no effort was made to coordinate formally with the instructors of those courses and they geared them, as they normally would, for Spanish majors who are generally nonnative speakers of the language.

Evaluation of the 1994 Spanish FLIP

In 1994, through the National Language Resource Center (NLRC) at the University of Minnesota, we began to conduct research on the Spanish FLIP. Initially, two research questions guided the project: 1) What level of language proficiency do students need upon entry into FLIP in order to pass FLIP courses with a grade of C or better? and 2) To what degree do students' foreign language skills improve in FLIP? To answer the second question, we developed academic assessment measures, observed classroom interaction, and developed an instrument for student self-assessment of target language ability and self-reported language use outside the classroom.

The assessment battery was developed by Carol Klee, Andrew Cohen, and Diane Tedick with the aid of Research Assistants Tomás Gonda, María Angeles Martín-Morán, and Lauren Rosen (Klee, Cohen, and Tedick 1995). The pre- and post-test battery was based on the University of California Language Ability Assessment System (LAAS, developed by Lyle Bachman and associates at UCLA to assess the language ability of students preparing for study abroad). We administered the LAAS as both a pre-test and post-test in 1993 in the hope that it might serve our purposes, but a study conducted by Loaiza-Arango (1993) revealed that the LAAS proved too difficult for the students. Based on these results, we designed a battery of assessments, less challenging than those found in the LAAS, which was administered at the beginning and end of the spring quarter in 1994 and 1995. Table 1 presents a brief description of the current battery. The battery was designed around one theme (women in Latin America), which contextualizes the test for students.

Modality	Current Battery
Reading	After reading an eight-hundred-word academic text in Spanish on the role of a democracy in Latin America, students answer, in English, seven open-ended comprehension questions (presented in English). Some of the questions involve inferencing. Answers to questions are scored on the basis of a point system for each correct idea unit contained in the reponse.
Writing	Students are asked to write a minimum of 150 words in response to a prompt (presented in Spanish) on whether the respondent foresees any change in men's and wome's' roles in Latin America in the future. The writing sample is scored by two raters using an analytic scale containing categories for content (thirty points possible), organization (twenty points), language use/grammar categories/morphology (twenty-five points), and mechanics (five points).
Speaking	Students participate in a twenty to thirty minute oral proficiency interview (OPI, based on ACTFL guidelines) with a trained interviewer.
Listening	Students listen to ten-minute video taped lecture by a native speaker on the contribution of women to the workforce in the colonial period of Latin America. During this task, students fill in a grid (in English) containing categories for organizing the information in the lecture. They also answer five open-ended comprehension questions (presented in English) before the lecture. Completion of the grid and answers to questions are scored on the basis of a point system for each correct idea unit contained in the response.
Grammar Development	Students complete a thirty-item rational deletion cloze task (i.e., specific grammatical items are deleted) on a text on sexism in society. Scores are based on student's ability to fill in the deletions with exact or equivalent responses. Students are presented with a six-sentence elicited imitation task, via audiotape, in which they listen to sentences and repeat them. The task yields scores for syntax, morphology, agreement (subject-verb and noun-adjective/determiner), and production of the exact or an equivalent phrase.

Table 1, The Spanish Academic Language Proficiency Battery

In the pilot year (1994) the assessment instruments, in the process of development, changed substantially between the first and second administration, so we were unable to accurately determine the true extent of improvement during the FLIP quarter. Furthermore, we tested only seven students. We found it difficult to recruit students to take the pre- and post-tests even though we offered a modest financial incentive. Eleven of the original eighteen students who had enrolled in the 1994 Spanish FLIP successfully completed it. We tested seven of the original eighteen, but only five completed the FLIP. The other two felt overwhelmed by the amount of work and had to drop one or more classes.

Case Study Data

The most interesting data from the 1994 cohort came from our case studies of three student volunteers of very different levels of oral proficiency who wrote weekly diaries on their language learning experience. The first student, who will be called Heidi, had spent a year in Bolivia and was very fluent in Spanish. Although we did not carry out ACTFL oral interviews that year, she was most likely in the Advanced range of the ACTFL scale. She was the only one of the three students who chose to write her diary in Spanish, indicating that she was much more comfortable with the language than either of the other two students, Linda and Frances. These two students each dropped one of the FLIP courses early in the quarter and could no longer be considered as fully enrolled in the program. However, they continued to take two or three courses in Spanish. Although both had participated in study abroad programs, their communication skills in Spanish were at a lower level than those of the first student.

Heidi had few academic or language problems during the FLIP quarter. Her journal usually began with the Anglicized phrase: *"Hoy es viernes y todo está yendo bien"* ["Today is Friday and everything is going well"]. During the fourth week of the quarter she felt overwhelmed by the quantity of work she had to complete, but her overall experience in the program was a very positive one. She completed her FLIP courses with a 4.0 average (the maximum GPA at the University of Minnesota). Her self-assessment of improvement in vocabulary and reading skills was confirmed by the results of the pre- and post-tests in reading in which she improved over thirteen percentage points in spite of the fact that the post-test was harder than the pre-test. In addition, her score on the essay section of the exam improved fourteen percentage points.

The second student, Linda, decided after three weeks of class to take only two of the four FLIP courses. She had studied Spanish for a year and a half and believed that her speaking skills were fine, although she admitted in her diary that she sometimes had to speak English in her FLIP classes to make herself understood. At times, she had trouble communicating with native speakers of Spanish on nonacademic topics, and she found it difficult to read, write, and understand academic Spanish. She mentioned in her diary that having to read material in Spanish was time-consuming and tedious and she found that many of the readings were over her head, observing "for the most part, my reading comprehension is lacking." Linda's difficulties with reading also affected her ability to write papers for her courses because she was unable to completely understand the readings.

Linda was frustrated that the prerequisites for FLIP (i.e., three third-year courses) did not adequately prepare her for the program. She believed it unfair "that those Spanish speakers with more experience can set the level for the class. The rest of us are left to 'struggle for air and to swallow gulps of water' as we try to stay afloat in this program." In spite of her considerable frustration and difficulties, she managed to complete the two FLIP courses with Bs. Again, although the tasks were not comparable in the pre- and post-tests of listening, she did show an eleven percentage point gain and her writing score improved by more than fifteen percentage points. Her reading score dropped by more than thirty-eight percentage points, most likely as a result of the type of texts on the pre- and post-tests. The pre-test text was less academic in nature while the post-test text was the type of scholarly text with which she had experienced immense frustration in her classes.

The third student, Frances, also experienced frustration. She had to drop the two-credit news coverage course, but continued in the other FLIP courses. Her greatest frustration was with the course on the History of Latin America. Her comments during the second week of class reflected a struggle with the quantity of reading material. When assigned forty-four pages in Spanish, she wrote, "I cannot simply get the gist of it and leave it at that because we will eventually be tested on the materials. Realistically, I do not see myself understanding this material enough to get tested and earn a good grade." Frances stayed in the history course, but received a C. She received a C and a B in the other courses, in spite of the fact that she had a 3.6 GPA going into the quarter. Based on her test scores, there seemed to be virtually no improvement in her language skills. In her self-assessment at the end of the quarter, she rated herself at the same level in all skills except for reading and writing, in which she rated herself at a lower level than at the beginning of the quarter.

The Third-Year Spanish FLIP Courses (1995)

Beginning in 1995, a call for course proposals was circulated to advanced graduate students who were interested in developing courses in Spanish. A small committee consisting of Professor Michael Metcalf, Director of the Institute of International Studies, Professor Carol Klee of the Department of Spanish and Portuguese, Silvia Lopez, the FLIP Coordinator, and Professor Diane Tedick of the Department of Curriculum and Instruction, reviewed proposals. The two courses selected were

"Religion and Social Change in Twentieth Century Latin America" and "Transformations of Latin American Social Movements."

The course on Religion and Social Change in Twentieth Century Latin America was taught by a Ph.D. student in Anthropology who was from the United States, but who had spent two years in Guatemala conducting research on his dissertation. The course was organized according to themes such as the poor and their reaction to injustice, popular religion, syncretic religions, spiritualism, and women and religion. Within these themes, different religions or religious perspectives were discussed and the class examined the reciprocal relationship of religion and society.

The instructor organized his class to insure active student participation. Following a brief introduction to the topic, students formed small groups to discuss the reading and discussion questions in the reading guide. The instructor circulated among the groups to answer questions. During the last part of the class period, students came together to report the results of their discussion. As the quarter progressed, the instructor, who was very responsive to student concerns, made two modifications. First, he reduced the number of themes studied, deciding to concentrate more closely on fewer themes. (The syllabus in Appendix B is based on the modifications that he made midway through the course.) He also discovered that the students, most of whom lacked background knowledge on the topic of religion, needed an overview of the topic, so he began to give twenty-minute lectures at the beginning of each class before students broke into their discussion groups.

The course on Transformations of Latin American Social Movements was taught by a Ph.D. in the Department of Anthropology who was from Chile. The class was divided into five parts. In the first, the "paradigms for the analysis of collective action," were introduced. The second part dealt with labor and peasant movements as exemplars of the "old social movements." The third part described the crisis of the old social movements and the proliferation of new social movements, the fourth was "collective action and political participation at the turn of the century in Latin America," and the final part was a broad discussion about the interrelationship of ideas, historical context, and social change as they relate to collective action and political participation. The readings and themes discussed in this course were highly theoretical, and students had great difficulty with the content. Class time was devoted to lectures that introduced the theoretical concepts, followed by small-group discussions of the readings.

The course on Foreign Language News Coverage of International Events was taught by a Panamanian Ph.D. student in the Department of Journalism.

She used a syllabus and teaching approaches that were very similar to those of the previous year.

Following the recommendations of the 1994 FLIP instructors that many students would benefit from having a tutor available, a Chilean Ph.D. student in the Department of Anthropology was hired. In addition to holding weekly office hours to work with students, she circulated brochures with information concerning activities in the Twin Cities (e.g., movies, lectures, art exhibitions) related to Latin America. She also organized a series of extracurricular activities that related to the content of the FLIP courses, such as lectures by guest speakers on social movements and religion in Latin America, and films (e.g., *In Women's Hands, The Burning Season, Conflicto en Chiapas,* and *La Lucha*).

Evaluation of the 1995 Spanish FLIP

In the spring of 1995, eleven students enrolled in the FLIP quarter, and eight were able to successfully complete it. Of those eight, six students agreed to take the pre- and post-test Spanish Academic Language Proficiency Battery and participate in the focus groups and exit interviews.

The limited quantitative evidence indicates that students' language abilities generally did improve, provided that their skill levels at the start of the program were at a certain threshold—a level yet to be firmly established. The paired t-test results were statistically significant for three of the subtests, the cloze test ($p < .05$), the elicited imitation task ($p < .05$), and the writing portion ($p < .01$). The cloze and elicited imitation had been added to the 1995 assessment package precisely because they had been found to be sensitive to gains in language proficiency even over just one quarter of immersion instruction. Students' reading comprehension improved substantially, as reflected by the mean scores and standard deviations (pre-test = 68.00 [25.09], post-test = 80.17 [14.23]) and approached significance ($p = .06$). (See Table D.1 in Appendix D for a summary of the mean pre- and post-test scores for the five subtests.) The listening comprehension section was the only section that did not reveal strong gains. Although there were few subjects and there was no comparison group, the improvement shown on four of the five subtests is encouraging. The improvement suggests not only that students' language skills are influenced by their participation in FLIP, but also that our instruments are sensitive enough to reveal change in a relatively short period of time (ten weeks).

The results of the self-assessment of language skills that were administered on a pre- and post-course basis reveal a slight tendency to indicate greater facility with the language. On a scale of 1 (minimum) to 4 (maximum), respondents rated themselves higher in vocabulary, discussion skills, and grammatical knowledge at the end of the quarter than at the beginning, although only the pre- and post-assessment for vocabulary were statistically significant using t-tests for dependent samples (see Table D.2 in Appendix D). Their comfort level in Spanish also increased, as indicated by the slight change in their responses to items 7 (conversation with native-speaking friends), 8 (handling telephone directions), 9 (asking professor to change exam grade), 10 (participating in class discussion), and 11 (going to a play or movie). It was reassuring to note that there is almost no change in attitude toward items like "knowing the language makes me a more educated person" (3.6 pre and 3.7 post). This indicated that the FLIP experience helped to maintain their initially positive attitudes.

Results of the Focus Groups and Exit Interviews

Two focus-group sessions were conducted with six of the 1995 Spanish FLIP students, the first during the second week of classes and the second during the sixth week. Although we had outlined a series of questions focusing on issues that we considered of interest, these were not followed rigidly. In addition to the focus groups, each student was interviewed individually at the end of the quarter. We also held a focus group with the instructors during the fifth week of the quarter to elicit their perspectives on the program and their perceptions of students' performance.

From the focus-group discussions and the exit interviews, a number of interesting issues emerged that provided us with feedback on the program. For example, we were interested in what motivated students to enroll in the Spanish FLIP. One student, who was planning to participate in a study-abroad program the following fall, felt that FLIP would be good preparation. A second student, who had not studied abroad, felt that she was at a disadvantage in comparison to other Spanish majors who had spent time abroad and that an immersion program would equalize things. She also mentioned that as a Spanish major she thought that it would be interesting to take courses in Spanish outside of the department. She thought this would be "more rounding" and give her a different perspective. Another student said, "I knew that I couldn't afford a study-abroad program, and so I wanted something that I can do here. I'm again trying to improve my Spanish . . . ." A fourth student enrolled in the program to "force myself to talk." One student mentioned that she decided to participate in FLIP because it was the only way to get into Spanish classes, which normally fill early. (FLIP students have priority for registration.)

Another observation that emerged was what students perceived as the strengths of FLIP. Most students felt that their language ability improved, especially in speaking and reading, and most felt more comfortable using Spanish than they had at the beginning of the quarter. In addition, most students reported learning a great deal about Latin American culture and society. One reported changing her views on American society and discovering biases in U.S. news coverage that she had not been aware of before. Another of the major strengths was the cohort: one student explained that "it made school seem so small . . . I saw the same people every day." Another student said that she liked having classes with the same group of students, all of whom had common goals, beginning with improving their Spanish.

We were also interested in knowing what students saw as the weaknesses of the FLIP. Most students complained that there was too much reading and, because of the quantity of work, students often came to class unprepared. We found that many students experienced difficulty reading academic Spanish. One of the instructors identified problems with "conceptual language." Several students complained that the themes or concepts were difficult, especially in the social movements class. One said, "I didn't feel I had a good enough base for some of the topics we talked about, especially in social movements." He mentioned that the material itself was difficult, but that "It wasn't necessarily all [due to] the Spanish." Another said, "Sociological jargon is a language in itself and you can translate most of the words pretty easily to English and I don't know that in English, I mean, 'epistemological' is not in my vocabulary." These comments seem to corroborate Adamson's (1993) claim that in addition to language proficiency, other factors, such as background knowledge of the subject matter, influence the degree of success that students experience in content-based instruction.

Students made a number of suggestions to improve FLIP. Most students recommended reducing the number of classes from four to three and having each course count for more credits. Some students recommended having a linked language course worth four credits in place of the news coverage course (which many found very valuable) and making the extracurricular activities and tutoring sessions a required part of that class, since otherwise, few students took advantage of these opportunities. We should point out that the University of Minnesota is an urban campus and that a majority of undergraduates commute and work at least twenty hours a week. They are, therefore, unable to spend much time on campus. Most students would have preferred to have only FLIPPERS in their classes and complained that they were not as comfortable with the "outsiders," especially with those who were native speakers of Spanish. Wesche (1985) has cautioned against placing nonnative speakers with native speakers in immersion courses, arguing that if all students are nonnative speakers, their anxiety will be reduced. She has also suggested that with native-speaking students in the class, instructors may make less use of sheltering strategies. Unfortunately, we have been unable to offer the courses exclusively to non-native-speaking students because of the increasing pressure in our institution to maintain larger class sizes. Our hope is to generate more interest in FLIP so that future course offerings may be open only to second language learners.

A number of students mentioned that they would like to have more structured contact with the Hispanic community as a formal part of their FLIP courses. Students also recommended that incoming FLIP students be prepared more completely for "what it is they're gonna go through" so that fewer students drop out during the quarter, suggesting the need for a better orientation.

What Have We Learned?

We begin our concluding remarks by addressing the questions that both prompted our research and emerged from it.

1) What are the effects of a quarter of immersion instruction on the students' academic language proficiency in Spanish?

The limited quantitative evidence that we reported earlier in this chapter indicates that students' language abilities generally did improve during one quarter of immersion instruction. Students' scores on the language proficiency assessment in 1995 improved significantly on the writing portion and the two subtests that reflect grammar development (cloze and elicited imitation). Students' scores on the reading comprehension subtest also improved, and the difference between the pre- and post-test scores approached significance. In the self-assessment of language proficiency and attitudes toward language, students rated their facility with language higher at the end of the quarter than at the beginning and also indicated that their comfort level with Spanish had increased.

The qualitative data from interviews, journals, and focus groups (in 1994 and 1995) suggested that students' proficiency did indeed improve over the quarter as long as their proficiency level at the beginning of the program was at a certain threshold. Our data tentatively suggest that students having a proficiency level lower than Intermediate High ACTFL at the beginning of the quarter experience extreme frustration in the FLIP courses, commonly having to drop one or more, and ending up with grades lower than their GPAs might predict. At the same time, we recognize that language proficiency is not the only factor that contributes to success in the program. This point leads to our next question.

2) What kinds of preparation do students need in order to pass FLIP courses with a grade of C or better?

All the students who remained as full FLIP participants in both 1994 and 1995 passed their courses with a grade of C or better. On initial examination it appears that the language prerequisite—namely, the equivalent of three years of university-level language study—is appropriate. However, only eleven of the original eighteen students successfully completed the Spanish FLIP program in 1994 and eight out of eleven in 1995. Many students had to drop one or two courses (as did the two students who wrote the diaries), thereby relinquishing their full participation in FLIP, and experienced major difficulty and frustration. Data from the journals, interviews, and focus groups suggest that at least two issues may be contributing to the difficulty and frustration that many students experienced—proficiency level and background knowledge of course content.

Threshold Proficiency

During both years of this study, the students whose initial scores on the proficiency assessment were the lowest encountered the most problems and also received the lowest grades in FLIP courses. It is our intention to use the assessment battery to determine the minimal scores that students must have in the various language modalities in order to succeed in the FLIP. The current prerequisites, based solely on seat time, are not sufficient. A score of ACTFL Intermediate High appears to be the minimum threshold for success in the FLIP.

Background Knowledge

Our data also suggest that the curricular content of the FLIP courses should be reexamined. It is possible that the actual course content is so advanced, requiring such a degree of background knowledge, as to make it very difficult for students, regardless of proficiency level. Adamson (1993), among others, has argued that students may compensate for lower proficiency levels in academic courses with high levels of prior knowledge of course content. The instructors were well aware of the need to provide students with background knowledge of the content and tried to do so by suggesting readings in English. However, students, who were short on time, tended to regard the English readings as unnecessary and did not take advantage of the support the readings would have provided. This suggests that, in addition to establishing minimum levels of proficiency for entrance into FLIP, we would also be wise to plan the FLIP curriculum in such a way as to make it possible for students to develop sufficient background knowledge about course content to help them to succeed in the courses. Shaw (Chapter 12, this volume) draws a similar conclusion.

In addition to these two factors—proficiency and background knowledge—which appear to contribute to students' success in FLIP, our data suggest that pedagogy is also an important factor. This third factor is addressed in our next question.

3) How do we best balance content and language learning?

Our fundamental goal in offering a FLIP quarter is to provide an experience for students that will enhance their language proficiency and at the same time increase their content knowledge. Such a goal requires well-prepared instructors and a program model that allows for a balance between content and language.

Our study of this CBI experiment revealed the devastating consequences on sheltered programs when the instructors are unwilling to employ sheltering strategies. Unfortunately, the instructor with whom we had the most problems had participated in a three-day seminar on how to make adaptations in his course for nonnative speakers of Spanish; however, he was unwilling to make the suggested adaptations. The question remains, then, of how best to prepare social scientists, who do not teach language classes, to participate as instructors in this program. Based on our experience over the past three years, it is clear that a three-day workshop is, in many cases, inadequate. We have frequently found ourselves in a role of troubleshooter, similar to the one Peter Shaw (1996) has described, as we attempt to gather ethnographic data on the students' experience in FLIP.

In the original FLIP model, we expected to involve social science faculty in teaching some of the courses each year. Unfortunately, given the current economic crisis facing public institutions of education and increasing pressures to teach high enrollment courses, departments are often not supportive of faculty who would like to teach a course that enrolls only twenty-five students, particularly when most of them are not majors in their discipline. In addition, faculty are reluctant to become involved because of the extra effort required to teach a FLIP course. For these reasons, we have tended to hire advanced graduate students to offer instruction in the program.

There are advantages to having graduate teaching assistants as FLIP instructors: 1) they often have more time than faculty members to spend on course development and preparation; 2) they are usually open to ideas and suggestions for improving instruction; and 3) some have received training in language instruction or have taught in language departments, making them more likely to understand and be sensitive to the challenges inherent in content-based instruction. The greatest disadvantage of hiring graduate students, of course, is that they eventually leave the university, creating the need to prepare new staff for teaching in the program each year.

Until now, the model we have been working with has focused on content instruction, but to strike a better balance between content learning and language learning, we need to establish firm goals for language learning within the context of these FLIP courses. One way to do this is with an adjunct language course in which students learn and practice the appropriate reading, listening, speaking, and writing strategies. We developed such a course for the 1996 program, are currently analyzing the data, and will report on the results at a later date.

Conclusions

Although the size of the sample and lack of a comparison group make it impossible to provide any definitive answers with regard to the pluses and minuses of the full immersion approach to content foreign language instruction at the university level, the results from two years of evaluating the University of Minnesota Spanish FLIP effort would suggest that there are numerous benefits. Pre- and post-test scores suggest that there are statistically significant gains in language proficiency at the end of the immersion quarter and that these gains seem attributable to the program. These gains have taken place while at the same time students have made progress through the subject matter of the respective courses.

Our detailed evaluation over the past two years has taught us that a number of issues need to be addressed concurrently. First and foremost, we believe (as does Klahn, Chapter 9) that administrative support is key to the success of programs like FLIP. Despite current budgetary constraints, we need to make the case for programs that contribute to the internationalization of the curriculum and strengthen students' proficiency in a second language. Second, we recommend that explicit program goals be established that emphasize the balance between content and language instruction. A related issue is the need to find instructors who are both able and willing to attend to both language development and content learning. One possibility is to employ graduate Teaching Assistants who have had experience teaching in language departments and who are familiar with the types of adaptations that must be made for second language learners. This, in fact, has worked quite successfully in the German FLIP.

A third issue to address is curriculum coordination. We believe that offering a consistent core of courses every spring quarter will allow students to plan for FLIP by taking subject-matter prerequisites that will allow instructors to assume a level of prior knowledge on the part of students. A consistent curriculum would facilitate course preparation since instructors would only need to update past syllabi rather than develop a course from scratch.

The final issue that needs to be addressed is target proficiency levels for entrance into the program. We hope that the assessment battery that we have developed will allow us to actually measure minimal levels of language proficiency for entrance into the program. Overall, in spite of continuing challenges, we are encouraged by the outcomes of the program and will continue to make modifications to improve the FLIP model and insure student success.

Carol A. Klee is Chair of the Department of Spanish and Portuguese and Associate Professor of Hispanic Linguistics. She has served as coordinator of research on immersion education in the National Language Resource Center at the University of Minnesota. She is President of the American Association of University Supervisors, Coordinators, and Directors of Language Programs (AAUSC) and has served on the Executive Council of the American Association of Teachers of Spanish and Portuguese (AATSP). Address: University of Minnesota, 34 Folwell Hall, 9 Pleasant St. SE, Minneapolis, MN 55455 (Email: Carol.A.Klee-1@tc.umn.edu)

Diane J. Tedick is Associate Professor of Second Languages and Cultures Education in the College of Education and Human Development at the University of Minnesota and is Coordinator of the Teacher Development Project of the University's National Foreign Language Resource Center. Address: University of Minnesota Second Languages and Cultures Education, 254 Peik Hall, 159 Pillsbury Dr. SE, Minneapolis, MN 55455-0208 (Email: djtedick@maroon.tc.umn.edu)

List of Appendixes

Appendix A: Foreign Language Immersion Program (FLIP) workshop for instructors

This appendix contains the outline of a yearly workshop given for FLIP instructors and a brief description of the topics that were presented and discussed.

Appendix B: Sample Syllabus for a Spanish FLIP course

This is the syllabus for a course on Religion and Social Change in Twentieth Century Latin America that was offered in the spring of 1995 by Chris Chiappari. For inclusion here the syllabus has been translated from the original Spanish. Note that the assignments include complete bibliographic information for the readings in Spanish as well as for the background readings in English.

Appendix C: Sample Reading Guide for a Spanish FLIP course

This is one of the reading guides for the course on Religion and Social Change in Twentieth Century Latin America. Note that the pre-reading section and the reading questions are in English to insure that students understand the assignment, while the post-reading (i.e., discussion) questions are in Spanish, as the discussion of the readings will be conducted in that language.

Appendix D: Assessment Results

Table D.1: Comparison of Pre- and Post-Test Means of the Spanish Academic Language Proficiency Battery of FLIP students (spring 1995).

Table #.2: Pre- and Post-Test Comparison for Self-Assessment in Language Skills and Attitudes of Spanish FLIP students (spring 1995).

Appendix A
Foreign Language Immersion Program
University Of Minnesota Workshop

Seminar leader: Carol A. Klee

Session I
Theoretical Foundations:
Discussion of the importance of input in second language acquisition.

Presentation of Courses to Be Developed:
Course content (syllabus), main themes, and objectives.

Syllabus Preparation:

Instructors are given sample syllabi from previous social science courses taught in a foreign language and instructors of these courses are invited to discuss how they planned their syllabus and what modifications they made based on their experience. Factors to take into account when designing the syllabus are discussed—learning goals, teaching modes, course texts, materials, and learning tasks.

Text Selection:

Instructors are asked to brainstorm examples of text types that they might use in their courses (e.g., biographies, comic books, diaries, editorials, essays, films, folklore, interviews, legal documents, manifestos, mass media, novels, oral literature, paintings, sermons, and speeches). The group discusses the advantages and disadvantages of various types of texts and ways to assess text difficulty, taking into account topic, genre, purpose of the text, vocabulary, and linguistic considerations.

Assignment for Session II:

1) Attempt to determine an overall course syllabus. Identify potential foreign language texts and identify criteria for selection of texts (e.g., type of text, length, and difficulty). Be prepared to report your results in Session II.

2) Read Carrell: "Fostering Interactive Second Language Reading"; Westhoff: "Increasing the Effectiveness of Foreign Language Reading Instruction" (Parts 1 and 2); and Smith: "Active Learning: Cooperation in the College Classroom."

Session II
Syllabus Development and Text Selection:

Report by course instructors.

Preparation of Reading Guides:

Instructors work through some foreign language texts and discuss top-down and bottom-up reading strategies. We then discuss the characteristics of the reader (e.g., motivation, ability to read in the native and foreign language, and experience with reading strategies), text (e.g., graphic layout, genre, conceptual message, linguistic considerations), and the task (e.g., the purpose of the task) that need to be taken into account when designing reading activities. Instructors are given reading guides used in previous courses and it is recommended that they follow a three-part structure. The first section, or the pre-reading activity, should prepare students for the task by providing linguistic, conceptual, and cultural background (including readings in English) and by suggesting appropriate reading strategies. The second section of the guide focuses on reading activities which include promoting an active hypothesis-testing and problem-solving approach to reading and providing students with comprehension checks including question/answer, charting information, and summaries or paraphrases. The final section of the reading guide should help students examine the insights they acquired while reading and relate the content to the topics studied previously.

Classroom Management:

Integration of reading, lecture, small-group work, and writing. We discuss how the classes should have a variety of formats—lectures, videos, small- and large-group work, class presentations, and active learning techniques to reach students with a variety of learning styles and levels of proficiency. Instructors view a video of the Sheltered Program at the University of Ottawa that provides examples of how instructors modified their lectures and syllabi for second language learners.

Types of Writing Assignments:

We discuss the need for frequent, briefer assignments rather than one long exam or term paper.

Assignment for Session III:
1) Choose a particular foreign language text for use in your course. Identify why this text is significant and demonstrate how this text might be prepared for student use (e.g., pre-reading, reading, and post-reading). Be prepared to report your results at Session III.
2) Read Brinton, Snow, & Wesche: Chapter 8, "Issues in Content-Based Evaluation"; and Ready and Wesche: "An Evaluation of the University of Ottawa's Sheltered Program: Language-Teaching Strategies at Work."

Session III
Presentation and Discussion of Reading Guides by faculty participants.

Discussion of Student Evaluation:

We recommend that students be evaluated frequently and discuss the relationship between language issues and content issues in student evaluation.

Course Evaluation:

Instructors are shown the instruments that would be given to students to evaluate their courses and are informed of the extensive program evaluation that would occur during the quarter.

Appendix B
Sample Syllabus
Religion and Social Change in Twentieth Century Latin America
(Translated here from Spanish)

Instructor: Chris Chiappari
Tutor: Debbie Guerra

In this course we will discuss the phenomenon of religion in the context of the social changes that the continent of Latin America has undergone in this century. We will focus on the Catholic and Protestant religions, along with some examples of indigenous and syncretic religions (that is, mixtures of Christianity with different religions, generally Christianity with an indigenous religion).

For convenience, the course is divided into sections by groups and by themes, although in reality it is often not possible to separate them so clearly: the poor (politics), indigenous (ethnicity) and women (gender). Within these themes and groups, there will be descriptions of different religions, perspectives of different religions or churches on certain themes, and analyses of certain religions and social phenomena. In this context we will examine the reciprocal effects between religion and society, that is, how religions (in their institutions, practices, and beliefs) change and have changed society, and also how society changes and has changed religions.

On a more general level, the emphases of the course are on the importance of religion as a social phenomenon in the world today, its complexity, and the variety of religious experience in Latin America.

The main readings will be in Spanish, but there are background readings in English in order to give a context to the readings in Spanish.

Course Requirements:
- Three partial exams (15 percent each of the total grade)
- An oral presentation (10 percent)
- A final exam (25 percent)
- Class participation (20 percent; it consists of regular attendance in class, preparation for discussion, and oral participation)

- Each student must consult with the instructor about the topic of his/her oral presentation, BEFORE OR DURING THE THIRD WEEK OF THE QUARTER. This presentation can be on any religious topic or person related to Latin America in this century. The presentation will be ten minutes long and, as part of it, the student must prepare a one-page summary of the presentation to be handed out to each member of the class.

Week 1: Introduction to the course; "The poor"

1. Tuesday 28 March: Introduction.
2. Thursday 30 March: Preferential option for the poor
   Reading: Consejo Episcopal Latinoamericano (CELAM). 1979. "Opción preferencial por los pobres." *Puebla: La evangelización en el presente y en el futuro de América Latina.* III Conferencia General del Episcopado Latinoamericano. 9a ed. Caracas: Ediciones Tripode. pp. 207-212.
   Background: Levine, Daniel H. 1986. "Religion, the Poor, and Politics in Latin America Today." *Religion and Political Conflict in Latin America.* Daniel H. Levine, ed. Chapel Hill: Univ. of North Carolina Press. pp. 3-23.

Week 2: "The poor and their reaction to injustice"

1. Tuesday 4 April: The study of the Bible
   Readings: Iriarte, Gregorio. 1991. *¿Qué es una Comunidad Eclesial de Base?: Guía didáctica para animadores de las CEB.* Bogotá: Ediciones Paulinas. pp. 7-25, 31-40, 47-52. Cardenal, Ernesto. 1983 [1978]. "La otra mejilla" en *El evangelio en Solentiname.* 3a ed. Managua: Nueva Nicaragua-Monimbó. pp. 72-76.
   Background: Levine, "Religion, the Poor, and Politics in Latin America" (the same as last week).
   Cook, Guillermo. 1994. "The Genesis and Practice of Protestant Base Communities in Latin America." *New Face of the Church in Latin America: Between Tradition and Change.* Guillermo Cook, ed. Maryknoll, NY: Orbis Books. pp. 150-155.
2. Thursday 6 April: Liberation theology
   Readings: CELAM. 1987 [1977]. "Justicia." *Los Textos de Medellín y el Proceso de Cambio en America Latina.*

3a ed. San Salvador: UCA Editores. pp. 25-32.

Richard, Pablo. 1987. "Como nace, crece y madura la Teología de la Liberación." *La Fuerza espiritual de la iglesia de los pobres.* Prólogo por Leonardo Boff. San José, Costa Rica: Editorial DEI. pp. 135-141.

Nuñez, Emilio A. 1988. "Conclusión: Un intento de respuesta." *Teología de la Liberación: Una Perspectiva Evangélica.* 3a ed. Miami: Editorial Caribe. pp. 255-266.

Thomas, Donald. 1993. *Lecciones de la Escuela Sabática para Adultos. Cartas a la iglesia: 1 Timoteo y Tito.* 98 (3): 62, 64, 80-81.

Background: Smith, Christian. 1991. "What is Liberation Theology?" and "Making Medellín." *The Emergence of Liberation Theology: Radical Religion and Social Movement Theory.* Chicago: University of Chicago Press. pp. 25-50; 150-164.

Week 3: "Popular religion"

1. Tuesday 11 April: The Catholic perspective and a Protestant case

    Readings: CELAM. 1979. "Evangelización y religiosidad popular." *Puebla: La evangelización en el presente y en el futuro de América Latina.* III Conferencia General del Episcopado Latinoamericano. 9a ed. Caracas: Ediciones Tripode. pp. 120-124.

    Jeter de Walker, Luisa. 1990. "El Salvador: II. Crecimiento Fenomenal 1950-90." *Siembra y Cosecha: Las Asambleas de Dios de México y Centroamérica.* Tomo 1. Deerfield, FL: Editorial Vida. pp. 78-94.

    Background: Luchetti Bingemer, Maria Clara. 1994. "Popular Religion and the Church: Hopes and Challenges at the Dawn of the Fifth Centenary." *New Face of the Church in Latin America: Between Tradition and Change.* Guillermo Cook, ed. Maryknoll, NY: Orbis Books. pp. 156-162.

    Escobar, J. Samuel. 1994. "Conflict of Interpretations of Popular Protestantism." *New Face of the Church in Latin America: Between Tradition and Change.* Guillermo Cook, ed. Maryknoll, NY: Orbis Books. pp. 112-134.

2. Thursday 13 April: The case of the Virgin of Guadalupe
    •••PARTIAL EXAM 1••• (25 minutes)
    Reading: Boff, Leonardo. 1990. "El Método Liberadora de la Virgen Morena." *Nueva Evangelización: Perspectiva de los Oprimidos.* Fray Guillermo Ramírez, o.f.m., trad. Bogotá: Indo-American Press Service-Editores. pp. 129-134.
    Background: Wolf, Eric R. 1958. "The Virgin of Guadalupe: A Mexican National Symbol." *Journal of American Folklore* 71: 34-39.

Week 4: "Syncretism"

1. Tuesday 18 April: Christianity and four different indigenous religions
    Readings: Marzal, Manuel M. 1985. "El Sincretismo Andino, Maya y Africano." *El Sincretismo Iberoamericano: Un estudio comparativo sobre los quechuas (Cusco), los mayas (Chiapas) y los africanos (Bahía).* Lima: Pontificia Universidad Católica del Perú. pp. 175-193.
    Bunzel, Ruth. 1981. "Para pedir perdón al inicio de alguna empresa." *Chichicastenango.* Francis Gall, trad. Guatemala: Editorial "José de Pineda Ibarra". 376-377.
    Background: Kselman, Thomas A. 1986. "Ambivalence and Assumption in the Concept of Popular Religion." *Religion and Political Conflict in Latin America.* Daniel H. Levine, ed. Chapel Hill: Univ. of North Carolina Press. pp. 24-41.

2. Thursday 20 April: Magic and witchcraft
    Readings: De Grial, Dr. Hugo. 1975. "Introducción." *Defensas Mágicas.* México: Publicidad Editora. pp. 6-11.
    "Brujería en la era espacial." 1993. *Crítica* (Guatemala) 68 (2761): 39-42.

Week 5: "Spiritism"

1. Tuesday 25 April: Allan Kardec
    Reading: Kardec, Allan. [1857]. *El Libro de los Espíritus.* NY: Studium Corporation. pp. 14-23, 45-47, 226-229.
    Background: Brandon, George. 1993. "Espiritismo." *Santería from Africa to the New World: The Dead Sell Memories.* Bloomington: Indiana University Press. pp. 85-90.

2. Thursday 27 April: A Catholic critique and one by the Jehovah's Witnesses
    Readings: Santagada, Osvaldo D., et al. 1988. "El Espiritismo." *Las Sectas en América Latina*. 6a ed. Buenos Aires: Editorial Claretiana. pp. 161-175.
    Franz, F.W. 1992 [1974]. "Los espíritus inicuos son poderosos." *Usted puede vivir para siempre en el paraíso en la Tierra*. México: Grupo Editorial Ultramar. pp. 90-98.

Week 6: "Afrocuban religions"

1. Tuesday 2 May
    Readings: Díaz Fabelo, Teodoro. 1983. "Pattakí del Principio del Mundo." *Cincuenta y Un Pattakíes Afroamericanos*. Caracas: Monte Ávila Editores. pp. 13-14.
    Pollak-Eltz, Angelina, 1977. "La Santería Cubana." *Cultos Afroamericanos (Vudu y Hechicería en las Américas)*. Caracas: Universidad Católica Andrés Bello. pp. 223-238.
    Background: Brandon, George. 1993. "Introduction"; "Cuba: Santería (1870-1959) [selection]." *Santería from Africa to the New World: The Dead Sell Memories*. Bloomington: Indiana University Press. pp. 1-8, 90-103, 123.
2. Thursday 4 May
    •••**PARTIAL EXAM 2**••• (25 minutes)
    Reading: Cabrera, Lydia. 1986. *La Regla Kimbisa del Santo Cristo del Buen Viaje*. Miami: Ediciones Universal. pp. 9-24.

Week 7: "Indigenous religions"

1. Tuesday 9 May: Maya (Guatemala), Zoques (Chiapas)
    Readings: Noj, Beleje. 1993. "Valores de la Religión Cosmogónica Maya"; "Aproximación a Temas Fundamentales en la Religión Maya y Cristiana." *Voces del Tiempo* No. 6: 16-20; 41-49.
    Aramoni Calderón, Dolores. 1993. "Iglesia, cultura y represión entre los zoques de Chiapas en el siglo XVII [selección]." *Catolicismo y Extirpación de Idolatrías, Siglos XVI-XVIII: Charcas, Chile, México, Perú*. Gabriela Ramos y Henrique Urbano, comps. Cusco: Centro de

Estudio Regionales Andinos "Bartolomé de las Casas". pp. 374-382.

Background: Quicaña, Fernando. 1994. "The Gospel and the Andean Culture." *New Face of the Church in Latin America: Between Tradition and Change.* Guillermo Cook, ed. Maryknoll, NY: Orbis Books. pp. 99-111.

2. Thursday 11 May: Perspectives

    Readings: Diócesis de Quetzaltenango. 1989. "Prioridad: Pastoral Indígena." *En Comunión y Participación: Plan Pastoral Diocesano, 1990-1994.* Quetzaltenango, Guatemala: Vicaría de Pastoral. pp. 91-94.

    "Palabras de hermanos Indígenas a sus Pastores." *500 años sembrando el Evangelio.* Carta Pastoral Colectiva de los Obispos de Guatemala. Guatemala: Publicaciones O.M. pp. 44-59.

    "Entrevista a Manuel Tun." *Voces del Tiempo* No. 6: 54-55.

    Zapata Arceyuz, Virgilio. 1982. *Historia de la Iglesia Evangélica en Guatemala.* Guatemala: Génesis Publicidad. pp. 183-185.

    García-Ruiz, Jesús. 1991. "De la Identidad *Aceptada* a la Identidad *Asumida*: El Rol de lo Religioso en la Politización de las Identificaciones Étnicas en Guatemala." *Estudios Internacionales* (IRIPAZ) 2(3): 68-79.

Week 8: "Women"

1. Tuesday 16 May: Perspectives

    a) K'iche' Maya

    Reading: Una mujer K'iche'. 1992. "El Ser de la Mujer K'iche'." *Voces del Tiempo* No. 3: 23-26.

    b) Catholic

    Readings: Consejo Episcopal Latinoamericano (CELAM). 1979. "La Mujer." *Puebla: La evangelización en el presente y en el futuro de América Latina.* III Conferencia General del Episcopado Latinoamericano. 9a ed. Caracas: Ediciones Tripode. pp. 172-174.

    Diócesis de Quetzaltenango. 1989. "Subcomisión: Pastoral de la Mujer." *En Comunión y Participación: Plan Pastoral Diocesano, 1990-1994.* Quetzaltenango, Guatemala: Vicaría de Pastoral. pp. 98-99.

    1992. *La Biblia Latinoamericano.* Madrid: Ediciones

Paulinas. 1 Corintios 11: 2-16; 1 Timoteo 2: 8-15 (notas de pie también).
c) Protestant
Readings: 1986. *La Santa Biblia.* Revisión de 1960. México: Sociedades Bíblicas Unidas. 1 Corintios 11: 2-16; 1 Timoteo 2: 8-15.
Chamorro Argüello, Graciela. 1986. "La Mujer Bautista: Perspectivas Teológicas y Consecuencias Pastorales." *La mujer en la construcción de la iglesia: una perspectiva bautista desde América Latina y el Caribe.* Jorge Pixley, ed. San José, Costa Rica: Editorial DEI. pp. 17-30.
d) Seventh Day Adventist
Reading: Thomas, Donald. 1993. *Lecciones de la Escuela Sabática para Adultos. Cartas a la iglesia: 1 Timoteo y Tito.* 98 (3): 30-32.
2.   Thursday 18 May: Experiences
   •••**PARTIAL EXAM 3**••• (25 minutes)
   Readings: 1992. "Vivencia de una Sacerdotisa Maya." *Voces del Tiempo* No. 3: 64-68.
   1993. "El sacerdocio de la mujer." *Latinoamérica Internacional* (Colombia) Edición 7: 12-16.

Week 9: Student presentations
   1.   Tuesday 23 May: Presentations
   2.   Thursday 25 May: Presentations

Week 10: Student presentations and wrap-up
   1.   Tuesday 30 May: Presentations
   2.   Thursday 1 June: Religion, social change and the contemporary world
   Reading: Marroquín, Enrique. 1993. "Perspectivas Posmodernas"; "Evangelización y Cultura." *La Iglesia y el Poder: Reflexiones Sociológicas sobre la Iglesia.* México: Ediciones Dabar. pp. 108-133.
   Background: Stoll, David. 1993. "Introduction." *Rethinking Protestantism in Latin America.* Virginia Garrard-Burnett and David Stoll, eds. Philadelphia: Temple University Press. pp. 1-19.
   Míguez Bonino, José. 1994. "The Condition and Prospects of Christianity in Latin America." *New Face of the Church in Latin America: Between Tradition and Change.*

Guillermo Cook, ed. Maryknoll, NY: Orbis Books. pp. 259-267.

Cook, Guillermo. 1994. "The Many Faces of the Latin American Church." *New Face of the Church in Latin America: Between Tradition and Change.* Guillermo Cook, ed. Maryknoll, NY: Orbis Books. pp. 268-276.

FINAL EXAM: Wednesday, 7 June, 10:30AM - 12:30PM

Appendix C
Sample Reading Guide
Religion and Social Change in Twentieth Century Latin America
Area Studies 3930, Section 1

Professor: Chris Chiappari

Sincretismo:

Jueves, 20 de abril: Cristianismo y cuatro distintas religiones indígenas

Lecturas: Marzal, Manuel M. 1985. "El Sincretismo Andino, Maya y Africano." *El incretismo Iberoamericano: Un estudio comparativo sobre los quechuas (Cusco), los mayas (Chiapas) y los africanos (Bahía).* pp. 175-179, 190-193.

Bunzel, Ruth. 1981. "Para pedir perdón al inicio de alguna empresa." *Chichicastenango.* 376-377.

Background: Kselman, Thomas A. 1986. "Ambivalence and Assumption in the Concept of Popular Religion." *Religion and Political Conflict in Latin America.* Daniel H. Levine, ed. pp. 24-41.

Terms and Concepts (in the Bunzel reading):

El Calvario: the Stations of the Cross (Vía Crucis)

El Mundo: the deity of the Earth; it is prayed to at any of the many shrines to it located in caves, mountains, and some lakes.

PRE-READING QUESTIONS:

Marzal:

1. How does Marzal define syncretism, and what are the four processes involved in it?
2. What are Marzal's three types of reinterpretation?

Bunzel:
1. What are the syncretic elements of this ceremony?
2. What is the relationship between the petitioner and his/her ancestors?

POST-READING QUESTIONS (Para la discusión)

Marzal:
1. ¿Es cristianismo una religión sincrética? ¿Por qué sí o no?
2. En su opinión, ¿es posible hablar de la religión sin hablar de la cultura? O sea, ¿hay religiones que son iguales en todas partes donde se las practican?

Bunzel:
1. ¿Por qué piensa Ud. que la persona que pide en la ceremonia tiene que ir a los tres lugares mencionados?
2. ¿Considera Ud. que la ceremonia descrita sería aceptada por la iglesia católica como una forma de la religión popular? ¿Por qué sí o no?

Appendix D
Assessment Results

Table D.1 Comparison of Pre- and Post-Test Means (1995)

(n=6)

	Mean	SD	t-value	signif.
Reading Comprehension				
Pre	68.00	25.09	-1.84	.06
Post	80.17	14.23		
Cloze				
Pre	49.00	14.72	-2.01	.05*
Post	57.67	17.56		
Lecture				
Pre	70.00	17.74	-0.76	.24
Post	75.17	10.82		
Elicited Imitation				
Pre	65.50	18.55	-2.40	.03*
Post	75.33	17.12		
Essay				
Pre	68.83	06.97	-4.39	.003**
Post	78.00	10.68		
*p<.05 **p<.01				

Table D.2 Pre- and Post-test Comparison for Self-Assessment in Language Skills and Attitudes

(n=6)

Language Skills and Attitudes	Pre-Test		Post-Test	
	Mean	S.D.	Mean	S.D.
1. Listening Comprehension	3.00	0	3.00	.632
2. Vocabulary*	2.75	.612	3.25	.418
3. Discussion skills	2.67	.516	3.08	.665
4. Grammatical knowledge	2.50	.548	2.67	.516
5. Reading comprehension	2.83	.753	2.83	.753
6. Writing & composition	2.67	.516	2.67	.816
7. Conversation with native-speaking friends	3.17	.753	3.50	.548
8. Handling telephone directions	3.17	.753	3.33	.516
9. Asking professor to change an exam grade	3.17	.753	3.33	.816
10. Participating in a class discussion on a familiar topic	3.17	.753	3.50	.548
11. Going to a play or movie	2.50	.548	2.83	.408
12. Reading magazines & newspapers	2.50	.548	2.50	.548
13. Watching a TV show	2.50	.548	2.08	.665
14. Knowledge of FL will be useful in future career	3.80	.447	3.80	.447
15. Knowledge of FL will help in getting to know NSs	3.83	.408	3.67	.516
16. Makes learner a more educated person	3.58	.665	3.67	.516

*p<.05

Part Four

CBI at
Advanced Levels
of Proficiency

8

The Mexico Experiment
at the Foreign Service Institute

Stephen B. Stryker

Editors' Note: The Mexico Program, designed by Stryker and his colleagues in the Spanish Section at the FSI, represents the ultimately "collaborative" model: it involved two language teachers, an area studies expert, and many guest lecturers. In keeping with the broad cultural, political, social, and economic knowledge that Foreign Service Officers need in order to be successful on the job, content modules were developed on a variety of topics such as the political system, the media, the family, migration, the role of women, the judicial system, and international trade issues for students assigned to diplomatic posts in Mexico. Initially, the curriculum was developed to take students from an ILR level 2 to a level 3 in both speaking and reading. For teachers interested in adapting this kind of curriculum model, the author describes how the modules were created and provides guidelines for designing the scope and sequence of the CBI curriculum. Although the learning out comes were very positive, an immense amount of time and effort was required for this program. Appendixes provide the reader with model lesson plans and a list of the resources and materials. The general framework of the FSI Mexico Program was adapted successfully by Professor Norma Klahn, who turned it into an innovative academic course at Columbia University's School of International and Public Affairs. Her adaptation is described in the following chapter. General references for this chapter are located in the bibliography at the end of this volume.

The Setting

The Foreign Service Institute (FSI), the training arm of the U.S. Department of State, is probably best known outside of the Department of State for its School of Language Studies, which provides intensive language training programs in more than forty languages. In addition to language training, the FSI provides comprehensive training in many areas related to the functions of the Foreign Service and other international agencies of the U.S. government. Training programs are offered by the School of Area Studies, the School of Professional Studies, the Center for Foreign Affairs, and the Overseas Briefing Center. The mandate of the School of Language Studies is to train students to predetermined proficiency levels in speaking and reading. In the majority of cases students are required to reach levels that the FSI has designated as Speaking (S)-3 and Reading (R)-3, described as "minimal professional proficiency." (Since the FSI levels have been adopted by the Interagency Language Roundtable [ILR], the levels will be referred to as ILR.)

The student population is made up of approximately 50 percent Foreign Service Officers; the remainder are employees of numerous other government agencies. Most programs at the FSI are highly intensive. Students are in class for up to six hours per day, five days a week, for periods ranging from six weeks for a "survival" course to forty-four weeks for a complete course in Russian, Greek, Polish, or Arabic. Classes are relatively small, with no more than six students per class. The language instructors are all "educated native speakers" (ILR-5) of the languages they teach.

The Spanish Program

The Basic Spanish Program at the Foreign Service Institute is a twenty-four-week course designed to bring students to FSI/ILR levels of speaking, S-3 and reading, R-3. Students aiming for the lower proficiency levels of S-2 and R-2 are enrolled for about 20 weeks. Since the FSI students are professional adults who are preparing for assignments overseas, most are highly motivated to learn; in some cases, their assignments depend on reaching a level 3. The length of time required for students to reach a given proficiency level varies, depending on individual factors such as language aptitude, previous language-learning experience, disposition, and motivation.

The Spanish Program consists of six hours per day of study in groups of five or six students, taught by language and culture instructors who are educated native speakers of the language. Teachers rotate weekly in order to expose students to a variety of accents and individual rhetorical and teaching styles.

The basic Spanish texts and accompanying audiotapes (the *Spanish Programmatic*, 1962, 1967) were developed at the FSI specifically for Foreign Service personnel. These texts, based on a classical audio-lingual model, have served as the core texts for more than three decades. Since foreign language writing skills are not required of Foreign Service personnel, writing skills per se are not emphasized, nor are they tested; however, written exercises are used regularly to reinforce the oral skills and vocabulary development. In the initial weeks of study, students are required to spend a portion of study time listening to the audiotapes; subsequent classroom exercises practice and reinforce the audiotape exercises. As the course progresses, increasing quantities of current periodical and media materials from Latin America and Spain are used to supplement the basic Spanish texts.

Toward Integration of Area and Language

In 1983 the Russian Section of the FSI began successful experiments CBI in their curriculum (see Leaver, Chapter 1). In the Spanish Section, the challenge of including a wealth of cultural information in the foreign language curriculum was complicated by the multiplicity of countries involved. The Spanish language is spoken in more than twenty different countries, and, although there may be a "standard Spanish" that is internationally accepted, great differences in regional language varieties and cultural characteristics separate the country-specific varieties. To teach a generic "Hispanic culture" to persons headed to Madrid, Buenos Aires, Mexico City, and Santo Domingo would be comparable to teaching "Anglo culture" to a group of ESL students going to London, Johannesburg, New York City, and Melbourne; the result would be gross misinformation and reinforcement of misconceptions and stereotypes.

At the FSI, the challenge of providing area and culture training for the countries in the Hispanic world was accomplished by overlapping courses in the School of Area Studies and the School of Language Studies. For example, once a week, for a three-hour block of time, students and language teachers attend area studies lectures given in English by experts on one of the five subregions: Mexico, Central America/Caribbean, Andean, Southern Cone, and Iberia. Following the lecture students and teachers, matched for regions, returned to language classrooms. During this Spanish-language portion of the program, teachers from the countries being studied based their language lessons as closely as possible on the area topic of the day. They often made use of newspaper articles, political cartoons, TV programs, scenes from films, photographs, songs, and other authentic materials from their countries.

Thus, for at least a part of the week (10 percent of class time), all the students in the Spanish Program received some content-based language instruction. Students and teachers alike responded enthusiastically to the activities based on real, current issues. These content activities were especially well-received by students in more advanced stages of the program, many of whom had become bored with predominantly grammar-based or situation-based activities.

These area/language portions of the curriculum provided us with a conceptual model for a much more ambitious CBI endeavor.

Goals, Objectives, and Curriculum Design

In 1985 the FSI School of Language Studies, in collaboration with the School of Area Studies, mounted a major curricular experiment in content-based instruction in Spanish. The goal of the curriculum was to accelerate growth in foreign language proficiency while simultaneously accelerating growth in area knowledge and cultural literacy. The country chosen was Mexico. The team that worked on the development of the program consisted of two Mexican language and culture instructors, a Mexican Studies specialist from Georgetown University, and the Head of the Spanish Section at the FSI (the author of this chapter). The goal of the CBI experiment was to achieve total integration of language studies and area studies, focusing on a specific region of the Hispanic world, and to produce a curricular model that could be adapted to other regions. Our specific objectives were 1) to accelerate students' proficiency growth in oral and reading proficiency from level 2 or 2+ to level 3 or beyond, 2) to provide students with a wealth of cultural and sociopolitical information about Mexico, 3) to familiarize students with the special variety of Spanish spoken in Mexico, and 4) to give students an understanding of the Mexican ethos and world view.

Our approach was to take the general topics of the FSI area studies program—political, economic, social, cultural, and foreign policy matters—and create a series of self-contained units of study, each requiring six hours of class time, or about one FSI day. We called these units "modules" because they were self-contained and independent of one another and could be presented in any sequence. Each module focused on a specific theme such as the family, the educational system, the press, migration, and music. The theme would provide both the unifying content element and the vocabulary domain. The plan called for the two teachers who prepared the modules to team-teach the course, i.e., to be in class together, constantly interacting, providing students with the double input that only "four-handed" instruction can provide.

Because we wanted to emphasize oral rather than literacy skills, we did not rely on written texts as our primary materials. We decided to have a "video event" as the centerpiece of each module. We built all of the activities of a unit around a video "text," in the same way as traditional language classes are built around a particular written text. Consequently, the video had to be our starting point in the preparation of each module: the content of the video served as our basic text as well as a point of departure for all the other activities related to that module. The video event served as the focal point; consequently, finding appropriate videos was of primary importance.

At first we sought material from Mexican television such as news and documentary programs, interviews on TV news magazines, such as the popular "24 Horas" ("Twenty-Four Hours"), and segments from certain "telenovelas" (soap operas). However, since much of the material was too long, irrelevant, or beyond the reach of our students, we had to edit segments down to digestible chunks of ten to fifteen minutes. The question-answer format of a short TV interview appeared to be ideally suited to our purposes. In cases in which we could not find appropriate interviews on the airwaves, we filmed them ourselves in the studio at the FSI. Some of our guests included the Mexican Cultural Attaché, the chief correspondent for the Mexico City Newspaper *Excelsior*, and a professor of sociology from Mexico City College. Segments from films and television broadcasts were used. For example, for the "Migration" module, we used the first thirty minutes of the film *El Norte*. For the "Natural Resources" module, we used a Mexican-made documentary on the history of PEMEX, Mexico's national petroleum company. In each case, the teachers carefully studied the video for both form and content and then designed a variety of activities to reinforce the concepts and recycle the vocabulary. (See Appendix B for the lesson plans of two modules and an example of a vocabulary guide for the film, *El Norte*.)

Figure 1, on the next page, presents the theoretical framework for the exploitation of the "video text" and also represents the sequencing of the different activities within a module. As shown in the diagram, each module was designed to begin with the receptive activities of reading and listening; the module ended with production activities of speaking, and to a minor degree, writing. Each module contained nine steps, as explained in the descriptions following the diagram.

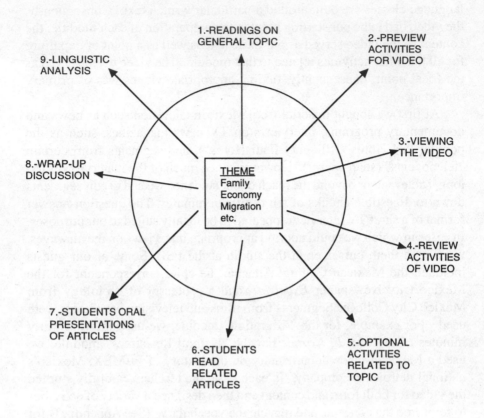

Fig. 1. Framework for sequencing of activities for each theme

Step 1: The student is given a packet of reading material for homework in order to "read into" the topic.

Step 2: The classroom activities begin with teacher-directed activities in preparation for the video, the most important exercise being a list of "key concepts" that present the main ideas or vocabulary in short sentences.

Step 3: The group views the video.

Step 4: The teacher directs activities as a review or analysis of the video.

Step 5: The teacher introduces other activities appropriate as follow-up to the video.

Step 6: The teacher gives each student a different article related to the content of the video. If the teacher does not have an article, she might tell the students to go to the library and find one that is pertinent to the topic. The students are given 20 to 30 minutes to prepare an oral presentation on their articles; teachers are available to coach, as needed. Students are encouraged to summarize and paraphrase.

Step 7: Each student gives an oral presentation of 4 to 5 minutes, using notes only. During the presentation the teacher takes notes of errors or problems for feedback later. If the students desire, they audiotape or videotape their presentations in order to critique their own performances.

Step 8: The teacher directs a wrap-up of the topic in the form of discussion, an informal debate, reviewing of the video, or viewing of a related video, depending on the topic, the students, and the materials available.

Step 9: The teacher leads a discussion of the linguistic problems observed in students' performance, addressing problems in phonology, morphology, syntax, vocabulary, or rhetorical style. The teacher takes whatever steps she thinks appropriate to help correct the problems, such as providing the students with written exercises on specific structures.

These nine steps represent the generic sequence for a CBI module. When translated into a class schedule, the sequence of activities became an eight-hour module, including approximately two hours of outside preparation and six hours of classroom work. Figure 2, on the next page, presents a chart of the generic eight-hour module with specific activities, materials, objectives, and timeframes.

STEP	ACTIVITIES	MATERIALS	OBJECTIVES	TIME FRAME
1	Students read in packet as homework	- A packet of reading material (10-20 pages) - Homework excercises - audio recording (if approriate)	To prepare for both language and content of the module	2 hours (homework the day before the module)
2	Teacher directs preparation and introductory activities	- List of key concepts - Audiotape - Cloze excercises - Readings from packet	To intrduce the key concepts and vocabulary for the video event	1 hour
3	All view the video	- Interview - Film - Lecture - Vignette - TV show etc.	To provide both text and context for topic	1/2 hour
4	Teacher directs review of video	List of key concepts (used in step 2)	To facilitate in-depth analysis of content of video and discussion of new vocabulary or expressions	1 hour
5	Teacher directs related activities	Cartoons, songs, short readings, videotape, audiotape (radio), cloze excercises	To provide teacher opportunity to expand upon either language or content, depending on group	1 hour
6	Students read articles and prepare oral summaries	Selected newspaper or magazine articles	To allow students to synthesize an article from a current periodical and prepare oral summaries	1/2 hour
7	Students make oral presentations ("briefings") on their article	Articles: same as above (tape recorder or video recorder as needed)	To practice oral presentation of a briefing from written sources	1 hour
8	Teacher leads wrap-up discussion	Possibly list of key concepts or other items from step 2, above	To synthesize the topic (content) of the module	1/2 hour
9	Teacher leads linguistic analysis	- Student questions - Notes taken during presentations - Audiotapes of presentations - Videotapes of presentations - Teacher materials	To discuss and correct problems in phonology, morphology, syntax, vocabulary, and rhetorical style	1 hour (may be done the following day)

Fig. 2. The Nine Steps in a Generic Eight-Hour Module

The outlines presented in Figures 1 and 2 above represent a flexible framework for the organization of our modules. In practice, each module was unique and the implementation process varied depending on the topics, the materials available, and the students.

Grammar and Error Correction

Questions arose during the planning phase concerning when and how correction of student errors should take place. Certain general principles were agreed upon. *Explicit* correction techniques, such as indicating the error and asking the student to repeat correctly, would only be used during teacher-directed activities aimed at grammatical analysis and during individual coaching sessions. *Indirect* correction techniques, such as echoing, restatement, and other natural rhetorical devices, would be used in all the student-directed activities. Thus, the general design of the curriculum placed heavy emphasis on the "acquisition process" but did not exclude "formal learning" of grammar and structure.

The Team-Teaching Approach

The plan called for "four-handed instruction" during large portions of the pilot program. This strategy was used to create interaction between two instructors and to maximize the students' exposure to native speakers speaking naturally and spontaneously. Usually one or the other would lead an activity and the other would assist. Frequently, the teachers would improvise a role play of a situation for the students. They were encouraged to engage in constant conversation with each other—even to engage in mock disagreements or arguments. This unique feature was designed initially as a luxury during the pilot programs as a way to help teachers develop the curriculum and to train new teachers in the approach. In actual practice, this "four-handed" component turned out to be one of the major pedagogical advantages of the program.

Materials Preparation

For each module we developed a packet of ten to twenty pages: assorted newspaper and magazine articles (some in English), political cartoons, transcripts of videos, songs, maps, charts, or photographs. (See the list of materials in Appendix C.) The collection and editing of the materials, filming of interviews, editing of videos, and preparation of support materials for a four-week program (120 hours of instruction) was a prodigious job. Dr. John Bailey from Georgetown University obtained much of the material. The Mexican teachers, Marisa Curran and Carmela Glover, worked full-time for three months, editing and preparing the material. A series of pilot programs, undertaken during 1985-1986, drew from the following modules:

El mosaico mexicano .... (The Mexican Mosaic)

Población y urbanización .... (Population and Urbanization)

La migración .... (Immigration)

Asuntos consulares .... (Consular Matters)

Fiestas y costumbres populares .... (Festivals and Customs)

La familia .... (The Family)

Los medios de comunicación impresos .... (Printed Means of Communication)

Los medios de comunicación electrónicos .... (Electronic Means of Communication)

Los recursos naturales .... (Natural Resources)

El sistema político mexicano .... (The Mexican Political System)

El sistema jurídico .... (The Judician System)

La educación .... (Education)

La Revolución .... (The Revolution)

Asuntos económicos .... (Economic Matters)

Las artes .... (The Fine Arts)

Evaluating the Program

The Mexico Program was piloted during 1985-1986. Class size ranged from four to six students; twenty-three students participated. The FSI proficiency test, used as both pre-test and post-test, was administered in the FSI testing unit by testers who were not involved with the Mexico Program. The results of the pilot groups were both encouraging and informative. Although there was no formal control group per se, the results of the tests could be compared to the norms accumulated over a period of decades, involving several thousand students: the norm for a half-point increase from 2+ to 3 in Spanish was about six weeks; a full-point increase from 2 to 3 in Spanish was about eleven weeks.

Of the twenty-three students who were tested in the four-week pilot programs, seven students moved up one full point. The other sixteen students moved up one half-point. (See Appendix A for complete student scores.) These initial results were very encouraging. It appeared that the new curriculum was indeed helping to accelerate students' growth in proficiency far beyond the long-established FSI norms. However, we evaluated these results with reservations, suspecting that the "Hawthorn effect"—results being affected by students' knowledge that they are participating in something special—might be partially responsible for the positive outcomes. Indeed, all seventeen of the students were very aware that the "programa piloto" was something out of the ordinary. They were also aware that they were given special attention: a new curriculum with splashy new materials, a country-specific program, teachers from Mexico, guest speakers, field trips, and, moreover, "great expectations." Still, the results were encouraging. The students achieved significantly higher proficiency scores in less time than ever before. Important as these statistical results were to us, the personal opinions by the participants were equally important. At the FSI, the students are all professionals who tend to be both demanding and outspoken concerning the quality of their training. Their training time is precious to them, and they are quick to complain if they think their time is being wasted. They were asked to be frank and critical of the program.

Student Feedback and Suggestions

Students' evaluations of the CBI curriculum were overwhelmingly favorable. At the same time, they provided many constructive comments concerning both the content of the modules and methods of instruction. The suggestions of each successive group helped the teachers to improve the procedures for the next group, and many modifications were made based on students' suggestions. For example, many students thought that audiotaping of their oral presentations and the subsequent "self-correction" (done on their own at home) was especially useful, but they had two suggestions: 1) students should be encouraged to make transcriptions of their oral presentations and then correct their errors on the transcriptions; and 2) these exercises should be done only once or twice per week, because they were so demanding and time-consuming. Both of these suggestions were subsequently incorporated into the program.

Another frequent comment was that students wanted more writing activities, not just to hone their writing skills *per se*, but to reinforce the other three skills and vocabulary learning. Consequently, more writing activities were included.

A majority of the students requested more explicit treatment of grammar during the course (as might be expected from educated adult students who were accustomed to audio-lingual grammar drills). Consequently, the teachers increasingly addressed discrete grammatical points— but always within the context of a given topic. For example, if students demonstrated consistent weaknesses in preterit-imperfect verb usage during their discussions and presentations, the teacher found newspaper articles from Mexican sources that were rich in those two tenses and used the articles as contexts in which to analyze and practice those forms. On other occasions, the teachers anticipated certain predictable linguistic problems and incorporated grammatical exercises into the module. For example, in the module entitled "la Revolución," the teachers focused on the past subjunctive/conditional tense usage (the contrary-to-fact if clauses) by using one of the best-known of the Mexican revolutionary songs, a "corrido" (ballad) called "Adelita:" "Si Adelita se fuera con otro, la seguiría por tierra y por mar . . ." (If Adelita were to leave with another, I would follow her by land and by sea . . ..) Frequently, the teachers focused on certain verb structures by using either a song, an advertisement, or popular proverbs as fill-in-the-blank exercises, in which the blanks were the verbs.

Students responded very favorably to the content-based approach. The enthusiasm of their responses, however, varied according to proficiency level, learning styles, and personalities. Students who entered the Mexico Program at the relatively high level of 2+ or 3 tended to have a more enthusiastic response than those entering at 2. A probable factor was their higher confidence level and ability to handle the large quantities of authentic oral and written language, whereas weaker students felt frustrated by the sheer quantity of material. It seems that when students felt the sensation of accomplishing a real communicative task in a classroom activity or on a field trip, they felt an increase in self-confidence. This phenomenon appears to lend support to the hypothesis proposed by Krashen and others that success in second language learning correlates positively with students' self-confidence and motivation.

Students who were "risk-takers" (those students who approached the second language learning experience in an uninhibited, confident way) also tended to respond favorably. One of the risk-takers who entered with a 2+ and finished with a 3+ wrote:

The move into a 100 percent Mexican environment came at just the right time. The fact that Spanish was being used as a medium for learning other things, rather than as an object of singular study itself, made it highly interesting and relevant to our professional needs. We learned both subjects: Mexico and Spanish. Essentially, we got two courses in one and each served to reinforce the other.

Another student, whose profile was similar to the one quoted above, wrote:

Being able to study with Mexicans who are enamored of their own country put a positive face on the place. Aside from the language benefit, I am now excited about going to Mexico.

These comments were typical of the responses of the majority of the students. There were, on the other hand, a small number of less proficient and less confident language learners (about 15 percent) who were concerned that the program was oriented too much towards content and not enough towards grammar and structure. These students felt overwhelmed by the quantity and complexity of the materials. Typical of the comments written by these students: "I did enjoy learning a lot about Mexico, but I personally would have preferred more grammar work and drills." It was interesting to note that such students held a strong conviction that "learning" the language meant grammar work and drills.

This reserved reaction was seen again more emphatically when we experimented to see if the program would be equally effective for a group of students entering at the 1+ proficiency level. We reduced the quantity and intensity of the content in an effort to adapt the program "down" to the lower proficiency of the group. The student response, again, was lukewarm. They also felt overwhelmed. Since that experience, we have been careful to choose students who were "ready" for the material, i.e., students whose proficiency levels were at least level 2 in both speaking and writing. (The question of the appropriate threshold of proficiency for a CBI curriculum is also addressed by Klee and Tedick in the previous chapter and later by Shaw in Chapter 12.)

By 1986, the Mexico curriculum was implemented at regular intervals throughout the year, and the Mexico prototype served as a model for two other regional instructional teams: Central American/Caribbean and the Andean regions. Those teams had to deal with the challenge of creating an area/language approach within multicountry, multicultural regions. They made this transition successfully by preparing a series of "regional modules" in which each theme (again, political systems, education, the family, roles of women in society, the press, etc.) was presented as a regional phenomenon. The students in the CBI class received reading materials that were either regional or specific to their country of destination. For example, students destined for Central America saw a video on "The Press in Central America." Following the activities based on that video, the students were assigned the task of finding articles in the periodical library that addressed that topic in El Salvador, Nicaragua, Guatemala, or the Central American country to which they were assigned. Each student was asked to prepare a summary of the article and give an oral presentation of that article as it related to the topic presented in the video. Results of the Central American and Andean regional CBI curricula were comparable to the results attained by the Mexico groups.

The Evolving Curricular Design

AS our original CBI model was adapted to other geographical regions in the Spanish Section at the FSI, several major changes affected the design of the program. Although the original design called for a four-week (120-hour) program, the nature of the FSI training schedules required that the program be implemented for periods varying from two to five weeks. The "self-contained" nature of each module facilitated changing the length of the program to suit each group. The fact that the modules were not designed to be presented in any particular sequence provided the flexibility of choosing different sets of modules for individual groups, depending on each group's interests and needs.

Over time each of the modules grew and changed, depending on the quantity and quality of materials available. On fluid topics, such as the topic of migration or political parties, materials became obsolete quite fast; teachers had to keep the materials up-to-date. Consequently, some modules were essentially "current events" courses, sometimes using newspaper articles from that very morning. For other topics, instructors amassed large quantities of useful materials, requiring as much as two days to implement.

Our original design called for a single video to be the "central event" in each module. However, as the number of videos in our library grew, we could incorporate two or more videos into the same module and use them in different ways. For example, in the Mexico module on "Demography and Urbanization," we had two excellent short interviews on video. We used one as the "central event" and the other as a comprehension activity later in the module. The use of a second video gave us more than just an opportunity to present a different point of view on a given topic. It frequently gave us the opportunity to provide the students with a linguistic "cold shower"—a one-time viewing of a video with no priming or preparation. Such "cold showers" served as excellent tools for students to test their listening comprehension skills.

The idea that the program would be taught "four-handed" turned out, of course, to be an ideal that was too expensive. Since the benefits that students derived were substantial, we arranged to have portions of the day team-taught. The logistics involved in training other teachers in the curriculum turned out to be one of the best ways to provide four-handed instruction: the new teacher was asked to participate by asking questions and helping students to understand the lessons.

The idea that the teachers had to be nationals of the country or region was another ideal that encountered personnel problems. A "native-born" teacher was not always available for a particular region. The Mexico curriculum, for example, was taught successfully on several occasions by teachers from other regions of Latin America who were highly knowledgeable of Mexico.

The idea that explicit correction would be confined to certain parts of the day was also slightly modified. Many students insisted on more explicit correction and explanation of grammatical rules. In such cases, the teachers did their best to meet students' needs without breaking the pace of the activity or seeming to digress from the topic at hand. The results of the student "self-correction" exercises were particularly interesting. Occasionally students audiotaped their oral presentations, took the tape home, listened and took notes, and critiqued their own performance. They were given guidelines on phonology, morphology, syntax, vocabulary use, and rhetorical style. It was interesting to note that many students, especially those students with higher proficiency, could identify and correct up to 80 percent of their own errors in production, indicating (according to the dichotomy emphasized by Krashen, Terrell, and others) that many rules and patterns had indeed been *learned* by the students but not yet *acquired*. Thus, certain structures had not yet been sufficiently internalized or acquired to be produced in spontaneous speech, for example, verb endings, noun/adjective agreement, cognates, stress patterns, and gender of words. In a series of informal error analyses conducted by instructors on two of the groups, many of these mistakes were found to have been corrected over a period of three to four weeks.

In actual classroom implementation, the sequence of the nine activities, outlined in Figures 1 and 2, became less and less rigid. In some of the modules certain steps were repeated and in others eliminated; some activities were lengthened, others curtailed.

Concluding Remarks

By 1990 a total of fifty students had completed at least three weeks of the CBI area/language program in the Spanish Section. Of the fifty, thirteen had increased their proficiency level by a full S-score and thirty-seven had increased by one-half an S-score. Ten of the fifty ended their training at FSI (averaging a total of twenty-four weeks) with S-3+, which has been generally recognized as the highest score achievable by a student in basic Spanish language training.

These results indicated that the CBI programs were effective in achieving the dual objectives of the program: 1) the acceleration of foreign language proficiency growth and 2) the acquisition of new area and cultural knowledge. Compared to the established norms for similar students in the

Spanish Program, the students in the CBI courses achieved higher proficiency scores in significantly shorter periods of time. The students also acquired a great deal of valuable area and cultural knowledge about the specific countries to which they were assigned. These positive results helped to persuade the administration (at least for a while) that the expenses involved in designing and delivering the CBI program were worth the payoff—many weeks of expensive training were saved, and many Foreign Service Officers went to post more knowledgeable and better qualified to "hit the ground running."

Motivation

The great majority of the students who experienced the CBI programs commented on their increased motivation to learn the language, as well as their increased appreciation of the culture of the areas they studied. Perhaps the term most used to by students was "relevance." One student, who started the Mexico Program at a low 2 and ended four weeks later with a 3+, wrote the following:

> I doubt very seriously whether I would have had the same result if I had stayed in the regular programmatic course—a rather tedious combination of seemingly irrelevant and often useless drills and sporadic use of old articles. It was difficult to muster-up proper motivation. It seemed that the time had come to actually speak Spanish in a more natural environment without the constant "set-ups" and drill environment.

None of the students in the course, even those who enjoyed minimal success in linguistic growth, failed to perceive the content as relevant to their needs—as exemplified by the student, quoted earlier, who observed that he "enjoyed learning about Mexico," even though he thought he would have "learned more Spanish through drills."

Grammar and Writing

The experiments in the Spanish CBI program indicated that literate adult students do perceive the need for some systematic study of explicit grammar and structure. In the early plans for the Spanish CBI program, relatively little formal study of grammar was anticipated. However, "by popular demand," the formal grammatical content of the program increased over time. Perhaps "pure acquisition" modes, such as those that have worked well in immersion programs for children, do not work as well with educated, deductively-oriented adults. There may be certain characteristics inherent in the learning styles of educated adult language learners that impede the use of a purely inductive, acquisition-oriented approach. Possibly, CBI enthusiasts should keep in mind the phenomenon observed by Swain and Lapkin (quoted in Chapter 1 of this volume) who noted that more mature learners are, in fact, very efficient language learners because they can apply their native language literacy skills—their ability to abstract, to classify, and to generalize—to their second language experience. Those of us involved in second language teaching to adults should mark these words and, instead of seeking to change the learning styles of our students (that is, force them to learn as children do), should capitalize on their cognitive skills, maturity, and experience, all of which can be advantageous in second language learning. Moreover, if adults can learn more efficiently with doses of explicit grammar and rules, then we should provide appropriate doses in our CBI curricula.

Related to the issue of adult learning styles is the crucial role of writing in the process of adult second language learning. Many years ago, when the FSI used audio-lingual approaches exclusively, writing was not recognized as part of the language-learning process and was therefore prohibited. However, over time it became more and more apparent that FSI students *needed* to write. It was a natural part of their acquired learning styles. Consequently, writing crept back into the classroom, and by the time the CBI curricula were in place, writing was accepted as a logical component in language development and a useful tool for adult learners to employ, not necessarily to develop writing skills *per se*, but as a reinforcer of the other three skills and as a means of processing information and as a memorization technique. All of the students that went through the CBI programs insisted on frequent writing exercises, even though they knew there was no writing required in the FSI proficiency test. Of particular interest was the student-inspired activity of writing transcriptions of their oral presentations (usually only three to five minutes in length). From their transcriptions they made their own corrections and, according to the teachers and other observers, could identify and correct 80 to 90 percent of their own mistakes. This suggests that the transcribing exercise was helpful to them in improving their grammatical and discourse competence. It may also confirm what Tracy Terrell concluded in his 1991 article: that formal grammatical activities—"learning"—are probably a good complement to and reinforcer of "acquisition" and a necessary part of any educated adult's learning process.

The Content

Appropriate content and materials are essential to the success of a CBI program. In the early stages of our experiment we had unwittingly overloaded the modules. Many of the videos were too long and too sophisticated for students at 2 to 2+ levels of proficiency, especially since a majority of those videos were essentially "talking heads." Many of the original articles and excerpts from books were also beyond the reach of the students; most frequently, the problem was in length, not in level of difficulty. Most students could handle dense prose (Octavio Paz, for example) when given a short passage, but they could easily become frustrated by too much such material. We learned to keep our video content brief (about 15 minutes), to use small doses of authentic reading material, and to use materials especially appropriate for language learners when available, for example, essays edited for students of Spanish or excerpts from Latin American secondary school texts.

We also learned, over time, to use visual reinforcement whenever possible (maps, charts, pictures, posters, and cartoons) and to emphasize "experiential" approaches over "expository" approaches. For example, rather than invite a guest speaker to come and lecture on the pros and cons of democratic elections in Central America, the guest briefly presented the topic, then the class divided into two teams, with the guest moderating a debate on the topic.

The success of the Spanish CBI program and similar experiments at the FSI in Russian, Indonesian, Arabic, and other languages indicates that a carefully designed, well-implemented CBI curriculum offers the potential of accelerating student proficiency growth, increasing motivation and self-confidence, and greatly enhancing students' cultural literacy as well. These multiple advantages, in the long run, suggest that the extra time, money, and human resources required, were well-worth the effort.

Epilogue

Since my departure from the Spanish Section of the FSI in 1990, cutbacks in funding for training and a subsequent reduction in enrollment at FSI have caused the number of students going through the CBI modules to be greatly curtailed. The CBI modules developed for Mexico, Central America, the Andean Region, and the Southern Cone are still offered systematically to selected groups of students in their final weeks of training. Similar modules are still being used occasionally in other sections of FSI.

Stephen Stryker, Professor of English, Adjunct Lecturer in Spanish, and TESOL Director at California State University, Stanislaus, was Head of the Spanish Language Training Section at the Foreign Service Institute in Washington, D.C. from 1984 to 1990. Address: Department of English, CSUS, 801 W. Monte Vista, Turlock, CA 95382 (Email: stryker @toto.csustan.edu)

List of Appendixes

Appendix A: Students' pre- and post-program scores from the pilot programs

This table presents the oral proficiency scores of students both before and after the pilot CBI programs. Scores are given for Speaking (S) and Reading (R). No tests are given in writing at the FSI. Students were tested in the FSI Testing Unit by a team of testers who were not involved in the CBI program in any way.

Appendix B: Daily lesson plans for two of the Mexico modules

Two (of the fifteen) modules are provided here as examples of the step-by-step format of the module design. In the second example, on "Migration," a sample vocabulary worksheet is included. Each module has several such worksheets and reading guides. They are translated here from the original Spanish.

Appendix B-1: Example Module: Daily Lesson Plan for "The Print Media"

Appendix B-2: Example Module: Daily Lesson Plan for "Migration" (including an example of the worksheet for the film El Norte)

Appendix C: Resources and Materials for the Mexico Program

This appendix contains lists of reading materials, films, newspapers, magazines, videotapes, songs, games, and documents used in the program.

Appendix A
Students' Pre- and Post-Program Scores from the Pilot Programs

STUDENT	AGENCY	STARTING PROGRAM SPEAKING/READING		ENDED PROGRAM SPEAKING/READING	
MAY/JUNE 1985					
1	STATE	S-2	R-2+	S-3	R-3+
2	STATE	S-2	R-2	S-3	R-2+
3	STATE	S-2+	R-2	S-3	R-3
4	STATE	S-2+	R-2+	S-3+	R-3
AUGUST 1985					
1	STATE	S-1+	R-1+	S-2	R-2+
2	STATE	S-1+	R-1+	S-2	R-2+
3	STATE	S-1+	R-1+	S-2	R-2
4	STATE	S-2	R-2	S-2+	R-2+
5	STATE	S-1+	R-1+	S-2	R-2
OCTOBER 1985					
1	STATE	S-2	R-2+	S-3	R-3+
2	US MARINE	S-2	R-2	S-2+	R-2
3	STATE	S-2	R-2	S-2+	R-3
4	STATE	S-2	R-2	S-2+	R-2+
JANUARY 1986					
1	DLI	S-2	R-2	S-3	R-3
2	STATE	S-2	R-2	S-3	R-3
3	STATE	S-2+	R-3	S-3	R-3+
4	DLI	S-3	R-3	S-3+	R-3
5	STATE	S-2+	R-3	S-3	R-3+
FEBRUARY 1986					
1	STATE	S-2+	R-2+	S-3	R-3
2	STATE	S-2	R-2	S-3	R-3
3	STATE	S-2	R-2+	S-2+	R-2+
4	STATE	S-2+	R-2+	S-3	R-3
5	STATE	S-2	R-2	S-2+	R-3

Appendix B-1
Example Module: Daily Lesson Plan for "The Print Media"

Preliminary preparation—"reading into" the topic: Each student receives a copy of the reference material describing the characteristics of the Mexican media, a list of general vocabulary, readings in Spanish, and Mexican political cartoons by Abel Quesada.

I. Introductions to the Mexican printed media: Each student is given a newspaper, ideally one from the city to which they will be assigned. They have approximately 15 minutes to browse through it. The teacher remains in the room with them and acts as advisor. The teacher leads a discussion of what the students found interesting about their newspapers, including layout, cultural notes, advertising, entertainment, etc.

II. Preview: The students are given a copy of the vocabulary corresponding to the videotape. The vocabulary is discussed in the form of questions and answers and/or formulation of sentences, NOT as a translation exercise.

III. Videotaped interview: All view the twenty-minute video of the interview with José Manuel Nava, Washington Correspondent for *Excelsior.*

IV. Review and discussion: The teacher leads a discussion of the video. Students are encouraged to recreate what was said in the video, using the vocabulary list as a guide.

V. Preparation of articles: Each student chooses an editorial from a Mexican newspaper or magazine and prepares a presentation of the editorial to the class. The student should comment on whether or not that particular editorial follows the editorial tendencies normally associated with that newspaper and/or magazine.

VI. Oral presentations: Each student presents a 3- to 5- minute oral summary of the article read. (Optional: These presentations may be audiotaped so the student can listen to the tape and make the necessary corrections, which he/she will discuss the next morning in class.)

VII. Wrap-up discussion: The teacher leads a discussion of the major issues brought up during the module. Reference to the students' articles, and the Abel Quesada reading might help focus the discussion. The teacher shows the students several cartoons and asks the students to give their interpretations.

VIII. Linguistic analysis (the next day): Students present and discuss their observations, critiques, and questions concerning grammar or vocabulary based on the notes taken while listening to their audiotaped presentations. This segment is devoted to analysis of any grammatical, stylistic, or lexical topic of interest to the students.

Appendix B-2
Example Module: Daily Lesson Plan for "Migration"
(including an example of the vocabulary worksheet for the film El No*rte*)

Preliminary preparation: **Each student receives a copy of the reference
material describing the terms of the Simpson-Mazzoli immigration
bill. The students should be acquainted with the terms of this bill
and be able to discuss how it affects U.S. - Mexico relations. The
students are given a copy of the U.S. poll results and copies of articles
published in American newspapers that address immigration issues.
In addition, the students are asked to read excerpts from Octavio
Paz's *El Laberinto de la Soledad*.**

    I. Linguistic analysis: Discussion of grammar and vocabulary based
on students' analysis of their oral presentations done the day before.

    II. Preparation for film: Teacher leads the study of the vocabulary
for the film *El Norte*, concentrating on such *"mexicanimos"* as the verb
chingar, and the words *la lana, el coyote*, etc. The teacher can ask questions
using the vocabulary or ask the students to formulate their own sentences
and/or questions. (See attached vocabulary worksheet.)

    III. Viewing of the movie *El Norte*: Since the movie consists of three
identifiable segments: Guatemala, Mexico, and the United States, only the
first two segments will be seen.

    IV. Discussion of the film: The teacher leads a discussion of the movie,
concentrating on migration and the social, economic, and cultural
circumstances surrounding the characters of the movie as well as the unique
dialects of Guatemalans and Mexicans.

    V. Discussion of the reading: The teacher leads a discussion of the
origin, meaning, and use of the verb *chingar* in the Mexican context
according to excerpts taken from the chapter "Los Hijos de la Malinche"
from Octavio Paz's *El Laberinto de la Soledad*.

    VI. Videotaped interview: With a minimum of preparation, students
see the short interview with Mr. Luis Acle on immigration matters. Students
should take notes of key points discussed and of useful vocabulary.

    VII. Discussion: The teacher or guest leads discussion of immigration
reform and what reaction there has been both in the United States and Mexico
to proposed changes to the current immigration law.

    VIII. Preparation of articles: The students are given an hour to read
their articles and prepare their presentations.

IX. Presentation of articles: These presentations may be taped and the students will be asked to listen to their tapes and to make their own corrections.

Optional: Students may also see a fifteen-minute segment of the PBS video on immigration to the United States.

Wrap-up discussion: The teacher (or a designated student) leads in discussion of the major issues discussed and presented.

Example of the Vocabulary Worksheet for *El Norte* (Migration Module)

The following are some of the key "mexicanisms" taken from the film. Before the film is seen, they are presented by the teacher in the following sentences, and their meaning and use are discussed. Translation into English is avoided in favor of finding equivalents or synonyms in Spanish.

Vocabulario de la película *El Norte*

1. No puedo comprar ese coche porque cuesta mucha lana.
2. La secretaria tiene media hora de estar platicando por teléfono con sus amigas y no trabaja.
3. Muchas personas tienen miedo a la oscuridad.
4. Necesito dinero y para conseguirlo no hay más remedio que vender mi carro.
5. Acaban de vender la fábrica y ahora el nuevo patrón es el Sr. González.
6. En esa sierra hay grandes montañas y barrancos de gran profundidad.
7. Hay que ser muy vivo para no pagar tantos impuestos.
8. Hay que tener maña para los negocios; estudiar no es suficiente.
9. En Guatemala, los chapines usan la palabra zompopo como sinónimo de hormiga o animal pequeño que se esconde en la tierra.
10. El diplomático recibió una amenaza de muerte. Su vida corre peligro (o está en peligro) y es mejor que salga del país.
11. La policía finalmente agarró a los criminales y los metió a la cárcel.
12. Los indocumentados cruzan la frontera ayudados por coyotes que les cobran mucho dinero y se aprovechan de su situación.
13. Tengo tanto trabajo que me estoy volviendo loca/a.
14. Hoy no traje el coche. ¿Puedes darme un aventón a casa?

15. Esa señora es <u>fayuguera</u>, vende ropa y aparatos eléctricos que tráe de <u>fayuca</u> de allá <u>del otro lado.</u>
16. A Enrique no le gusta su trabajo y quiere <u>probar suerte</u> haciendo otra cosa.
17. Ese individuo es un vago, no tiene educación ni aspiraciones, es vulgar y grosero y ni hablar de su aspecto físico. Es un verdader <u>naco</u>.
18. Yo no quería ver a mi jefe hoy después de la discusión que tuvimos el otro día y, para colmo <u>me topé</u> con él en el elevador.
19. Con tanta tierra y tanto viento, ¡qué <u>polvero!</u>
20. Tan pronto llega la primavera los pájaros empiezan a hacer sus <u>nidos</u> en los árboles.

Appendix C
Resources and Materials for the Mexico Program

1. Reading materials:

Atlas Cultural de México. 1987. México, D.F.: SEP, Instituto Nacional de Antropología, y Grupo Editorial Planeta.

Banco Nacional de México. 1988. *Review of the Economic Situation of México.* LXVI:754, September.

Bernal, Victor Manuel y Eduardo Torreblanca, coordinadores. 1988. *Espacios de Silencio: La Televisión Mexicana.* México, D.F.: Nuestro Tiempo.

Cumberland, Charles C. 1972. *The Mexican Revolution: The Constitutionalist Years.* Austin, TX: University of Texas Press.

Colegio de México. 1977, 1981. *Historia General de México.* 2 vols. México, D.F.: El Colegio de México.

Enciclopedia de México. 1987. México, D.F.: Secretaría de Educación Pública.

García, Manuel. 1988. *México y Estados Unidos: Frente a la Migración de Indocumentados.* México, D.F.: Porrúa.

Langly, Lester. 1988. *Mex-America: Two Countries, One Future.*

Méxicoen el Arte. 1987. Nos. 1-18 (1982-88), México, D.F.: Instituto Nacional de Bellas Artes.

Meyer, Lorenzo and Josefina Vazquez. *Mexico frente a los Estados Unidos. Un Ensayo Historico.* Mexico: El Colegio de Mexico.

Riding, Alan. 1985. *Distant Neighbors: A Portrait of the Mexicans.* New York: Alfred A. Knopf.

Secretaría de Educación Pública, México, D.F., textbooks for secondary schools: *Ciencias Sociales, Historia, Matematicas,* Grades 7-10.

Silva Herzog, Jesús. 1960. *Breve Historia de la Revolución Mexicana.* Vol. I & II. México, D.F.: Fondo de Cultura Económica.

Smith, Peter H. 1980. *Mexico: Neighbor in Transition.* Headline Series. New York: Foreign Policy Association.

Trejo Delarbre, Raul, coordinator. 1985. *Televisa: El Quinto Poder.* México, D.F.: Claves Latinoamericanos.

2. Commercial films:

Así Es Mi Tierra (Cantínflas)
El Norte
Flor Silvestre
Los Abañiles
Los Olvidados
Macario
The Ballad of Gregorio Cortéz

3. Newspapers:

El Excelsior   (Mexico, D.F)
El Informador   (Guadalajara)
Novedades   (Mecico, D.F.)
El Universal   (Mexico, D.F.)

4. Magazines:

Impacto
Nexos
Proceso
Siempre
Uno mas Uno
Vuleta
Vision

5. Videotaped interviews:

Interviews with leading personalities, intellectuals, and political leaders were either taken from the television or filmed in the studios of the FSI.

6. Music and songs:

A large selection of Mexican music and songs included selections from Trio los Panchos, Javier Solís, Pedro Infante, Armando Manzanero, El Ballet Folklórico de México and Mariachi Vargas.

7. Games:

"La Lotería," (the Lottery)—available commercially in Mexico
"Fiesta de Palabras" (Scrabble)—available commercially in Mexico
"Trivia"—made up by students and teachers on specific topics in the modules
"La Horca" (Hangman)—a game for practicing spelling
"El Gato" (Tic-Tac-Toe)—a game for practicing grammar
"Who Am I?"—a game for practicing identifying famous people
"Where Am I?"—a game for describing places
"Twenty Questions "—a game for practicing any information such as persons, places or things

8. Examples of formal communications:

Business letters
Invoices
Invitations
Birth certificates
Marriage certificates
Death certificates
Work permits

9

Teaching for Communicative and Cultural Competence: Spanish through Contemporary Mexican Topics

Norma Klahn

Editors' Note: Norma Klahn describes her successful adaptation of the FSI Mexico program for the School of International and Public Affairs (SIPA) of Columbia University. Professor Klahn, working almost single-handedly, with strong administrative support and funding from Exxon and the Pew Charitable Trusts, designed and taught an intensive course aimed at bringing students from an ACTFL Intermediate level to ACTFL Advanced level while focusing entirely on Mexican literature, society, and culture. As was the case in Vines' French program at Ohio (Chapter 6), there was a focus on developing all four skills as well as on fostering academic knowledge and cultural literacy. Students who took her course demonstrated significant increases in their Spanish proficiency and wrote rave reviews of the program. In describing her experience developing and teaching the course, Klahn emphasizes that any teacher who undertakes this kind of CBI project must be an experienced language teacher who understands teaching for proficiency and is very knowledgeable about literature, history, geography, laws, economy, politics, current events, and culture. Although Klahn has left Columbia University, the course lives on, and she has developed a similar course for graduate students of literature at Santa Cruz, which has been offered since 1993. Her new course, as well as other interesting developments since 1990, are discussed at the end of her chapter. General references for this chapter are located in the bibliography at the end of this volume.

Introduction

Between 1987 and 1990, the School of International and Public Affairs (SIPA) of Columbia University (N.Y.C.) developed a new content-based, graduate-level Spanish language course entitled, "Spanish Immersion through Contemporary Mexican Topics." The course was developed with funding from Exxon and the Pew Charitable Trusts. The goal of the new course was to integrate area and language studies in such a way as to lead students to increased Spanish language proficiency by immersing students in the study of Mexican society and culture.

The course was proposed as a result of a commitment on the part of the directors of SIPA to the concept of the integration of language and culture. In order for students in the U.S. to conduct significant research about other countries, extensive knowledge of the culture, the politics, the economics, the literary history, and the sociology of those countries is essential. It was felt that this could best be accomplished by studying language as the concrete expression of a society. Mexico was chosen because of its special relevance to students in the United States whose specialization within the area of Latin American studies focused on Mexico or United States-Mexico relations from different disciplinary approaches. The signing of the North American Free Trade Agreement (1993), with its economic, social, and political consequences and cultural implications on both sides of the border, added to the growing Mexican-origin populations in the United States, especially in the Southwest, makes this a fundamental course for any Latin American or global studies program today.

The course at SIPA was modeled on a course created in the Spanish Section of the Foreign Service Institute (FSI), described in the previous chapter. The success of the FSI program suggested that language students at an ILR level 2 of proficiency could benefit from the study of subject matter, rather than advanced grammar, syntax, and phonology.

The FSI program caught the attention of SIPA during the time when some language departments at Columbia University were moving toward proficiency testing as the best way to judge the degree of communicative and professional competence in a foreign language. The FSI, in an effort to improve its curriculum preparing Foreign Service personnel to serve in the American Embassy and consulates in Mexico, experimented with a "Mexican Spanish Course" as early as 1984. Statistical results between 1984 and 1986 showed that students who had already reached oral and reading proficiency levels of Speaking and Reading-2 could increase their levels to Speaking and Reading-3 in a significantly shorter period of time and, in addition, students were more culturally competent to work and live in Mexico (Stryker, Chapter 8).

Through a partnership established between the FSI and the SIPA, the FSI Spanish Section cooperated with the author by sharing models, methods, and materials from its four-week immersion "Mexico Program." Although a course at Columbia had to take into consideration the goals of university students and an academic semester, the two fundamental goals of the FSI program remained the same at Columbia: language competency and cultural literacy. Attention was directed to achieve total integration of language studies and area studies by focusing on a specific country, while raising students' Spanish proficiency. In order to adapt the FSI course to a university setting a rethinking had to occur that took into consideration the level of content preparation of the graduate students and the particular programs in which they were enrolled. This reconceptualization brought about several changes, some major and others of a more technical nature.

One of the changes made in adapting the FSI model to Columbia was to use a valid yet more cost-efficient proficiency testing instrument. At the FSI the official oral proficiency test requires two testers and takes about ninety minutes to administer. Furthermore, the format and content of the FSI test is tailored to the Foreign Service population. For these reasons, the ACTFL proficiency test in Spanish was adopted for use in the SIPA pilot courses. It was generally agreed that the ACTFL test met acceptable scientific standards and was much more economical—a fifteen- to thirty-minute exam administered by one individual (Liskin-Gasparro 1984).

Since growth in oral proficiency was one of the central goals of the SIPA course, students' proficiency was measured both before and after the course. The requirement for admitting students to the course was set at ACTFL level 2, although nine of the thirty-six initial participants entered at the 1+ (Intermediate-High) level. (See Chapter 1 for ACTFL level definitions.)

The Columbia course also differed from the FSI course in the teacher-student ratio and the intensity of the course. Whereas the FSI classes averaged six students and met for six hours a day, the Columbia course averaged twelve students and followed an eight-hour week in a fourteen-week academic program of study. Out-of-class reading was extensive: students were expected to do about seven to ten hours of homework a week.

Whereas the FSI program included little emphasis on formal writing, it was seen as an essential part of the Columbia course to reinforce vocabulary and grammar, and to improve overall language skills.

Goals and Objectives of the Course

The course on Mexico at Columbia was designed to fulfill the foreign language requirement for advanced-level language and literature for either the certificate or regional specialization in Latin American and Iberian studies for students in the School of International and Public Affairs. Students who took the course were graduate students studying for a master's degree at SIPA, Ph.D. students in history, political science, or anthropology, graduate students in Columbia Teachers College, law students, journalism students and other advanced undergraduate students who met the entrance requirements. The Mexico course also became a favorite course for Chicano students who had reached an advanced level of Spanish but who had little formal knowledge of the history, culture, or political system of Mexico. Chicano students especially appreciated the final topic of the course on United States-Mexico relations and Mexican-Americans in the United States.

The Philosophy and Organization of the Course

The Mexico course was designed to provide language students (especially graduates) with an alternative to upper division language courses that focused purely on grammar or on literature. The course was carefully designed to emphasize the acquisition of language through activities focused on themes, topics, and content; there was little focus on explicit rule learning or overt correction of errors. Every effort was made to assure that the content of the course was sequenced in such a way as to facilitate student comprehension. This was accomplished by carefully controlling the quantity and quality of the content of the material so that each lesson guided the student to a higher level of competence. To facilitate student comprehension, all lessons were focused on specific topics, and a great deal of extralinguistic information was presented, especially visual stimuli. Each topic included at least one video component.

Receptive skills were initially emphasized in the design of the course so that in the beginning of each module, students were provided with both listening and reading activities on the specific topic. They were then required to present oral reports, to engage in discussion and debate, and finally to produce an essay, commentary, or editorial. Frequently, a study of a particular topic culminated with a visit to the class by a guest lecturer who led discussion and conversed with the students on the topic. Visitors to the class included many Mexican nationals visiting the New York area and Mexican graduate students from other departments at the university. The participation of Mexican guests was an essential component of the course, providing the students with "authentic" exchanges with a broad variety of Spanish-speakers on current, relevant, and ongoing debates. When possible, the colloquia of the guest speakers was filmed. The videos were used to review the discussion the following day or to introduce the same topic in a subsequent course the following semester.

The formal study of morphology, phonology, syntax, semantics, and vocabulary was not overlooked. Discussion of grammatical topics, always in the context of the specific content activities, were an ongoing part of the curriculum and were always conducted in Spanish. For example, if students manifested problems using certain complicated verb structures in expressing their views and opinions, the correct usage of that structure was discussed within the specific communicative context, and not as an abstract topic per se. Correction techniques in the classroom were confined to unobtrusive, informal, and indirect methods and focused only on errors which interfered with communication. Attention to grammatical errors was more explicit in teachers' responses to written work, which was either corrected or discussed individually with students.

In the organization of the course content, every effort was made to orient the topics to the students' needs and specializations within the university curriculum. The topics were taught in a specific sequence, using the ACTFL proficiency guidelines to establish an order of gradual language acquisition. Although the Spanish instructors at the FSI felt that the order in which the topics were presented was not crucial, at Columbia this instructor became aware that the different topics lent themselves to the performance of certain linguistic tasks and that, studied in a specific order, they facilitated students' progress from 1+/2 to 2+/3. Thus, the topics were sequenced as follows: 1) The History of Mexico, 2) The Political System, 3) Means of Communication, 4) The Mexican Economy, 5) Geography and Demography, 6) The Arts, 7) Popular Culture, and 8) US-Mexican Relations. (See Appendix C for a complete list of topics.)

We began with history and used this topic, rich in facts and description, to emphasize narration and description in the past using, naturally and authentically, the preterit, imperfect, and other past verb forms. Literature was presented as reading material only after students had some insight into the overall cultural context which had produced the texts. A selection of some of Mexico's most important literature was studied after the students had a good grasp of the history, culture, and literary tradition of the country and were closer to a 2+ level of proficiency. It was at this point that the study of literature became "comprehensible input" and a careful reading of the works of Juan Rulfo, Carlos Fuentes, Martin Luis Guzman, or Elena Poniatowska took place. The topic of the Mexican world view and current US-Mexican relations (Appendix D) was saved for last because it required students to demonstrate a high degree of abstract and analytical thinking, defending of opinions, and hypothesizing—activities associated with level 3 proficiency.

Course Materials and Activities

All the materials used were examples of authentic Mexican discourse. They included historical, biographical, and autobiographical accounts, newspaper and magazine articles, editorials, film reviews, economic predictions and graphs, political speeches, poems, short stories, popular traditions, interviews, business letters, recipes, and tourist brochures. Some of the audio-visual materials included excerpts taken from the radio, popular songs, authors reading their works, movies, television programs, documentaries on the Mexican Revolution, interviews of prominent Mexican personalities, commercials, soap operas, slides and photographs. These materials formed the "text" of the course and, as such, required constant revision, addition, deletion, and editing. The focus on current events was an important factor in maintaining a high degree of student engagement. There were, of course, basic information topics, such as history and geography, that formed the core of the course, while other topics were updated on a regular basis in order to maintain maximum relevancy.

Materials were selected and, in some cases, edited so that they became progressively more difficult and challenging. Listening activities began with videotaped interviews directed to a general audience on very specific topics and progressed toward films such as Luis Buñuel's *los olvidados,* a complex view of Mexico City in the fifties, in which the characters, representing different sectors of society, speak in their respective dialects.

Reading activities ranged from straightforward news articles and reporting of facts and events to interpretative articles in specialized journals and, only in the final weeks, to literary fiction and the highly metaphorical languages and imaginative structures of poetry and popular expressive forms.

Speaking activities were designed to progress, over the course of the semester, from oral reports on factual information or events to defending the differing positions on controversial topics such as the "English Only" movement, the *maquiladora* industry (border assembly plants), the one-party system of government, the debt crisis, current social movements, and the environment. Using different speech registers and styles, students reported the news, sold a product, promoted a tourist attraction, reviewed a film, described a painting, interpreted a poem, gave a political speech, acted as advisor to the president, justified a foreign loan from an international bank, or took a position in the current debates on neoliberalism, democracy, and social justice.

Writing activities were structured so that students began by summarizing factual descriptions and ended by advancing an analysis of the bilateral relations between the United States and Mexico. There were many assigned readings and miniresearch projects. To complete assignments, it was essential that the students use Mexican periodicals such as *La Jornada, Excelsior, Nexos,* and *Proceso.* (These publications are available at most university libraries and on the Internet. Today we would add *Reforma, El financiero* and *Ojarasc*a.)

The Outcomes

Results of the pilot course offered in the spring semester of 1987 were very positive. Students were pre-tested and post-tested using the ACTFL proficiency scale. The six students in that course demonstrated proficiency gains of one full point on the ACTFL scale. Four students who pre-tested at the Advanced level (2) scored at the Superior level (3) at the end of the course. The other two students began the semester at Intermediate High (1+) and ended with Advanced Plus (2+). Subsequent classes conducted from 1987 through 1990 showed similar gains, with the great majority of students advancing one full point on the ACTFL scale. Of the thirty-six students enrolled during this period, twenty-two improved their proficiency one whole point on the ACTFL proficiency scale, and all of the remaining students increased their proficiency by one-half point on the scale. (See Appendix A for students' pre- and post-test scores, and Appendix B for selected student comments.)

Student comments and evaluations of the course were extremely favorable. One student wrote:

As we became more engrossed in Mexican issues, we forgot about trying to speak perfect Spanish and instead concentrated on making ourselves understood. I think that the switch from the traditional method of learning Spanish by studying disjointed material and literature, to immersion in one topic, allowed us to gain a deeper and more workable knowledge of the language.

And another student wrote:

The intensive Spanish-Contemporary Mexico pilot course was, by far, one of the most dynamic and informative courses that I have taken here at Columbia. This type of seminar offered the combination of intensive foreign language training and the introduction of a new culture.

Concluding Remarks

Overall, this course had very positive results in the cognitive, linguistic, and affective domains. The statistics given above, combined with the overwhelmingly favorable student reactions to the course, were very encouraging. Student evaluations demonstrate the potential for a course of this kind to achieve the goal of greater socio-cultural understanding through increased foreign language fluency.

A course of this nature should be taught by a native or near-native speaker of Spanish who is highly knowledgeable of culture and current events in Mexico and Latin America. An "integrated" course of this kind also requires a teacher who has extensive experience in foreign language teaching, including teaching and testing for oral proficiency (although an oral proficiency tester could perform a pre- and post-test). It is, essentially, a content-based foreign language course requiring the full integration of fields that are traditionally taught in separate "departments" at a university.

An interdisciplinary course of this kind does require the enthusiastic support from department and college administrators since it attracts students from many different departments. It requires qualified faculty prepared to engage in newer approaches. It might be offered as an option for faculty whose regular assignments in Spanish Literature or Modern Language Departments require they teach a Spanish grammar course. A course such as this might also be co-taught by a language instructor and an area studies specialist.

Thanks to the strong administrative support of SIPA at Columbia University, the funding provided by Exxon and the Pew Foundation, and the excellent results achieved by the students in this course, "Contemporary Mexican Topics" now serves as a model for area/language courses in Russian at Columbia and in Portuguese at New York University.

Epilogue: An Evolving Model

Shortly after my departure from Columbia University in 1990, courses modeled on Contemporary Mexican Topics were begun in Russian at Columbia and in Portuguese at New York University. In 1991 the course received national attention in an article by Karen E. Breiner-Sanders entitled, "Higher-Level Language Abilities: the Skills Connection." It was also featured as a story, "Programa Mexico del Instituto de Estudios Latinoamericanos e Ibéricos de la Universidad de Columbia," by Miguel Angel Flores, in *Proceso* (No. 630, 28 de noviembre de 1988), a well known Mexican weekly news magazine.

At Columbia University the course continues to be offered by Dr. Ruth Elizabeth Borgman with great success and popularity. Every semester at least twenty students interview and twelve are selected. In the summer of 1994, Dr. Borgman used the model to develop an immersion course for Spanish teachers at Columbia's Teachers College. That twenty-hour course was funded by an NEH grant and was titled "Mexican Culture and Language Skills for the Classroom."

At Knox College, Professor Timothy Foster, my former graduate assistant at Columbia, has used the model (and funding from the Lily

Foundation) to develop an intermediate language course called "Area/ Language Studies: Mexico."

At the University of California at Santa Cruz (UCSC), I have developed a graduate Spanish immersion course for entering graduate students in the field of literary and cultural studies. Following the course at Columbia, it was also grounded methodologically on the integration of area and language, but in this case the students were aiming to reach a Superior level (ACTFL). This intensive course lasts for three weeks, meets three-and-a-half hours per day, and requires up to six hours of preparation in reading. It is an Introduction to Spanish-American Literature taken by incoming graduate students just before the regular quarter begins. The syllabus dedicates a single day to a single Latin American author—Jorge Luis Borges, María Luisa Bombal, Julio Cortázar, Rosario Castellanos, Manuel Puig, Juan Rulfo, Elena Poniatowska, Gabriel García Márques, Isabel Allende, Carlos Fuentes, Mario Vargas Llosa, Luis Rafael Sánchez, Luisa Valenzuela, and Rosario Ferré. The course is conducted entirely in Spanish. The students prepare for the class by reading an interview with the author, a short story by that same author, and a critical essay on the work. The stories are chosen for their variety of form, content, and semantic areas. Both the stories and critical articles are arranged in ascending order of difficulty. Vocabulary in context is introduced the day before the readings are assigned. A videotape of the interview is seen after the students have familiarized themselves with the written version and before discussing the story and its interpretations. Toward the end of the course, more abstract and theoretical articles are assigned. This course has been very successfully implemented since 1993 and similar courses have been developed at UCSC in French and Italian.

∽ ∾

Norma Klahn is currently Associate Professor of Spanish in the Literature Department, and Co-Director of the Chicano/Latino Research Center at the University of California at Santa Cruz. She was Assistant Professor in the Department of Spanish and Portuguese at Columbia University (New York City) from 1978 to 1989. Address: 59 Merrill College, University of California, Santa Cruz, CA 95064 (Email: norma_klahn@macmail.ucsc.edu)

List of Sources for the Mexico Course

Atlas Cultural de México. 1987. México, D.F.: SEP, Instituto Nacional de Antropología, y Grupo Editorial Planeta.
Ayala Blanco, Jorge. 1986. *La Aventura del Cine Mexicano: 1931-1967.* 1968; *La Búsqueda del Cine Mexicano: 1968-1972.* 1974; *La Condición del Cine Mexicano: 1973-1985.*

Banco Nacional de México. 1988. *Review of the Economic Situation of México.* LXVI:754, September.

Bqueiro López, Oswaldo. 1986. *La Prensa y el Estado.* México, D.F.: Fondo de Cultura Económica.

Benitez, Fernando. 1967. *Los Indios de México.* México, D.F.: Ediciones Era.

Berdan, Frances. 1982. *The Aztecs of Central Mexico: An Imperial Society.* New York: Holt, Rinehart, and Winston.

Bernal, Victor Manuel y Eduardo Torreblanca, coordinadores. 1988. *Espacios de Silencio: La Televisión Mexicana.* México, D.F.: Nuestro Tiempo.

Bilateral Commission on the Future of United States-Mexican Relations. 1989. The *Challenge of Interdependence: Mexico and the United States.* Lanham, New York and London: University Press of America.

Brenner, Anita. 1971. *The Wind that Swept Mexico.* Austin: University of Texas Press.

Constitución Política de los Estados Unidos Mexicanos. 1988. México, D.F.: Editorial Teocalli.

Cumberland, Charles C. 1972. *The Mexican Revolution: The Constitutionalist Years.* Austin, TX: University of Texas Press.

De la Rosa, Martín and Charles A. Reilly, coordinadores. 1985. *Religión y Política en México.* México, D.F.: Siglo Veintuno.

El Colegio de México. *Historia General de México.* 2 vols. México, D.F.: El Colegio de México, 1977, 1981.

El Colegio de México. 1973. *Historia Mínima de México.* México, D.F.: El Colegio de México.

Enciclopedia de México. 1987. México, D.F.: Secretaría de Educación Pública.

Fem. Fem: 10 Años de Periodismo Feminista. Mujeres en su Tiempo. 1988. México, D.F.: Planeta.

Fernández Chrislieb, Paulina e Rodriguez Araujo, Octavio. 1986. *Elecciones y Partidos en México.* México, D.F.: Ediciones el Caballito.

García, Manuel. 1988. *México y Estados Unidos: Frente a la Migración de Indocumentados.* México, D.F.: Porrua.

Garza E., Humberto, ed. 1986. *Fundamentos y Prioridades de la Política Exterior de México.* México, D.F.: El Colegio de México.

Hart, John Mason. 1988. *Revolutionary Mexico.* Berkeley: University of California, Berkeley.

Iturriaga, José. 1951. *La Estructura Social y Cultural de México.* México, D.F.: Fondo de Cultura Económica.
Kandell, Jonathan. 1988. *La Capital: The Biography of Mexico City.* New York: Random House.
Klahn, Norma y Jesse Fernandez. 1987. *Lugar de Encuentro: Ensayos Críticos Sobre Poesía Mexicana Actual.* México, D.F.: Katun.
Krauze, Enrique. 1987. *Biografía del Poder* (series). México, D.F.: Fondo de Cultura Económica.
1. *Porfirio Díaz: Místico de la Autoridad.*
2. Francisco I. Madero: Místico de la Libertad.
3. Emiliano Zapata: El Amor a la Tierra.
4. Francisco Villa: Entre el Angel y el Fierro.
5. Venustiano Carranza: Puente Entre Siglos.
6. Alvaro Obregón: El Vértigo de la Victoria.
7. Plutarco E. Calles: Reformar desde el Origen.
8. *Lázaro Cárdenas: General Misionero.*
Lafaye, Jacques. 1976. *Quetzalcóatl and Guadalupe: The Formation of Mexican National Consciousness, 1513-1813.* trans. Benjamin Keen. Chicago and London: Chicago University Press.
Merida, Carlos. 1987. *Escritos de Carlos Merida Sobre Arte: El Muralismo.* México, D.F.: Centro Nacional de Investigación, Documentación e Información de Artes Plasticas, INBA.
Méxcio en el Arte. 1987. NOs. 1-18 (1982-88), Méxcio, D.F.: Instituto Nacional de Bellas Artes.
Meyer, Lorenzo, Rafael Segovia y Alejandra Lajous. 1978. *Historia de la Revolución Mexicana: Período 1928-1934. Los Inicios de la Institucionalización. La Política del Maximato.* México, D.F.: El Colegio de México.
Meyer, Lorenzo and Josefina Vazquez. 1982. *Mexico frente a los Estados Unidos. Un Ensayo Histórico.* Mexico: El Colegio de Mexico.
Monsivaís, Carlos. 1987. *Entrada libre: crónicas de la sociedad que se organiza.* México: Ediciones Era.
Ojeda, Mario. 1976. *Alcances y Límites de la Política Exterior de México.* México, D.F.: El Colegio de México.
Paz Octavio. 1950. *El Laberinto de la Soledad.*
Poniatowska, Elena. 1969. *Noche de Tlatelolco.*
Prieto, Guillermo. 1987. *Primer Foro de Cultura Contemporánea de la Frontera Norte de México.* México, D.F.: SEP.

Riding, Alan. 1985. *Distant Neighbors: A Portrait of the Mexicans.* New York: Alfred A. Knopf.

Rodas Carpizo, A. R. 1987. *Estructura Socioeconómica de México.* México, D.F.: Limusa.

Ruiz Castañeda, María del Carmen, coordinadora. 1987. *La Prensa: Pasado y Presente de México: Catálogo Selectivo de Publicaciones Periódicas.* Méxcio, D.F.: Universidad Nacional Autonoma de México.

Salvador, Gabriel. 1987. *Historia de la Música en México.* México, D.F.: Gernika, SEP.

Schavelzon, Daniel, compilador. 1988. *La Polémica del Arte Nacional en México. 1850-1910.* México, D.F.: Fondo de Cultura Económica.

Sefchovich, Sara. 1987. *México: País de Ideas, País de Novelas: Una Sociología de la Literatura Mexicana.* México, D.F.: Grijalbo.

Silva Herzog, Jesús. 1960. *Breve Historia de la Revolución Mexicana.* Vol. I & II. México, D.F.: Fondo de Cultura Económica.

Smith, Peter H. 1980. *Mexico: Neighbor in Transition.* Headline Series. New York: Foreign Policy Association.

Trejo Delarbre, Raul, coordinator. 1985. *Televisa: El Quinto Poder.* México, D.F.: Claves Latinoamericanos.

Tuñon Pablos, Julia. 1987. *Mujeres en México.* México: Planeta.

Uno Más Uno: Diez Años. México. 1987. D.F.: Editorial Uno.

Valdez, Luz María. 1988. *El Perfil Demográfico de los Indios Mexicanos.* México, D.F.: Siglo XXI para Coordinación de Humanidades. UNAM, y Centro de Investigaciones y Estudios Superiores en Antropogía y Sociología.

Womack, John Jr. 1969. *Zapata and the Mexican Revolution.* New York, NY: Alfred Knopf.

List of Appendixes

Appendix A: Summary of results of ACTFL scores of students in the Columbia course from 1987 to 1989

Appendix B: Selected student comments

Appendix C: List of course topics as they appeared in the course syllabus (in Spanish)

Appendix D: Detailed description of three sample modules as they appeared in the course syllabus (translated from the original Spanish)

Appendix E: List of popular magazines, periodicals, and films used in the course

Appendix A
Oral Proficiency Exams—ACTFL/ETS Results

STUDENT (MAJOR)	BEGAN	ENDED
SPRING 1987		
Student 1 (SIPA)	1+ Intermediate High	2+ Advanced Plus
Student 2 (SIPA)	2 Advanced	3 Superior
Student 3 (SIPA)	1+ Intermediate High	2+ Advanced Plus
Student 4 (Journalism)	2 Advanced	3 Superior
Student 5 (SIPA)	2 Advanced	3 Superior
Student 6 (SIPA)	2 Advanced	3 Superior
FALL 1987		
Student 1 (SIPA)	1+ Intermediate High	2+ Advanced Plus
Student 2 (SIPA)	2 Advanced	3 Superior
Student 3 (SIPA)	1 Intermediate	2 Advanced
Student 4 (SIPA)	2 Advanced	2+ Advanced Plus
Student 5 (SIPA)	2 Advanced	3 Superior
Student 6 (SIPA)	2 Advanced	2+ Advanced Plus
Student 7 (SIPA)	2 Advanced	3 Superior
Student 8 (SIPA)	1 Intermediate	2 Advanced

SPRING 1988

Student 1 (Urban Studies)	2+ Advanced Plus	3 Superior
Student 2 (Education)	2 Advanced	3 Superior
Student 3 (Law)	2+ Advanced Plus	3+ Superior Plus
Student 4 (SIPA)	2 Advanced	3 Superior
Student 5 (SIPA)	2 Advanced	2+ Advanced Plus

FALL 1988

Student 1 (Political Science)	1+ Intermediate High	2 Advanced
Student 2 (Undergraduate)	2 Advanced	2+ Advanced Plus
Student 3 (Undergraduate)	2 Advanced	3 Superior
Student 4 (Anthropology)	2 Advanced	3 Superior
Student 5 (SIPA)	2 Advanced	2+ Advanced Plus
Student 6 (Law)	1+ Intermediate High	2+ Advanced Plus
Student 7 (SIPA)	1+ Intermediate High	2+ Advanced Plus
Student 8 (History)	1+ Intermediate High	2+ Advanced Plus
Student 9 (Political Science)	2+ Advanced Plus	3 Superior

SPRING 1989

Student 1 (Undergraduate)	2+ Advanced Plus	3 Superior
Student 2 (SIPA)	1+ Intermediate High	2 Advanced
Student 3 (SIPA)	2+ Advanced Plus	3 Superior
Student 4 (SIPA)	2+ Advanced Plus	3 Superior
Student 5 (SIPA-Journalism)	2+ Advanced Plus	3 Superior
Student 6 (General Studies)	2 Advanced	3 Superior
Student 7 (SIPA)	2 Advanced	3 Superior
Student 8 (Journalism)	2 Advanced	2+ Advanced Plus

Appendix B
Selected Student Comments

Student A:

"This course has undoubtedly been one of the most rewarding experiences I have had in my two years at the Columbia University School of International Affairs. Unfortunately, there have been few other instances in which I worked with professors and students of such uniformly high caliber. By virtue of the course's format, the professor and the students were consistently able to cooperate to help each other improve both their language skills and their understanding of Mexico. Discussions in class were typically interesting and intense, putting the course on a par with most of my English-language ones in terms of the amount of knowledge students gained and the quality of intellectual analysis they undertook."

Student B:

"I felt that my fluency in Spanish improved in all areas; oral, written and reading. Since we approached the theme of Mexico from a number of directions, the course certainly widened the scope of my Spanish vocabulary to include more specialized terminology. Most importantly, the language seems to flow with greater ease after having worked intensively with it for 4 months."

Student C:

"As we became more engrossed in Mexican issues, we forgot about trying to speak perfect Spanish and instead concentrated on making ourselves understood. I think the switch from the traditional method of learning Spanish by studying disjointed material and literature, to immersion in one topic, allowed us to gain a deeper and more workable knowledge of the language."

Student D:

"I was a Spanish major at Georgetown University, but graduated several years ago and had forgotten much vocabulary, etc. After having taken this course, I can say that I am comfortable with my Spanish and feel confident enough to use it at my job if needed. My Spanish has 100% improved."

Student E:

"The Intensive Spanish-Contemporary Mexico pilot course was, by far, one of the most dynamic and informative courses that I have taken here at Columbia. This type of seminar offered the combination of intensive foreign language training and the introduction of a new culture. In short, the thought process, introduction of new material and vocabulary, as well as the practice of formulating and defending an argument in a foreign language was the greatest benefit the seminar offered."

Appendix C

This is the list of topics as it appeared on the course syllabus. Each number represents one week in the course. Some topics took more than one week to cover. The students were pre-tested in week one and post-tested in week thirteen.

1. Introducción/La Historia de México
2. La Historia de México
3. El Sistema Político
4. El Sistema Político
5. Los Medios de Comunicación
6. La Economía Mexicana
7. Geografía/Demografía
8. Geografía/Demografía
9. Artes (Literatura/Arte)
10. Las Artes (Literatura/Arte)
11. Cultura Popular
12. Mexcanidad
13. Relaciones Estados Unidos-México

Appendix D

The following arethree sample modules—1, 6, and 13—taken from the course syllabus (in translation from the original Spanish).

Module Number 1: The History of Mexico
(Pre-Columbian to 19th Century)
Preliminary step: Read: *El español en México*.
　　　　　Study and get familiar with the map of Mexico.
　　　　　Hear and read the national anthem and its history.
Step 1: Introduction to the course.
　　　　　Introduction of the students.
　　　　　Listen to the national anthem and discuss its history. Compare it to other anthems.
　　　　　Work with vocabulary of "Mexicanisms."
　　　　　Homework: Read *Los aztecas*. Discuss the pre-Columbian era.

Step 2: Discussion of Los *aztecas*.
See the video and slides on the Aztecs.
Review homework.
Homework: Reading: *175 años de historia*. Prepare a brief
presentation on sections assigned.

Step 3: Reports on *175 años de historia*.
Assignments: Prepare brief oral biographies on Cuautehmoc,
Moctezuma, Cortés, Bernal Díaz del Castillo,   Santa Ana,
Juárez, Maximiliano, Carlota, Fray Servando, Padre Hidalgo,
Morelos, etc.

Step 4: Presentation and discussion of the oral biographies.

Module Number 6: The Economy

Preliminary step: Read "La Desigualdad Económica." Note the
highlights and bring to class ten sentences or words that were
unfamiliar to you.

Step 1: Work with the key vocabulary list from "La Desigualdad
Económica." Discuss the article.
Work with the Mexican expressions concerning money and
finances.
Assignment: Prepare the practice sheet on the various tenses:
past, present, future, preterit-imperfect.
Students prepare brief oral reports on articles dealing with
finance taken from various newspapers.

Step 2: Review the assignments concerning tenses.
Students present their oral reports.
Work with the vocabulary dealing with the economy.
Assignment: Read "El Estado y la Economía Mixta." Prepare
the practice sheet on the verbs.

Step 3: Discussion of the article.
Correct and discuss grammar exercises.
Work with the vocabulary on the economy.
Guest lecturer on the Mexican economy.
Assignment: Students prepare articles on various topics
concerning the Mexican economy.

Step 4: Discussion of the lecture.
Work with key vocabulary and terms concerning the economy.
Student presentation of articles.

Module Number 13: U.S.-Mexican Relations

Preliminary step: Reading: Alan Riding, *Distant Neighbors.* Read the critique by Enrique Krauze. Each student will do a report on assigned chapters.

Step 1: Discuss Riding and Krauze.

Assignment: Read "Los hijos de la Malinche," from *Laberinto de la Soledad* by Octavio Paz.

Step 2: Discuss Paz in relation to Riding and Krauze.

Assignment: Read selections from *La Jaula de la Melancolía* by Roger Barta. Each student reads an article on U.S.-Mexico relations and presents it in class for discussion.

Step 3: Presentation of articles.

See the video: *La Frontera.*

Assignment: Each student reads an article on the topic.

Step 4: Presentation of articles

See video on "El Chicano."

Assignment: Read various articles on "relaciones Estados Unidos-México."

Step 5: Discuss the different topics.

See film *El Norte.*

Assignment: Write an essay on the U.S.-Mexico relations and the current political scene in Mexico.

Step 6: General discussion and overview.

Appendix E
Magazines and Newspapers

El Excelsior
FEM
La Jornada
Nexos
Plural
Proceso
Revista de la Universidad de México
Siempre
Uno mas Uno
Vuelta

Films

Los Abañiles
Ahí Está El Detalle (Cantínflas)
Así Es Mi Tierra (Cantínflas)
The Ballad of Gregorio Cortéz
Flor Silvestre
Frida: Naturaleza Viva
Macario
El Norte
Los Olvidados
El imperio de la fortuna

10

Content-Based Instruction:
An Indonesian Example

Jijis Chadran & Gary Esarey

Editors' Note: The Indonesian program desribed by Chadran and Esarey is an intensive thirty-six-week course, in which students are in class for up to five hours per day, five days a week. Classes are relatively small, with an average of six students per class. For three hours per week students attend an Indonesian area studies course, taught in English in the School of Area Studies. The CBI component is woven into a highly eclectic tapestry of different approaches that include grammar-translation, audio-lingual drills, Total Physical Response (TPR), Delayed Oral Response (DOR), role plays, and Community Language Learning (CLL). Small units of CBI are introduced early in the language training to complement lectures from the area studies program; then, in the final phase of training, the curriculum becomes a series of "Advanced and Specialized Job-Related Modules." One of the unique aspects of Chadran and Esarey's CBI design is the attention given to differences in students' learning styles. The modules have been designed to cover the broadest possible spectrum of student learning styles, and in order to achieve this, the authors have adapted the "4-MAT system," in which the sequence of activities accommodates eight different cognitive styles. As in the other CBI experiments at the FSI, the development of students' oral and reading proficiencies was reported to have accelerated during the CBI phase of training. They point out, however, that not all of their experiences with CBI were positive. General references for this chapter are located in the bibliography at the end of this volume.

Introduction

In this chapter we describe the "Advanced and Specialized Job-Related Modules" of the Indonesian curriculum at the Foreign Service Institute (FSI). The content-based portions of the Indonesian course are contained principally in these modules. Before examining this phase in detail, however, we offer a brief overview of the entire thirty-six-week course in order to put these modules into perspective.[1]

Phase One: Delayed Oral Response and Community Language Learning

Phase One, the introductory phase of the basic course in Indonesian, which lasts five days (approximately thirty hours), combines aspects of Community Language Learning (CLL) methodology and Delayed Oral Response (DOR). Although these two approaches are "opposites" in the sense that CLL is production-oriented and DOR is comprehension-oriented, they complement each other well in the day-long intensive language learning environment of the FSI.

CLL, developed in 1972 by Father Charles Curran, was introduced to the FSI by Earl Stevick in the late 1970s. In Community Language Learning, students take the initiative in communication, guided by a bilingual instructor who provides them individually with the appropriate foreign language phraseology. The Indonesian program at FSI has adapted the classic model of CLL to the needs and desires of its students. The Indonesian teachers begin by eliciting key phrases that students would like to use in conversation. These phrases are written on the blackboard in Indonesian. Students practice them, working on pronunciation and intonation. The students practice the model conversation in groups of three to six. The instructor explains grammar points, cultural implications, and lexical usage. The students and teacher jointly analyze individual phrases and expand on the original key phrases.

Although aware of published work on the importance of comprehension to the development of speaking proficiency (e.g., Winitz and Reeds 1973; Postovsky 1974; Winitz 1981; Gary and Gary 1981; Krashen and Terrell 1983), language program faculty at FSI were first inspired to experiment with DOR by the work of J. Marvin Brown, who demonstrated it at FSI in the early 1980s (see Brown and Palmer 1987). Under the leadership of Madeline Ehrman, the FSI Turkish program experimented with an adaptation of Brown's approach. After the success of this experiment in Turkish, other language programs, including Indonesian, began their own adaptations.[2]

In the Indonesian Section of the FSI, two native-speaking instructors implement DOR using pictures and realia. Speaking Indonesian, they discuss families, geographical features, and places of interest. Students are tasked with listening. Comprehension exercises require students to respond by nodding, shaking their heads, pointing, or picking up objects as the phrases are heard. In addition students listen to authentic or simulated newscasts. Working in small groups, they complete a variety of tasks, such as underlining words they recognize, listening for specific information, or expressing the general "gist" of the report. Other listening exercises include identifying colors, spatial relations, numbers, family members, and greetings. Many of the exercises are adapted from those developed by the FSI's Turkish program for the DOR phase in their forty-four-week training program.

The CLL and DOR components of Phase One of the Indonesian curriculum are carefully integrated. The topics of the CLL sessions parallel the listening activities. Students are encouraged to produce sentences in English that recreate the topics presented in the listening hours. For example, they would produce sentences describing the family. When possible, these are cast in dialogue form. The topics are not restricted to their own experience, but the content tends to be familiar and personal.

Other Phase One activities include reading for global comprehension (authentic newspaper passages and captions with heavy cognate content) and Total Physical Response (TPR) activities, involving moving around the room, touching objects, or pointing to different colors in response to teacher cues. Some of these activities are carried out in small groups, some in large groups.

There are several advantages to an approach combining CLL and DOR. In this phase students hear a great deal of Indonesian vocabulary modeled by native speakers. By making the listening activities a group effort in which all students are involved, but none singled out, initial classroom anxiety is reduced, especially among those with little language learning background. Furthermore, such activities encourage members of the group to become acquainted and to support one another in a mutual effort. The CLL activity, which allows students to try to form their own sentences in the target language in a nonthreatening environment, addresses the students' eagerness to produce the language they are hearing—an eagerness which is common among most adult language learners.

Phase Two: Notional Functional and Grammar-Based Approaches

Phase Two lasts approximately sixteen weeks (480 hours). The materials used in the beginning of Phase Two are based on the FSI's Familiarization and Short Term (FAST) course textbook which was introduced in 1982. The FAST text consists of lessons aimed at creating limited fluency in common social situations. Later in this phase, students move to *Sentence Patterns of Indonesian* (Dardjowidjojo 1984), a commercial textbook for beginning Indonesian students, containing grammar, drills, cultural notes, dialogues, and readings.

A selection of authentic reading materials is introduced at the same time as Dardjowidjojo's text. These readings, derived from Indonesian newspapers and magazines, are divided into five content categories: General Current Interest, Culture and Society, Business and Economics, Political and Military Affairs, and Science/Agriculture and Technology. Articles are chosen on the basis of several criteria. They must contain simple grammatical structures, many cognates, straightforward information, and must relate clearly to the world knowledge which students already possess.

Initially, Phase Two was characterized by heavy use of CLL techniques in order to elicit student-generated language. Because the rotating teaching staff used somewhat different techniques from hour to hour, students complained that the classes lacked focus and continuity. They also expressed a desire for firm guidance from a textbook or textbooks that offered linear progression as well as the fundamentals of grammar. In order to accommodate these expressed student needs, Phase Two was rewritten to include a strong element of grammar-based materials.

The Phase Two text introduces much cultural material and information about daily life in Indonesia via dialogues, drills, simulations, and cultural notes. The content is derived from publications such as *Indonesia Handbook* (Dalton 1991) and *Introducing Indonesia* (American Women's Association in Jakarta 1982) and from interviews with students who have returned from assignments in Indonesia and have expressed a need for more skills in dealing with the realities of transportation, marketing, and domestic help.

Students reach the Speaking-2/Reading-2 levels ("Limited Working Proficiency") by the end of this phase. At this level of proficiency they engage in social conversation with some facility and grasp the main ideas of newspaper articles in a variety of topics. In addition to discussing in general terms the topics presented in area studies lectures on religion, culture, geography, and history, the students are required to do some in-depth reading. After reading they deliver detailed oral reports and translate selected paragraphs. They engage in elaborate simulations, called "bridges," requiring them to cope with practical, job-oriented communication tasks such as typical challenges for a duty officer at the American embassy in Jakarta or the American consulate in Surabaya, East Java. These situations involve functions such as responding to requests and conducting interviews. At twelve weeks students obtain facts and information over the telephone in a mock crisis situation.

Other Phase Two activities include the use of audio and video listening comprehension materials. Some are produced in-house, and some are more "authentic" such as newscasts from Indonesia. Both contrived and authentic reading materials are used in class. Reading exercises emphasize scanning and skimming skills rather than verbatim translation.

Exposure to the culture is enhanced by attending local cultural events and taking fields trips to the Indonesian embassy, Voice of America studios, and private homes. In-class cultural activities introduce students to Indonesian dance, food, parties, and gamelan music by the Javanese and Balinese musical ensemble.

Phase Three: Emphasis on Grammar

Phase Three, lasting about two weeks (sixty hours), is a comprehensive review of Indonesian grammar. The rationale for this phase is practical. Normally, Phase Three begins after a holiday break in December. At this time students often feel they have regressed and forgotten their Indonesian. During the review sessions, individual problems are addressed. In-house materials are sufficient to allow individualized instruction. Small groups concentrate on specific grammar points. Students are encouraged to develop their own skills in self-diagnosis. The teachers' role becomes that of a coach.

During this phase a third simulation promotes the organization of job-related knowledge in the presentation of a "briefing"—an activity that is an integral part of the job of a Foreign Service Officer. In this "briefing" students write, edit, and deliver short oral reports on topics selected by students in accordance with their future work requirements.

Phase Four: A Content-Based Approach

Phase Four, the most CBI-oriented section of the Indonesian course, integrates area studies with language study to address the need of students for a fairly sophisticated understanding of the culture, customs, traditions, and values of the country to which they are being assigned. This phase consists of several units that are variously termed "content-based modules" or "area studies content modules" or "job-related core modules." The topics of the modules are not narrowly job-related. They are oriented toward broad cultural and area studies topics.

The objective of this phase is to develop one-way and two-way oral skills. One-way skills include presentation of reports on what students have seen, read, or "overheard." Two-way skills include discussions and interviews of native speakers. Listening comprehension activities include practice with Indonesians speaking at a natural tempo, with a variety of regional accents, and in a variety of registers. The topics involve realistic, professionally relevant situations. The seven modules that were developed by 1990 included:

Religion: "Islam in Indonesia"
Politics 1:   "The Soekarno Era, or the Old Order"
Politics 2:   "The Soeharto Era, or the New Order"
Military: "The Dynamics of the Indonesian Armed Forces"
Economics: "Economic Developments in Indonesia"
Culture: "The Hindu Influence in Indonesia through the Wayang Culture"
Politics 3:   "General Elections in Indonesia"

Some general sources of information on the above topics are identified in the list of reading material at the end of this chapter.

The modules begin after the students complete Phase Three or by the time they reach the Speaking/Reading-2 or Speaking/Reading-2+ proficiency levels. Use of cultural content in the language curriculum provides a vehicle for developing advanced, professional language skills. Through these modules our students learn more advanced, job-related, formal language and also become more familiar with subtle uses of the language, including innuendoes, hints, allusions, nonverbal language, and idiomatic expressions.

Another important outcome is that students become more familiar with regional accents. Indonesia is a very multilingual environment, and local languages clearly influence the way people communicate in the national language, Bahasa Indonesia.

Throughout the CBI modules students complete extensive, in-depth readings on their own, both in English (as background reading) and in Bahasa Indonesia. Most of the readings in Indonesian require reading skills beyond the Reading-2/2+ level. Therefore, students use the reading skills— skimming, scanning, "gisting," and in-depth, intensive reading—that they develop earlier in the basic course.

The 4-Mat System

The CBI modules adopt, in principle, the structure of the "4-MAT system" developed by Bernice McCarthy (1987), which is based on the notion that students have preferred learning styles. McCarthy chose to use the four categories of learner types proposed by David Kolb (1979). These types are those who perceive through:

1. Concrete experience and process through reflective observation;
2. Abstract conceptualization and process through reflective observation;
3. Abstract conceptualization and process through active experimentation; and,
4. Concrete experience and process through active experimentation.

In the 4-MAT system, the learning process is described as a sequence of steps which reflect these four different styles. Thus, McCarthy believes that all learners should start with Type One and follow through to Type Four. McCarthy also found that left-hemisphere-dominant students and right-hemisphere-dominant students displayed different learning characteristics and needs. Therefore, she separated left and right hemisphere dominant processors in each of the four categories, yielding eight subtypes. Based on these eight types, McCarthy further divides activities into four basic steps to reflect tasks that correspond to right- or left-brain dominance. For example, left-brain-dominant students might be asked to analyze a reading assignment. Right-brain-dominant students might be asked to discuss a hypothetical situation.

Since the learning process in this model follows a sequence that reflects the way in which individual students learn, all types of learners are able to develop their own natural abilities when they are working in accordance with their own learning preference. At the same time, McCarthy claims, they can develop their ability to work successfully in other, nonpreferred learning styles.

The 4-MAT system proved to be suitable for Phase Four of the Indonesian basic course curriculum. The process presented a natural and progressive sequence of activities from the more passive to the more active and exposed students to a variety of learning styles. At this relatively advanced stage of formal learning, students benefited from learning through different approaches; they were able to handle many kinds of experiences and break away from the spoon-feeding of pattern drills, direct teacher assistance, and graded readings. In Phase Four, students had the chance to study independently part of the time, and the role of the teacher changed, depending on the activity and where it fitted into the 4-MAT model. For example, in Step One, the teacher served as a "motivator," in Step Two as an "information giver" in Step Three as a "coach" or "facilitator" and in Step Four as an "evaluator" or "remediator."

The four steps outlined above provided a useful and workable framework for sequencing activities in the language training modules for Indonesian.

That sequence is:

Step 1: Introduction of the topic through film or video, followed by discussion and reflection on the learners' own experiences. In this step the role of the teacher is that of **motivator and stimulator** of discussion.

Step 2: Introduction of basic concepts and practices associated with the topic followed by listening to a discussion by native speakers who are active participants in the activities associated with the topic. Students are then questioned about the content of what they have heard and seen. In this step the role of the teacher is the traditional one of **imparter of information**.

Step 3: Intensive practice in the language forms and vocabulary associated with the topic, followed by student-directed reading and research on a particular aspect of the topic. This may include interviews of native speakers. In this step the role of the teacher is that of **coach.**

Step 4: Student fieldwork (e.g., interviews) and design of a format of presentation of their findings. Finally, students present the results of their work and answer questions about it. In this step the role of teacher is that of **evaluator and remediator.**

For example, the "Islam in Indonesia" module demonstrates how the 4-MAT model was used in Phase Four of Indonesian. Islam was selected as an initial topic because of its relevance to the professional needs of the students. In a country where Muslims make up more than 90 percent of the population, Foreign Service Officers must have a thorough understanding of the beliefs and practices of Islam in order to function effectively in the community. Religious beliefs and precepts are central to relationships among Indonesians and must be taken into account by outsiders if they are to correctly interpret the way Indonesians act. (Specific sources of information about this subject are included in the references at the end of this chapter.)

A Model Module: "Introduction to Islam in Indonesia"
In the introduction to the module, the teacher explains the 4-MAT process to the students, as well as the activities to be undertaken. The

purpose of the orientation is to provide the students with an overall understanding of what will take place during the 4 to 5 days that they will be studying religion in Indonesia.

Before students begin the module in the classroom, they are given reading assignments about Islam in Indonesia. These readings come from English-language sources, such as Johns (1984) and the American Women's Association in Jakarta (1982). Relevant articles were also selected from the *Far Eastern Economic Review* or *Asia Week*. The readings are completed at home and were discussed in Step 1-A, the first hour of the class meeting:

Step 1-A

Discussion: The class is divided into small groups. Each group reports and discusses in Indonesian the English-language reading assignments, which have been completed at home. In this way the information is shared among class members as the students practice expressing the content in Indonesian.

Film: The class is regrouped. Students view the film, *Moslem Students in Aceh* (North Sumatra), which they discuss afterwards in Indonesian.

Field Trip: The class takes a field trip to the Islamic Center in Washington, D. C., where they are given a tour of the mosque. Afterwards, the leader of the Islamic Center answers student questions. The tour and the discussion are in English, because staff members there are from the Middle East. Later, in class, students review their experience—in Indonesian.

Step 1-B

Personal Experience: Students ask questions of teachers about Islamic practices which the teachers have experienced in their hometowns in Indonesia. Students then work in small groups, reflecting on their own experiences and what they learned from the film, field trip, and the teachers' accounts, drawing conclusions and making generalizations, as appropriate.

Group Presentations: Students prepare for group presentations on the contrasts and similarities of religious life in the United States and Indonesia (or other countries where they have lived). Each group gives a five-minute oral presentation. Questions and answers follow each presentation.

Step 2-A

Exhibit: For this activity the class is combined. Students browse through a small exhibit of Islamic items of everyday life in Indonesia, such as pictures of mosques, wall-hangings, jewelry and other objects that the teachers bring in. They also listen to the *azan* (call for prayers) and short verses from the Koran on audiotape.

Interview: Students interview an invited guest on her or his pilgrimage to Mecca.

Step 2-B

In-class Reading: For this activity the class is divided into small groups. Each group reads an article entitled "Agama di Indonesia" from *Vocabulary Building in Indonesian* by Dardjowidjojo. Students then answer oral questions on the reading passage. New vocabulary contained in the reading is introduced through discussion of new words, phrases, and idioms, followed by drills and practice.

Step 3-A

Drills: For this activity the class is again divided into small groups. Students continue to practice using the new phrases, structures, and idiomatic expressions they learn from their reading assignment. They quiz each other on the new vocabulary or play games using the new words or phrases. If necessary, grammar or structure drills are conducted by the teacher.

Step 3-B

Article: Teachers provide other Indonesian reading materials on Islam in Indonesia. Students select and read one of the articles, then prepare a five- to ten-minute oral report on the reading.

Report: For the reports, the class is recombined. Each student reports to the class. Questions and answers follow each report.

Step 4-A

Video: For this activity the class is combined. Students watch a videotaped panel discussion on Islam in Indonesia prepared by visiting scholars from Indonesia. The video is then discussed.

Interview Preparation: Students brainstorm more questions on Islam in Indonesia. They prepare to interview Indonesians outside of class. The preparation includes practicing the format of the interview, the appropriate introductions, and opening and closing remarks.

Step 4-B

Interviews: Students conduct interviews, prepared in class, with Indonesians in the Washington community. The interviewees include officials from the Indonesian embassy or the Voice of America, Indonesian exchange students, and others. Upon completion of the interviews, students make a final presentation to the class. A question and answer period follows.

Wrap-Up: The module ends with a group wrap-up discussion on the activities that have been completed by the students.

Evaluation of the CBI Modules

Although complex modules such as the introduction to Islam in Indonesia generally worked well in the curriculum, not all of our experiences with the content-based modules were positive. Some of the problems were student-centered; others were logistical.

Some students felt overwhelmed by the amount of vocabulary introduced in the modules. This seemed to some degree to be a function of proficiency. Students who were clearly at the 2 or 2+ level managed best to absorb the massive amounts of new vocabulary associated with a module. Students who had not progressed so far in general skill level were sometimes unable to participate fully in the exercises. These observations echo those of several other contributors to this volume—Klee and Tedick (Chapter 7), Stryker (Chapter 8), and Klahn in the previous chapter, for example.

Students who did not display a fair amount of initiative in locating reading materials and assimilating them were often not able to perform well in interviewing and discussing. In fact, since the CBI modules placed much responsibility on the student, complaints were sometimes heard that the course lacked structure and direction. Those who relied on the aid of a textbook were rarely comfortable with the modules. It might have helped in such cases to have been explicit with students about the variety of learning styles and to have urged them to try out nonpreferential ways of learning and acquiring new information. It may also be necessary for the teachers to intervene with some students and assign specific reading passages.

The Phase Four CBI modules presented special problems to the instructional staff. First, they required more resources than ordinary classroom teaching. The development of the Indonesian CBI modules consumed a great deal of time and required extensive content research, especially since there were very few relevant materials available. Completion of the original four modules required more than 250 hours. In addition, materials for certain topics, such as politics, had to be revised continually. The materials, therefore, required a substantial commitment of instructor time even after they had been used for several years.

The investment of preparation time did pay off, however. After the initial efforts, instructors kept up a package of materials. Also, since the responsibility for discussion fell more heavily on students, instructors found less pressure on themselves to prepare classroom lectures or exercises.

Instructors had to plan each module carefully. Even if it had been taught many times before, it was necessary to recruit outsiders and coordinate their involvement as interview partners or lecturers. This was especially difficult when time-sensitive and controversial issues were on the agenda.

One way that such coordination time might be reduced is to make frequent use of videotaping. Whenever a guest consents to visit the class, the session could be taped for use in future modules. Furthermore, when guest lecturers are scarce, the instructors might make use of native-speaking friends or family to organize and tape role plays.

Library resources adequate to the task of a comprehensive CBI curriculum are likely to be too limited. Much of the basic reading materials have to be selected by the instructors from Indonesian newspapers and magazines. Information involving current events or economic data has to be updated regularly. The Indonesian embassy can been helpful in locating or providing needed materials. Instructors must continually update their collection of newspaper and magazine articles, videotapes and films.

Planning events and coordinating activities while following the sequence of steps required by the 4-MAT model was difficult and time-consuming. Each exercise was somewhat individualized, and this fact multiplied the effort and time needed on the part of staff to provide guidance, feedback, and materials to the students. Instructors had to adjust their roles accordingly by providing guidance and increasing the responsibility of the students themselves in preparing their presentations.

For some topics, such as economics, obtaining realia and videos that were relevant and informative was difficult. This was partly due to the fact that the economic situation in Indonesia was constantly changing. In addition, few videos have been made on this topic. To overcome this difficulty, in some instances the FSI Indonesian Section made in-house videos, using the services of visiting scholars, Indonesian embassy officials, and other authorities.

Students reported that they felt more comfortable using Indonesian in work-related and realistic cultural situations as a result of the activities they undertook in the CBI modules. The "culture shock" experienced by their predecessors was reduced for the students who studied in the CBI modules.

Results from the FSI proficiency tests indicated that students who had taken the CBI training scored higher than their predecessors in the final oral proficiency interviews. In particular, significant improvement was found in the areas of breadth of vocabulary and general discourse competence. The listening comprehension ability of most students also improved. Most of the students who experienced the CBI curriculum reached the Speaking-3 and Reading-3, levels or even higher, by the time they reached the last of the CBI modules.

In conclusion, the Indonesian instructors felt that, in spite of the difficulties inherent in developing the CBI modules, the approach was successful in forcing the students to use the language to deal with the kinds of issues and events that they will face on the job. The Indonesian modules represented a step toward fashioning an environment in which issues and events were dealt with in a similar milieu to that which the students will experience after training.

Endnotes

1. We would like to express appreciation for suggestions by Madeline Ehr-man and Frederick Jackson of the Foreign Service Institute, who helped us to clarify sections of this chapter. We also want to express our thanks and appreciation to the colleagues in the FSI Indonesian program who

have worked with us to implement this and other programs, with special gratitude to Andeny Rampen and Senior Instructor Andang Poeraatmadja.

2. Important research was conducted on students of Russian by Valerian Postovsky at the Defense Language Institute (Postovsky 1974). He claimed that students who had been exposed to massive listening input, with minimal requirement for speaking during the first six weeks of language instruction outperformed the control group that began speaking the first day of class.

Jijis Chadran is Language Training Supervisor for Bengali, Burmese, Indonesian, Malay and Tagalog at the Foreign Service Institute. Address: NFATC, SA-42, 4000 Arlington Blvd., Arlington, VA 22204 (Email: jijis.chadran@dos.us-state.gov)

Gary Esarey is the Director of the Language Learning Center at Whitman College, Washington, and was Language Training Supervisor for Indonesian at the Foreign Service Institute from 1988 to 1990. Address: Whitman College, Division II, Olin Hall, Walla Walla, WA 99362 (Email: esarey@whitman.edu)

Materials and Sources for Indonesian Modules

Books:

American Women's Association in Jakarta. 1982. "Religion in Indonesian Life." In *Introducing Indonesia* . 18-20. Jakarta. American Women's Association in Jakarta.

Dardjowidjojo, Soenjono. 1984. "Agama di Indonesia." *Vocabulary Building in Indonesian: An Advanced Reader.* 205-226. (Monographs in International Studies, Southeast Asia Series, No. 64). Athens, Ohio: Ohio University Center for International Studies.

Johns, Anthony H. 1984. "Islam and Cultural Pluralism." In *Islam in Asia*, vol. 2, eds. Raphael Israeli & Anthony H. Johns. 202-228. Boulder, Colorado: Westview Press.

Noer, Deliar. 1978. *Administration of Islam in Indonesia*. (Cornell Modern Indonesia Project). Ithaca, New York: Cornell University.

Periodicals:

Popular news magazines provide occasional articles on religion in Indonesia. Relevant articles may sometimes be found in *Far Eastern Economic Review* or *Asia Week*. Two useful sources for information in Indonesian are the Indonesian news magazines *Gatra* and *Tiras* and the Indonesian listserve *apakabar@clark.net*. Magazine articles include:

"Tak Ada Islah untuk Abu Hasan." 1996. *Gatra*. 27 (January):48-52.

Yarmanto, Widi and Sapto Waluyo. 1995. "Metode Zikir Itu Go Internasional." *Gatra*. 9 (September):100-101.

Newspapers:

Two informative sources are *Kompas*, and *Suara Pembaruan*.

Brochures:

See publications of The Islamic Center, 2551 Massachusetts Avenue NW, Washington DC, 20008.

Additional Sources on Indonesian Culture and Society:

Dalton, Bill. 1991. *Indonesia handbook*. Fifth edition. Chico, CA: Moon Publications.

Draine, C. 1986. *Culture shock: Indonesia*. Singapore: Times Books International.

Evans-Smith, William. 1983. *Indonesia: A country study*. Fourth ed. (Foreign Area Studies Series). Washington, DC: The American University.

Jenkins, David. 1984. *Soeharto and his generals: Indonesian military politics 1975-1983*. (Cornell Modern Indonesia Project). Ithaca: Cornell University.

McDonald, Hamish. 1981. *Soeharto's Indonesia*. Honolulu: The University Press of Hawaii.

Sarumpaet, J.P. and H. Hendrata. 1986. *A modern reader in Bahasa Indonesia*, Book 1. Sixth ed. Singapore: Tien Wah Press Pte., Ltd.

Sarumpaet, J.P. and H. Hendrata. 1987. *A modern reader in Bahasa Indonesia*, Book 2. Fifth ed. Singapore: Tien Wah Press Pte., Ltd.

Wilhelm, Donald. 1985. *Emerging Indonesia*. Second edition. London: Cassell Ltd.

Part Five

Foreign Languages Across the Curriculum (FLAC) Programs

11

Language-Based Content Instruction

H. Stephen Straight

Editors' Note: The CBI models in the previous chapters have all focused primarily on development and growth in foreign language proficiency. The focus has been on content-based language instruction. H. Steven Straight turns this concept around and labels his variation "language-based content instruction." The foreign languages across the curriculum (FLAC) approach focuses on the use of language as a tool for study in nonlanguage disciplines. In this model, implemented at SUNY-Binghamton, students who possess a minimum Intermediate level reading ability in a foreign language use that skill to do a portion of their reading and research in their regular academic classes. More than thirteen hundred students have participated in Binghamton's "languages across the curriculum" (LxC) programs since 1991. The LxC option is available in a dozen languages in more than fifty courses that participate in this university-wide program. The FLAC program has been established as part of the university's mission of becoming a "fully internationalized institution." Straight describes all aspects of the LxC programs, including the philosophical underpinnings and rationale, the curricular design and implementation, the recruiting of students, the use of graduate students as "language resource specialists." He evaluates the pros and cons of the Binghamton model and offers assistance to other educators who might want to adopt the LxC model. Appendix B ((Practical Advice for Language Resource Specialists) provides excellent guidance for any CBI instructor. General references for this chapter are located in the bibliography at the end of this volume.

Introduction

The idea behind SUNY-Binghamton's languages across the curriculum (LxC) program emerged as a result of a chance conversation early in 1990 between the director of the linguistics program—who was searching for ways to enable students other than his own majors (whose needs he was already meeting) to make meaningful use of their skills in languages other than English in their various fields of academic interest—and the director of the Office of International Student and Scholar Services—who remains vigilant for opportunities to maximize the impact of international students in the educational activities of the campus. Since fall 1991 LxC has employed international graduate students as language resource specialists (LRSs) to prepare substitute assignments utilizing non-English materials in dozens of courses in all of the academic divisions of Binghamton's Harpur College of Arts and Sciences and in both undergraduate and graduate courses in Binghamton's School of Management. LxC "substitute assignments" replace 10 to 20 percent of the assignments that students might otherwise perform, and LxC-acquired information and insights inform term papers, oral reports, class discussion, essay exams, and other grade-determining English-medium course requirements.

Binghamton's highly selective undergraduate admissions profile guarantees, in a state that requires three years of foreign language study for its high school graduates, that a sufficient proportion of Binghamton's students possess both the intellectual disposition and the intermediate-level reading skills necessary to participate in optional LRS-led study groups focusing on LxC assignments.

The LxC model of languages across the curriculum not only makes room for students with widely varying levels of language skill—as long as they all possess at least intermediate-level skill in reading—it also makes use of languages other than English independent of the multilingual capacities of individual course instructors and of the availability of language faculty in the languages included in the program. By using the students' primary language (usually English) as the medium of discussion in the weekly LRS-led study-group meetings for each course/language pair, and by supplementing the non-English materials with background materials, glossaries, and other ancillary aids in English, students of only intermediate-level reading ability find that they can successfully perform LxC assignments. And by employing as LRSs international graduate students with superior skills in the LxC-supported languages and requisite levels of disciplinary knowledge for each LxC-supported course, the program has supported as many as eight different languages in a single course, whether or not the course instructor had any skills whatever in the supported language, and whether or not the university offered any instruction in the language or had any faculty who knew the language.

More than thirteen hundred students have participated in LxC options at Binghamton since they were first introduced in fall 1991, in Chinese, French, German (Modern), Greek (Modern), Hebrew, Italian, Japanese,

Korean, Russian, and—predominantly, because of its ascendancy at the high-school level—Spanish. LxC study groups, in which the LRSs discuss their respective substitute assignments—usually in English—with participating students, have been supported in courses in accounting, anthropology, art history, biology, comparative literature, English, environmental studies, history, international business, Judaic studies, Latin American and Caribbean area studies, linguistics, marketing, philosophy, political science, psychology, sociology, theater, and women's studies. Appendix A contains a complete list of LxC-supported courses and the number of LxC participants in each.

The following account of the rationale, design, implementation, and evaluation of Binghamton's LxC program provides an overview of the program as a whole, with no more than a cursory examination of the broader conditions and pedagogical considerations that have motivated and shaped the program (though most of these underlie all of the programs described in this book); this account also contains only brief examples and thumbnail characterizations of LxC course syllabi, learning materials, assignments, and learning outcomes. Readers interested in more details on these and other matters may wish to consult fuller published treatments.[1]

Program Rationale

Unless they major in language or area studies, college and university students in the United States typically lack curricular opportunities to employ their existing competencies in languages other than English within their areas of academic interest, despite wide recognition of the increasing multilingual language needs of college graduates. The primary premise of the LxC program is that in order to increase the effective use of language skills by students, we must maximize the employment of non-English materials in courses across the spectrum of students' highly varied subject-matter interests (Straight 1990). Furthermore, the increasing prominence of "content-based language instruction" in language programs (Brinton, Snow, and Wesche 1989; Crandall and Tucker 1990; Krueger and Ryan 1993), along with evidence that a focus on meaning results in improved language acquisition (Swaffar, Arens, and Byrnes 1991; Ryan 1994), mesh well with efforts to infuse materials in languages students know as widely as possible into their academic work.

On the other hand, Binghamton's LxC program does not fit easily into the category of "content-based language instruction (CBLI)" or "discipline-based approaches to language study" (Wesche in Krueger and Ryan 1993). Not an approach to language study, nor a method of language instruction, LxC might better be termed "language-based content instruction (LBCI)"—

that is, the use of materials in various languages to further the ends of content instruction in various nonlanguage disciplines. The label inversion requires some clarification: while CBLI focuses on content as a way of pursuing language study, LBCI does not focus on language as a way of pursuing content study. Rather, both approaches adopt a focus on content.

LBCI, however, uses the learners' existing language skills as a way of furthering the intercultural breadth and depth of their study of whatever subject matter they may choose, while CBLI uses the learners' existing knowledge of and interest in specific areas of content as a way of furthering the specificity and effectiveness of their study of a language. The means employed by these two approaches are often identical, although CBLI typically evaluates its success primarily, though not exclusively, in terms of learners' improvements in receptive and expressive language performance in the target content domain, while LBCI evaluates its success primarily, though not exclusively, in terms of learners' ability to bring the content of what they have studied in their nonprimary language to bear on what they have studied in their primary language, whether or not they exhibit any measurable gain in their receptive or expressive ability in the nonprimary language.

In keeping with their labels, then, CBLI—as I am defining it in this context—is, in the end, a method of language instruction while LBCI—as I have somewhat playfully dubbed it—is, in the end, a method of content instruction, even if their respective pedagogical techniques often overlap. They both focus on the meaning rather than the structure of the target text; they both eschew drills, error correction, grammatical exposition, and vocabulary memorization; they both encourage students to use their background knowledge and growing familiarity with the subject matter as touchstones for the interpretation of new material and for the formulation of questions and conclusions.

The contrast between CBLI and LBCI emerges most clearly in CBLI's typical requirement that students participating in a given CBLI activity all possess comparable levels of language skill and that discussion and sometimes also written work take place in the target language. Students with low receptive or expressive fluency will hamper discussion, while students with clearly superior fluency will not only intimidate their lesser skilled peers and either monopolize discussion or find it tediously halting, but they will also have little to gain from the language-instruction aspects of the experience.

LBCI, on the other hand, welcomes participants of widely varying levels of skill, provided they all possess at least intermediate-level reading ability. Discussion takes place in the target language only to the extent that individual participants possess the necessary fluency to do so; otherwise, the discussion, and with rare exceptions all written work, employs the participants' primary language to the extent necessary to achieve a full understanding of the target language material relative to the subject-matter area. Students with low fluency or even low literacy in the target language participate effectively in the discussion as a function of their subject-matter knowledge and their capacity for critical thinking.

In the long term, LxC seeks to foster a campus-wide expectation that both faculty and students will make meaningful use of the foreign languages they know in every aspect of their study, research, and creative work at every level everywhere in the university curriculum. This overarching purpose of Binghamton's LxC program thus derives from the university's institutional mission to become a fully internationalized institution in which the "instructional, research, and outreach programs must incorporate extensively the knowledge and perspectives of other countries" (A Plan for the Future: *State University of New York at Binghamton* 1996, 1).

LxC serves all of this goal either directly or indirectly. Specifically, by employing international graduate students to provide support for student and faculty use of materials in languages other than English in a large number of different courses throughout Binghamton's academic programs, LxC broadens and deepens the international scope and global perspectives represented in the teaching and research activities of the university, helps prepare students for international education experiences, fosters enhancement of student abilities to make meaningful use of languages other than English, and involves international students immediately in the enrichment of the university's primary educational activities.

Making Room for LxC in a Course

The semester-by-semester cycle of operations for the LxC program begins with the recruitment of faculty who are interested in enriching and enlivening the content of an upcoming course through the optional use of course-specific materials in languages other than English by students in that course. To make room for LxC, faculty must design (or, in most cases, redesign) the course syllabus with a "thread" of assignments that will not be required of LxC participants in the course, along with guidelines for the preparation of the substitute LxC-prepared threads to be performed by LxC participants. Even faculty who have no facility in any language likely to be supported by the LxC program have proven more than willing to include LxC in their courses, as long as the LxC staff accepts the responsibility of offering LxC study groups only in languages for which they can find disciplinarily qualified LRSs. To date, the program has never failed to find such LRSs for all language/discipline pairs in which student demand warranted a study group. (See comments about study-group size in the Recruiting Student Participants section below.)

Because LxC study groups meet for an hour a week from the fifth to the fifteenth (or last) week of the semester, LxC participation adds about eleven hours to the forty-five to sixty hours of classroom time that students normally commit to each of Binghamton's four-credit courses. LxC participation thus constitutes approximately 15 percent of a participating student's in-class time commitment to a course. Consequently, the LxC staff asks that course instructors make the LxC-replaceable "thread" of course assignments amount to 10 to 20 percent of the total assignments in the course.

Recruiting Student Participants

Participating students, who need have only intermediate reading proficiency in the LxC-supported language in order to perform LxC assignments unassisted, indicate their interest in LxC participation during classroom visits by LxC staff to LxC-adapted courses in the first two weeks of the semester. First, the course instructor describes the content goals of the envisioned LxC substitute assignments and explains exactly what assignments they replace and how LxC participation will figure in the evaluation of student performance in the course. Then the visiting LxC staff member provides an overview of the purpose and structure of the program, putting special emphasis on the points that LxC is a program for course-specific language *use* rather than language *instruction* and that LxC assignments replace rather than increase the total assignment load. Moreover, because LxC assignments substitute for the English-based assignments they would otherwise perform, and because the LRSs—and other study-group members—provide assistance to participants who have difficulty performing LxC assignments on their own, LxC-participating students should not, except for the weekly study-group meeting, experience a greater workload than that of nonparticipating students in the same course.

Finally, the LxC staff member invites students to indicate what languages they would like to have supported in the course. Study-group scheduling forms are distributed to groups of six or more students interested in a specific language, with instructions to complete and submit the forms no later than the end of the second week. Although the LxC staff will immediately begin to seek a qualified LRS for each such language, no appointment will be made, no assignments prepared, and no study-group time established, until at least six forms have been received from interested students in a given course. (For the sake of experiment, we allowed the minimum allowable study-group size to drop as low as three during the FIPSE-funded program-development period. However, with the greater cost-consciousness that has come with institutionalization of the program, the minimum has risen to six, with a concomitant reduction in the number of supported languages and the total number of study groups and increases in the average study-group size and in the cost-effectiveness of the program.)

Recruiting and Appointing Language Resource Specialists

The first four weeks of the semester are the busiest for the LxC staff. Even before the LxC recruiting visits to targeted courses have been completed, international graduate students are encouraged to indicate their interest in serving as LRSs. They fill in a brief application form on which they indicate which of the semester's LxC-targeted courses they feel competent to work in, and how they acquired that competence (undergraduate or graduate courses, nonacademic training, or work experience). They also complete a Linguistic Facility Questionnaire on which they indicate the contexts and durations of their use of languages other than English. Finally, they participate in a one-on-one interview with one of the LxC program directors in which their aural/oral ability in English is informally assessed: it must be fluent in order for them to lead the weekly study-group discussions.

As soon as specific course/language pairs have been tentatively identified (by a show of hands during a class visit), the LxC staff surveys the field of qualified applicants in search of potential LRSs. If need be, the program director consults with the Director of International Student and Scholar Services and the Director of the Translation Research and Instruction Program for help in locating additional possible LRS candidates and inviting them to apply. As likely study-group prospects emerge, the directors ask individual candidates to consult with the course instructor to obtain a course syllabus and an overview of the instructor's expectations, and—if that interview is favorable to both parties—to come to the LxC office for copies of the student scheduling forms in order to identify a maximally convenient study-group meeting time or times. (As long as groups have at least six and no more than twelve members, LRSs are free to establish multiple meeting times in order to accommodate the schedules of as many participants as possible.)

Once the appropriateness and feasibility of a particular study-group assignment has been assured (through consultation with the course instructor and by the establishment of a meeting time), the LRS is formally appointed as an hourly employee of the program and given detailed instructions and assistance in the preparation of the initial course assignments. The number of paid hours required to fulfill the duties of LRS for a single course for a given semester has ranged from as few as thirty-six to as many as 120, with a median of about seventy.

Training LRSs to Prepare and Administer LxC Assignments

Appendix B contains the "Practical Advice" handout with which the program begins the training of new LRSs—and by means of which it reminds veteran LRSs of the key elements of the LRS role. This handout summarizes key points in the selection of materials, construction of study tasks, and discussion of assignments in the weekly LxC study-group meetings with participants.

The selection of course-appropriate materials and the preparation of course-specific assignments based upon those materials occupy the single largest portion of an LRS's program duties. The program remains vigilant regarding the maintenance and expansion of the University library's periodical and other literature relevant to LxC courses, but LRSs must often turn to interlibrary loan, their own and others' personal libraries, and even the holdings of friends and family abroad in order to find appropriate material for LxC assignments. The LxC program budget reimburses long-distance calls, mailing expenses, and fax charges incurred to obtain appropriate materials.

In keeping with its overarching goal to internationalize curricular content, the LxC program instructs its language resource specialists to utilize materials that express the point of view of members of cultures for which the LxC language is primary. Although this criterion rules out the use of materials translated from English, LxC materials typically parallel non-LxC materials in a course. LxC study groups in an environmental studies course in which magazine articles serve as foci for student commentary on the relative accuracy and technical depth of the treatment of environmental issues in the popular press, employ comparable materials in magazines published in Argentina, Belgium, Germany, or Korea. A course on immigration and ethnicity in U.S. history, in which personal correspondence and diaries serve as primary sources, makes ready use of such materials in the myriad of languages known by the culturally diverse immigrants to the United States Study groups in a course on the history of human services cull statistics from official government reports to compare health policies and the patterns of health care delivery in various places in the world.

In some cases LxC assignments contain material with no direct parallel in the non-LxC portion of the course. Even here, however, cross-cultural contrasts typically come to the fore. Study groups in an international business course do side-by-side comparisons of U.S. and non-U.S. materials such as advertisements, want ads, articles from newspaper business sections, and corporate reports. Study groups in a developmental psychology course discuss the assumptions about early childhood development that can be inferred from materials distributed to young parents, teachers, and the children themselves. Study groups in a course on the history of American musical theater explore the reactions of non-U.S. drama critics to American musicals exported to other parts of the world.

In addition to one-on-one consultation with LxC staff—including veteran LRSs—LRSs enroll in (and are paid to attend) a zero-credit seminar led by one of the program directors to obtain background knowledge about the program, receive guidance in the performance of their duties, and share ideas about how to maximize the effectiveness of their LRS activities. Special emphasis is given to prereading tasks that can help participants employ their background knowledge to understand assignments, strategies that participants can be taught to use in order to make sense of what they read, and techniques for effective discussion leadership.

Scheduling and Monitoring Study-Group Meetings

By the third week of the semester, the LxC office begins entering study-group meeting times and places into the university's computerized registration system as zero-credit "LxC" class sections (e.g., "LxC 264F: French Study Group in HIST 264"), thus ensuring both that the program can formally track its use of university facilities and support and that the students will receive official transcript notations for their participation in the program. The groups begin meeting in the fifth week of the semester and continue at the rate of one hour per week to the end of the fifteen-week semester.

Study-group discussion focuses predominantly on relating the content of LxC assignments to the broader content of the course to which they are attached. Although LRSs and student participants employ the language of the assignment frequently in the course of the discussion, most questions and answers take place in English unless all participants can communicate fluently in the language of the assignment—a rarity except in languages like Korean in which most participants have high oral fluency (in some cases, effective discussion requires that the assignment be taped by the LRS or read aloud so that participants with limited reading skills can understand it). LRSs receive frequent and detailed reminders that LxC aims for language-based content instruction, not content-based language instruction. Discussions of areas of vocabulary or strategies for syntactic analysis can in some instances serve content-instruction ends, but sustained attention to these would undermine the integrity of LxC as a *language-use* as opposed to a *language-learning* program.

As a gauge of individual LRS effectiveness, and as a way of staying informed regarding the nature of the LxC experience from the participants' point of view, the LxC directors observe every LRS at least once each semester, and new LRSs more often than that. The LRS receives a formative evaluation after each visit, replete with statements on the pattern of "You do X very well but you might try techniques of type Y in order to succeed better at Z" and covering every aspect of performance from materials selection and assignment format to study-group time allocation and discussion leadership style.

Evaluating Student Performance

LxC participants exhibit the benefits of their study-group work in a variety of ways. Students in the theater and psychology courses write end-of-term reports on the cross-cultural perspectives they have gained. Students in the international business and human services courses give in-class presentations in which they share responsibility for informing the rest of the students in the course regarding cross-national differences in the business and human-services policies and practices. Students in the history course base their answers to one of the final take-home essay exam questions on the insights they have gained from the study of non-English immigrant sources. Students in the environmental studies course submit individual journals in which they comment on the scientific accuracy and complexity, and the cross-cultural differences in perspective, of the LxC-provided magazine articles on environmental topics.

Students receive no separate letter grade for LxC participation, though—as indicated in the previous paragraph—in most cases their LxC-based oral or written work contributes in a clear and direct way to their grade in the LxC-supported course. However, participants do receive a zero-credit official transcript notation, with a grade of "Pass," for regular and meaningful attendance at LxC study-group meetings. LRSs submit the attendance and participation records upon which these notations are based both to the LxC office and to the course instructor. Students who have participated in a prepared manner in fewer than three quarters of the study-group discussions do not receive the transcript notation; no record at all of their LxC enrollment appears in the academic record.

Discussion

The results of semester-by-semester evaluation of LxC's success, as gauged by feedback systematically collected from students, LRSs, and LxC faculty, show a very high level of perceived value of the program as a way of enriching the subject-matter knowledge acquired by students (Straight [in press]). Measures of reading comprehension administered before and after LxC participation demonstrate a small but discernible positive effect (Gaddis Rose, reported in Straight [in press]). Preliminary transcript analysis and anecdotal feedback—pending the conclusion of a mail survey of LxC participants and nonparticipants in the same courses to be completed in 1997—shows that LxC participants do better than average in courses in which they pursue LxC, that they would not otherwise have maintained or increased their language skills through college course work, and that LxC increases their interest in further language study, study abroad, and international careers.

To better integrate LxC into Binghamton's curriculum, the program—which received continuing budgetary support from the university when external funds expired in 1995—is engaged in the following efforts:

- Expanding the number and range of LxC courses, with special emphasis on the inclusion of high-enrollment, first-year courses in SUNY-Binghamton's newly instituted General Education program;
- Consolidating gains in the most active LxC departments by working with faculty to make LxC a regular component of selected core courses;
- Compiling a Language Resource Specialist Handbook for use in LRS training, especially in the LxC Seminar;
- Constructing a revised set of end-of-semester participant and LRS survey forms that will facilitate systematic comparison of the effects—both in content learning and language acquisition—of LxC with languages across the curriculum efforts at other colleges and universities;[2]
- Reversing losses in LxC enrollments in languages other than Spanish by working with other campuses to employ distance-learning technologies (telephone, fax, audioconferencing, videoconferencing, and the Worldwide Web) to share both student demand and LRS supply in a wide variety of languages in LxC-style virtual study groups;

- Raising the level of language use possible in an LxC study group by employing these same distance-learning technologies and study-group formats to place LxC participants with high-level language skills into multiinstitutional virtual groups.

Obviously, the LxC program at SUNY-Binghamton cannot serve as a universally applicable model for revitalization of the role of languages in postsecondary education. Not only does it need improvement—as outlined above—in order to function most effectively in its own context to achieve its specific goals, but also its unique structure (especially in its dependency on international graduate students) and its delimited purposes (especially as revealed by its almost exclusive deployment of reading skills in the target language) may not serve the needs or desires of other students, faculty, programs, or institutions. Nevertheless, LxC has demonstrated the feasibility and worth of the use of qualified international graduate students as resource specialists for content-focused employment of materials in languages other than English as the basis for substitute course-specific assignments and weekly small-group discussion conducted in English in existing courses throughout the university curriculum. We have developed effective mechanisms for the restructuring of course syllabi, the training and compensation of resource specialists, the recruitment and reward of student participants, and the funding and administration of the program. We hope that others will follow our lead by implementing variants of our LxC model of "Language-Based Content Instruction" appropriate to their particular institutional context and educational goals. We stand ready to assist in these efforts in any way we can.

Endnotes

1. Fall 1995 first-year students at Binghamton had combined (Verbal/Quantitative) SAT scores of 1,223 (recentered; national average: 902), a mean high school average of 92.1 percent, and very high standings in the high school graduating classes: 59 percent in the top tenth, 89 percent in the top fifth ("Binghamton University Facts and Figures." http://www.binghamton.edu:80/about BU/facts.html, updated/reviewed 01/18/96).
2. Eleven essays describing the background and structure of the LxC programs and putting it into theoretical and operational perspective within the growing languages across the curriculum movement in the United States appear in *Languages Across the Curriculum: Invited Essays on the Use of Foreign Languages throughout the Postsecondary Curriculum* (Straight 1994). Fifteen essays that provide both overviews and course-by-course specifics of a number of examples in both Binghamton's LxC program and a different but similarly motivated languages across the curriculum program at the State University of New York College at Oswego

appear in *Using Languages Across the Curriculum: Diverse Disciplinary Perspectives* (Fichera and Straight in press).

3. Wolf (1993) reports that her own research on reading comprehension and eight other studies dating from 1979 to 1991 have shown—with no known conflicting findings—that "even at the very advanced levels of target language experience, learners' ability to demonstrate what they understand suffers when assessed in the target language" (Wolf 1993, 476). In accordance with these findings, even participants with relatively advanced skills in the LxC-supported language find that they must employ English to express their fullest understanding of LxC materials. Moreover, even participants with native proficiency in the language—as is typically the case for heritage-student study groups in Chinese or Korean—will be required to employ English to exhibit what they have learned. They do this in classroom discussion, in-class examinations, presentations, or written assignments, all done in English. LxC study groups must therefore use English in at least the summing-up portion of their discussion time, to ensure that everyone sees how to express that summing-up in English. Indeed, participants can often do this better than the LRSs, for whom English is, in most cases, a second language.

4. The American Council on Education's "Next Steps" and "Net Gain" projects—funded by NEH and FIPSE, respectively—have created a growing set of LAC-committed colleges and universities with which Binghamton is collaborating in this evaluation effort. The National Research Agenda prepared by Richard T. Jurasek, H. Stephen Straight, Gail L. Riley, and Andrew D. Cohen for the Next Steps conference in 1995 provides a relatively comprehensive outline of the variables that might be included in program evaluation, and the Net Gain institutions will presumably develop shared evaluation measures as part of their 1996-99 project, the last year of which will specifically focus on systematic project evaluation.

✑ ✑

H. Stephen Straight (Ph.D. in Linguistics, The University of Chicago, 1972) is Professor of Anthropology and of Linguistics and director of the linguistics program at the State University of New York at Binghamton University. He is the founding director of Binghamton's languages across the curriculum (LxC) program, which began in 1991. Straight has served as Associate Dean for Academic Affairs in Binghamton's Harpur College of Arts and Sciences and as Director of Graduate Studies in Anthropology. Address: Dept. of Anthropology and Program in Linguistics, Director of Languages Across the Curriculum, SUNY-Binghamton, Box 6000, Binghamton, NY 13902-6000 (Email: straight@binghamton.edu)

List of Appendixes

Appendix A: LxC courses from fall 1991 to spring 1996

Appendix B: Practical Advice for Language Resource Specialists

Appendix A
Binghamton University (SUNY):
LxC Courses, Fall 1991-Spring 1996

Fall 1991	TITLE	NUMBER OF PARTICIPANTS/LANGUAGES[1]
BLS 411	Business and Society	6/1
ENG 280	Modern British and American Literature	3/1
ENVI 101	Environment and Man/Woman: Ecological Perspectives	28/2
IBUS 311	Introduction to International Business	45/5
PHIL 441H	Gender and the State	3/1
PLSC 120	The Practice of Rights	9/2
QMMG 111	Statistics for Management	11/1
		105/5

Spring 1992		
IBUS 520	Introduction to International Business (graduate course)[2]	30/5

Fall 1992		
IBUS 520	Introduction to International Business (graduate course)	25/3

Spring 1993		
COLI 212	Literature and Music	5/1
ENVI 102	Environment and Man/Woman: Physical Aspects	13/3
IBUS 311	Introduction to International Business (two sections)	87/5
IBUS 520	Introduction to International Business (graduate course)	13/3
LING 214	Language, Sex, and Gender (two sections)	23/3
MKTG 570	International Marketing (graduate course)	23/4
SOC 263	History of Human Services	5/1
		169/5

Fall 1993		
ACCT 455/555	Advanced Accounting Theory (two sections)	119/6
ENVI 101	Environment and Man/Woman: Ecological Perspectives	7/1
HIST 106	Introduction to East Asian Civilizations	5/2
HIST 380F	AIDS	4/1
IBUS 311	Introduction to International Business (two sections)	101/6
IBUS 520	Introduction to International Business (graduate course)	21/6
PSYC 220	Developmental Psychology	4/1
THEA 101	Introduction to Musical Theater	11/2
		272/6

Spring 1994[3]

ACCT 581B	International Accounting (2-credit graduate course)	10/3
HIST 264	Immigration and Ethnicity in U.S. History	28/4
IBUS 311	Introduction to International Business	56/6
IBUS 520	Introduction to International Business (graduate course)	20/6
LA&C 385	Environmental Problems in Latin America	3/1
PLSC 113	Introduction to Comparative Politics (two sections)	3/1
PSYC 220	Developmental Psychology	12/2
PSYC 473Q	Psychology from a Cultural Perspective	2/1
SOC 360	Religion, Self, and Society	4/2
WOMN 380Z	Latin American Women and Their Communities	4/1
		142/9

Fall 1994[4]

ENVI 101	Environment and Man/Woman: Ecological Perspectives	33/3
HIST 264	Immigration and Ethnicity in U.S. History	11/3
IBUS 311	Introduction to International Business (two sections)	56/7
IBUS 520	Introduction to International Business (graduate course)	25/5
PLSC 113	Introduction to Comparative Politics (two sections)	13/3
PLSC 220	Developmental Psychology	107/2
SOC SCI	Social Sciences Study Group (graduate students)	5/1
SOC 263	History of Human Services	6/1
THEA 101	Introduction to Musical Theater	17/2
		273/10

Spring 1995

ENVI 201	Environment and Man/Woman: Psychological Aspects	3/1
ENVI 320	Energy and Environment	6/1
IBUS 311	Introduction to International Business	47/3
IBUS 520	Introduction to International Business (graduate course)	13/4
PSYC 220	Developmental Psychology	53/3
		122/5

Fall 1995

ENVI 101	Environment and Man/Woman: Ecological Perspectives	33/2
HIST 106	Introduction to East Asian Civilizations	2/1
HIST 264	Immigration and Ethnicity in United States History	7/2
IBUS 311	Introduction to International Business	14/2
IBUS 520	Introduction to International Business	18/4
THEA 101	Introduction to Musical Theater	37/2
SOC 340	Women and U.S. Criminal Justice System	4/1
		115/5

Spring 1996

BIOL 104	Diversity of life	7/2
ENVI 201	Environment & Man/Woman: Physical Aspects	12/2
ENVI 320	Energy & the Environment	9/1
HIST 186A	Modern World History	7/2
PLSC 113	Intro to Comparative Politics	7/2

PLSC 117	Intro to World Politics	11/2
SOC 240	Women of Color in the US	4/1
SOC 100	Intro to Women's Studies	3/1
IBUS 520	Intro to International Business	10/2
		70/3
	GRAND TOTAL	1323/11

[1] X/Y, where X = number of participants and Y =number of languages. When Y =1, the language was Spanish; when Y=2, the languages were Spanish and French. The total number of different languages supported has to date been eleven: Chinese, English (as a second language), French, German, Greek, Hebrew, Italian, Japanese, Korean, Russian, and Spanish.

[2] LxC in IBUS in spring 1992 was supported entirely by the School of Management, largely through the contributed efforts of George Westacott, who has taught an LxC course every semester since fall 1991.

[3] The fall-off in participation between the fall 1993 and spring 1994 semesters is largely a result of the reduction from 241 to 86 enrollments in the School of Management. Number of participation in the Harpur College of Arts and Sciences, in fact, nearly doubled, from 31 to 56.

[4] From fall 1991 through spring 1994, LxC participation was required of all students enrolled in IBUS 311 and IBUS 520. Beginning in fall 1994, participation was optional for all students, regardless of course.

Appendix B
Practical Advice for Language Resource Specialists

Getting Clear About How LxC Works in a Specific Course

1. LRSs need to ensure that participants have a clear understanding of exactly what LxC participation will require of them. They will need to communicate the following details to all participants:
- How the LxC assignments will relate to the non-LxC course material and the syllabus;

- How participants will share their LxC-derived subject-matter knowledge with others in the class (participation in discussion, special presentation in lecture);
- What role attendance at LxC meetings and performance of LxC assignments will have in calculation of the final grade;
- What role the LRS will play in assigning grades, monitoring attendance, writing examinations, or evaluating participant papers;
- How and when participants can stop participating without any penalty.

2. Consult widely and frequently!
- If you have any uncertainties regarding the points in item 1 above, you should seek clarification from the course instructor(s).
- LRSs should consult with course instructors concerning the possibility of attending meetings the instructors may have with Teaching Assistants, if any.
- LRSs should also invite course instructors to attend one or more of their LxC study-group meetings, if possible.
- When a course has more than one LRS, LRSs working on the same course should meet periodically with each other to share ideas about what materials to use for assignments and how to construct and implement LxC assignments.
- LRSs working in the same language in different courses should talk periodically with each other to share ideas about how to deal with linguistic and cultural issues that may arise regardless of the discipline of the supported course.

3. LRSs must become knowledgeable about the content of the course.
- *Remember, LxC is not a language- instruction program.* You should therefore focus your attention at all times on how the content of each LxC assignment relates to topics treated in the course.
- Whenever appropriate, you should attend the course lectures and/or regular course discussion of your study-group participants. The more you know about what's going on in the course, the better you can relate LxC assignments to it.
- In addition to attending occasional lectures or discussions, you should become familiar with the course syllabus and do some of the required reading.

General Suggestions for the Preparation and Implementation of LxC Assignments

1. Choose materials on the basis of their linguistic and cultural authenticity as well as their relevance to course content.

- You will probably find the most appropriate and accessible materials in the popular media (newspapers and magazines), but you may also be able to use governmental documents or other more specialized materials.

- You should look closely at the required readings for the course to find passages that you might include (or refer to) in LxC assignments. These can provide a context for the LxC-specific material. In this way, LxC participants can more readily relate what they learn in their weekly study-group meetings to the rest of the content of the course, and share their insights with the instructor and with other students in the course.

- Do NOT use materials specially written for language students or nonnative audiences. In particular, you should generally avoid language textbooks, which usually contain only highly edited and sometimes very unauthentic materials. If you do find something in a language text that seems authentic, use it in its original published form if at all possible.

- Do NOT use materials that have been translated from English or some other language. Remember that LxC seeks primarily to provide international perspectives and cross-cultural insights. A text translated into the LxC-supported language necessarily fails to provide such insights and perspectives. On the other hand, when you find something that contains, in part, translations from English, provide the English original in your assignment.

2. *Always* **give full citations of the sources of your LxC materials.**

- Everything you use, no matter how short and no matter in what language, should contain a full citation. If you prepare something yourself (such as a glossary or background information), put your own name and the date on it, as well as full citations of any reference books (dictionaries, encyclopedias) from which you have drawn. (If you use the same dictionary repeatedly, you can abbreviate the citation in later assignments, but never leave the citation out entirely.)

- Even when the source contains clear but indirect indications of its origin (as when the title and issue date of a magazine article appear in the margin), you should provide a citation in standard format as a model for the development of good habits of scholarship.

3. LRSs should strive to match the assignments to the appropriate place in the course syllabus, or at least to take topics up in the same order they come up in the course.

- When you cannot do exactly this, you should at least strive for a logical progression from assignment to assignment. You should try to make the LxC experience cumulative and coherent, whether topically or regionally.
- As you discuss new materials, always relate their contents back to previous assignments and, if possible, to the contents of forthcoming assignments. It's easier to keep track of where you are when you think periodically about where you've been and where you're going.

4. LRSs should distribute each assignment at least one week in advance of the date when the study group will discuss it.

- At the time you distribute an assignment, or the week before the group will discuss it, you may want to engage participants in a preassignment discussion (or "prereading activity") to explore their preconceptions or background knowledge relative to the assignment topic.
- LRSs may also provide a brief oral description of the larger cultural or historical context for the target material. (You can also do this in writing, in English or in the target language. Remember to give full citations of any sources you draw on!)
- If you have found more material than you can use for future assignments, describe it to the study-group members and let THEM make the choice.

5. LRSs should provide informal feedback to participants regarding their progress with the assignments and with the language.

- Acknowledge individual and group accomplishments: good questions, clear statements, successful handling of an assignment.

- If you ask participants to hand in written work (responses to readings, summaries of major points, answers to study questions, fill-in-the-blanks exercises), give it back to them with written comments no later than the very next study-group meeting.

6. Draw out *every* study-group participant. Everyone has something important to say!

- *Always* sit in a circle. Eye contact has a wonderful way of forcing people to take notice of others and to respond to what others say.
- Make participants take turns writing main discussion points on the board. Don't let yourself get into an "I'm the teacher and you're my students" mode!
- Remember that you're the study-group leader, they're the participants, and together you're seeking to relate the assignment to the course content. The participants, especially those who understand the assignment least, may often have more to go on than you do regarding how best to achieve this goal!
- Participants who do not volunteer comments will almost always respond with something useful when asked "What did YOU think about this assignment?" Even if they respond with a dismissive remark, such as "It was boring," you can pick up on this by asking "How would you have made it more interesting?" If you convince them that you CARE what they think, participants will almost always respond by TELLING you.

7. Don't hesitate to inject your own personal experience into the study-group discussion.

- Remember that we chose you as a language resource specialist not only for your linguistic and disciplinary expertise but also because we believe that your personal background will contribute directly to the learning experience of LxC participants.
- Remember also that things you may take for granted regarding the historical and social context may surprise or confuse some LxC participants. Try to anticipate these "cross-cultural moments" and help participants learn from them. (Be prepared, however, for some surprises of your own!)

Tips on Meeting the Linguistic Needs of LxC Participants

1. LRSs should provide contextually appropriate glosses (NOT simply dictionary definitions) for words, phrases, or sentences that participants may have trouble understanding.

- You should be on the lookout especially for items of popular slang or technical jargon that may not appear in the dictionaries available to participants.
- *Don't forget to provide a full citation for any dictionary or other reference source you use, and to take credit where appropriate for your own creativity.*

2. LRSs should allow participants who can speak the language moderately well to do so either in the study-group meeting or outside of it. However, LRSs must remain sensitive to the fact that *all* participants must in the end understand all of the points that come up in study-group discussion.

- You can achieve this by providing summaries (not translations) of what has been said periodically during the study-group discussion.
- Some participants may want to hear the text read aloud, and even to do the reading themselves. However, you should never spend more than ten minutes of your weekly hour on this activity. Reading aloud does not foster reading for comprehension. Indeed, the reader often understands less of what he or she is reading than does an attentive listener.
- Do NOT correct pronunciation unless the participants request that you do so. It impedes discussion.

3. LRSs should remember that many participants can benefit from hearing the spoken language.

- LRSs may wish to read aloud some of the assignment to the class, so that they can hear how the language sounds.
- LRSs can also tape a reading of the assignment so that the participants may listen to it in the library language lab.

4. In the regularly scheduled study-group meetings, LRSs should focus on the content of the assignments, not on vocabulary or grammar.

- You can address these linguistic concerns by providing glosses or inviting participants to talk to LRSs privately about their linguistic problems or confusion.

5. *Never* focus on translation, either in take-home work or study-group meetings. Translation is a separate skill.

- Translation can distract participants from the main task, which is understanding.
- It can also distort their understanding by forcing them to arrive at an incomplete and inflexible rendering of what is an essentially open-ended and contextually rich cultural artifact. You should help them explore the significance of that artifact from as many different angles as possible.
- Except for occasional reminders of the approximate translation of unfamiliar words or idioms, use rough paraphrases or inferences rather than translations to help participants understand difficult phrases or sentences.

12

With One Stone:[1]

Models of Instruction and Their Curricular Implications in an Advanced Content-Based Foreign Language Program

Peter A. Shaw

Editors' Note: Peter Shaw provides an ideal final chapter to this series of case studies in CBI. First, his program at Monterey Institute of International Studies (MIIS), funded by a grant from the Pew Charitable Trusts, represents a veritable synthesis of the models that we have seen in previous chapters. The program, implemented through collaboration between the School of Language Studies and the School of International Policy Studies, experimented with five different models—direct content, team content, subsidiary content, supplementary content, and adjunct—each of which has appeared in one form or another in earlier chapters. Second, the various models represent a blending of CBI and FLAC approaches in that some are oriented more toward "total immersion in the target language" and others toward the use of the target language as a supplement to courses taught principally in English. Third, Shaw's insightful comments concerning the linguistic, cognitive, affective, and pedagogical issues that emanated from the MIIS experiments serve as an excellent overview of the core issues raised by many of the other contributors. Especially valuable are his suggestions for student assessment and program evaluation, for improving teacher preparation, and his idea for a "learner training workshop." General references for this chapter are located in the bibliography at the end of this volume.

Introduction

This chapter describes the development of new courses at the Monterey Institute of International Studies (MIIS) in which subjects in the International Policy Studies (IPS) Division were taught partly or wholly through the medium of the students' foreign language (Arabic, Chinese, French, German,

Italian, Japanese, or Spanish). The project was funded by a grant from the Pew Charitable Trusts. In five sections, the chapter discusses the background to and rationale for the new curriculum (Introduction), the nature of the new courses (Designing the Curriculum), the ensuing adaptations (Implementing the Curriculum), the method of teaching the Pew courses (Pedagogy), and consequences for various aspects of the program (Evaluation and Conclusion).

The Monterey Institute of International Studies is an academic community committed to preparing innovative professionals to provide leadership in cross-cultural, multilingual environments. The basic goal of MIIS programs, therefore, is to provide the necessary language proficiency, cultural understanding, and content mastery for success in the fields of International Policy Studies, International Management, Translation and Interpretation, and Second and Foreign Language Teaching. For the kinds of reasons discussed in the first chapter of this book, the institute has selected CBI as one significant basis of its approach, embracing a philosophy which suggests that the advanced level language learner can best proceed to even higher levels of proficiency by addressing the language as a means of communicating ideas rather than as an object of study. Practice is provided in all four skill areas and learning is boosted by the interest and motivation generated by the subject matter. In terms of pedagogy and of syllabus design, this is a broad educational approach where language study is allowed to feed into the curricular mainstream rather than being dammed into grammatical or literary backwaters. The result is a splendid economy: the subject-matter owl and the linguistic parrot attacked with the one stone.

The degree program which has hatched and raised the new courses is International Policy Studies (IPS), which consists of a core of courses in policy analysis, economics, international relations, and area studies. Students select a specialization, either a regional expertise appropriate to their foreign language, or a functional focus, such as economics. The program description asserts that the goal of the division is to produce graduates who can do policy research in at least two languages. The faculty believe that this emphasis is appropriate for students aspiring to international careers that require analytical research and writing skills in addition to pertinent knowledge.

The background and experience of the faculty in this program are consistent with these aims. Because of hiring criteria in recent years, many IPS professors are able to teach in two or more languages, while, in a complementary development, faculty for the School of Language Studies are increasingly likely to have a specialization in some real world enterprise (economics, law, government, or education) rather than in literature.

Given this trend in faculty interests and specializations and the concerns of students for relevant language training, a needs analysis was conducted among two cohorts of IPS and IM students. The first step involved loosely structured interviews with groups of students, during which input was sought in various categories: for what future purposes were they studying a foreign language? what features did they seek in their language classes? and so forth. These interviews were recorded and transcribed and the contents analyzed for frequently occurring items, which were then formalized in a written questionnaire. This was then completed by 151 students. The main findings were as follows: 1) students expected to use their foreign language in both professional and social situations; 2) students intended to either live abroad or travel extensively; 3) students felt a much stronger need to further develop their communicative abilities than to know more about the language; 4) students preferred a focus on fluency to one on accuracy; 5) students wanted classroom activities to focus on content rather than on language form; 6) the content of choice was directly related to the interests and career plans of students, featuring economics, politics, and current events.

Designing the Curriculum

One of the outcomes of our early thinking and planning was the realization that the most effective deployment of resources (in particular, the knowledge and skills of the faculty) would involve multiple instructional formats rather than one particular type of course.

This section describes five instructional models which have been deployed at the institute during the development of the CBI program.

Type 1: Direct Content Model

Subject matter is delivered entirely in the students' second language (where "second language" means "not the mother tongue"—many of our students are multilingual and the language of instruction might be their third or fourth language; also, these descriptions refer to American students, not to the international students who also took these classes.) All readings, all classroom discussions, and all assignments are in this second language, which may be the instructor's mother tongue (Type 1A) or a second language for the instructor (Type 1B).

Type 2: Team Content Model

In this model, the subject matter is again taught in the students' second language. However, there are two instructors: one from the subject-matter field and one a specialist in the language of instruction. They combine in a team-teaching format which would aim to maximize learning opportunities for pupils by utilizing to the full the combined knowledge and talents of the teaching team. Again, all readings, texts, classroom interactions, and assignments are in the target language.

Type 3: Subsidiary Content Model

The major subject matter is delivered by a subject-matter professor in English. Related subset content is taught in one or more of the students' second languages by the language faculty. Thus, in the first session of the week (in English), a new topic is introduced and its scope examined, often across a number of cases. It is then studied with greater specificity, often in only one case, in the second language session.

Type 4: Supplementary Content Model

The subject matter is taught in English by a teacher from the relevant discipline. The same, or parallel, content is then covered by a language instructor in the students' second language. Both instructors are present in class sessions and the subject-matter teacher has at least a fluent understanding of the foreign language, while the language specialist is also sufficiently conversant with the subject matter. Parallels with this model may be drawn with approaches to bilingual education where, for example, material is previewed and reviewed in one language and taught in another (though normally by the same bilingual teacher).

Type 5: Adjunct Model

Subject matter is presented in the students' second language; a separate but related language class is offered to develop the necessary skills and proficiency in the language to be successful in the main course. Subject matter is not introduced in the adjunct class except as the basis for language practice. This model is currently restricted to adjunct ESL classes for international students in International Management (IM) and International Policy Studies (IPS), with a dominant focus on writing. This type is not accorded further discussion here. A sample of courses from the other four types are shown in Table 1, on the next page.

COURSE	TITLE	MODEL TYPE	LANGUAGE
Latin American Studies	Social Movements in Latin America	1B	Spanish
Western European Studies	Comparitive Politics of Western Europe (emphasis: Spain)	3	Spanish
Western European Studies	Comparitive Politics of Western Europe (emphasis: Germany)	3	German
Western European Studies	Comparitive Politics of Western Europe (emphasis: France)	3	French
Western European Studies	Comparitive Politics of Western Europe	4	English
Asian Studies	Economic Development in the People's Republic of China	4	Chinese, English
Francophone Studies	Francophone Africa	2	English, French
Near Eastern Studies	Politics of the Near East	3	Arabic, English
Latin American Studies	Redemocratization in the Southern Cone	1B	Spanish
Asian Studies	Women in Development: China	4	Chinese, English
Western European Studies	Italian Politics and Culture	2	Italian
Asian Studies	The Internationalization of Japan	1A	Japanese
Near Eastern Studies	Politics of the Near East	3	Arabic, English

Table 1: Sample Content Courses Taught in a Foreign Language at MIIS

In terms of content, language and instructional procedures, the instructional models listed above may be broadly characterized as in the following cases:

The Internationalization of Japan. Type 1A. This class is noteworthy for two things: first, the difficulty of the readings (all in Japanese) for the American students; and, second, the prominent role of the native speakers of the language of instruction. This class more than any other thus features, on the one hand, extensive periods of direct discussion of set readings, with the instructor and the native Japanese students helping the American students, and, on the other, dialogues between the two groups of students. Given the topic, the Internationalization of Japan, this seemed particularly apposite as the Americans, many of whom had resided in Japan for considerable periods, supplied the outsider's view to counterbalance the Japanese students' views of their own culture. (Several of the Japanese students commented in their diaries how surprised they were to learn so much about their own country in their own language in a class at the Monterey Institute.) Students selected and researched a chosen subtopic and wrote a paper in Japanese, presenting their findings in class.

Social Movements in Latin America and *Redemocratization in the Southern Cone.* Type 1B. All course materials, class proceedings, and assignments were in Spanish. The instructor led a discussion of the week's readings, often providing necessary background information through short lectures. Variety was provided by the use of documentary films and, later in the semester, by student presentations on prepared topics. There were guest speakers—natives of one of the countries being studied—who delivered short lectures and were questioned by the class.

Francophone Africa. Type 2. The team in this case consisted of an IPS professor specializing in African issues (a fluent French speaker) and a French professor with expertise in Francophone African literature. The syllabus was constructed around the main Francophone countries of Africa and a series of topics (the legacy of colonialism, the role of Islam); information about relevant political, social, geographical, historical, and economic issues was provided by presentations (the IPS professor), readings, and documentary films; against this factual background were then set discussions of a series of short novels, the real-world themes of which had already been identified. In addition, each student selected a poem by a Francophone African writer and made a short presentation about it. These literature sessions were led by the French instructor (although each teacher would add comments in classes chaired by the other, lending a truly collaborative air to the whole course). In addition to the poetry presentations, students wrote a series of short papers in French.

Italian Politics and Culture. Type 2. Very similar to the Francophone Africa course in concept and execution, this class also paired an IPS specialist with fluency in the language of instruction (Italian) with a language instructor who could contribute significantly to the subject matter. This course had no literature component, however, and was organized more simply, with readings on a series of topics covering government, politics, and current social issues and class discussions incorporating additional information from both instructors. The language instructor also provided feedback (usually in the form of written notes) to participants on their performance in spoken Italian and provided extensive help with their written papers. There was more direct attention to the language of instruction in this class than in any other; as its number suggests, it was of a more introductory and preparatory nature than the others (Comparative Politics of Western Europe, for example), while an introductory IPS class is an advanced language course.

Comparative Politics of Western Europe. Type 3. Two class meetings per week: in the first, all students attend the same plenary session in English. This serves two functions: the first part concludes the topic initiated the previous week by allowing students to interact in small groups, integrating material they have studied separately and reaching common conclusions. These conclusions are shared with the whole group and the instructor adds his own remarks. In the second part, the new topic is introduced by the instructor, who lectures, for example, about parliamentary systems in Western Europe, drawing examples from several different countries. Students have already read about this topic in English. The second class meeting of the week takes place in three separate sections: the languages of instruction are French, German, and Spanish, and the content focus, respectively, France, Germany, and Spain. Students read materials in the foreign language about the country of study; their discussion of the French parliamentary system, for example, is thus embedded in their general understanding gained from the first session. Their specific expertise is then taken to the first part of the next plenary session, where they instruct some of their colleagues in the French system, being in turn informed about details of the German and Spanish parliaments.

Class 1:

Plenary: in English (Monday).

Previous topic concluded: - Small groups share material from previous Wednesday

                                           - Groups report results of integration

                                           - Instructor's concluding remarks

New topic: - Instructor's introductory lecture on new topic

                              - Instructor and class discuss readings on new topic

[Students read foreign language materials on specific country; prepare for participation in class]

Class 2:

Separate sections: French, German, Spanish (Wednesday)

Instructor leads discussion of topic with specific reference to country of specialization.

Students make prepared presentations, discuss specific questions in small groups, participate in discussion, ask questions about readings.

[Students read materials in English about next topic; prepare for participation in small groups]

Class 3:

Plenary in English; continues on in Monday above.

Politics of the Near East. Type 3. The pattern is similar to that of Comparative Politics of Western Europe: in a plenary session, the lead instructor introduces the topic of the week by lecture, discussion of readings and, often, by documentary film material. The topic is then discussed in more detail in the second class session: those with sufficient proficiency in the language form an Arabic section, which is led by an Arabic instructor who is also well-versed in the subject matter. The remaining students join a discussion section in English, guided by the lead instructor. Insights formed in the discussion groups are often shared at the outset of the following plenary.

Economic Development in the People's Republic of China and *Women in Development: China.* Type 4. These two classes were the only cases in this experimental period in which it could not be predicted which language would be in use at any given time. The instructional team consisted of an economist whose understanding of Chinese was sufficient for her to easily follow discussions in that language and a Chinese instructor with a strong background in economics such that she could lead discussions of material and add her own perspective. Material was presented to the students through a variety of means: readings in English and Chinese, short lectures in English (the economist), documentary and feature films in Chinese, and commentaries in Chinese (the language instructor). This material was discussed largely in Chinese, but with frequent switches to English, particularly when the economist interjected comments. Students made individual and panel presentations and wrote short papers, all in both languages.

Implementing the Curriculum

The Curriculum Level

The most obvious curricular implication of a move towards CBI is that the foreign language courses have to be integrated into the overall sequencing of courses in the degree program: introductory or survey courses (Italian Politics and Culture or Comparative Politics of Western Europe, for example) must be offered early in the sequence; seminar or special topics (Redemocratization in the Southern Cone, for example) later; there may be prerequisites for a CBI course to be scheduled appropriately; and so on. These are program-specific concerns, however, and here I shall focus only on the sequencing of language courses. This is followed by some thoughts about the role of formal language study when CBI becomes the dominant mechanism for advancing students' proficiency. Finally, there is a short discussion of curricular resources, including the role of international students and other native speakers of the foreign languages concerned.

Sequencing Language Courses in the Curriculum

To return to basic principles for a moment, one of the basic arguments for CBI involves the importance of schema theory, of building on learners' existing knowledge, experience, and expectations. Our experience suggests very strongly that there are certain key conditions for a successful CBI course:

1) Students have the necessary background knowledge in terms of facts, ideas, and concepts;
2) Students have the necessary proficiency in the second language in terms of syntax, lexis, and discourse;
3) Students have the necessary basis of analytical and thinking skills upon which the instructor proposes to build;
4) Students' expectations of the learning/instructional process match the instructors' intentions.

When the Pew course instructors were debriefed, they were asked to identify what deficiencies, if any, they had identified in these four areas. In every case the area mentioned as a problem, ranging from slight to serious, was condition #1: students were consistently cited as being ignorant of basic historical, geographical, and sociological information. The instructor of Redemocratization in the Southern Cone noted that the most significant obstacle to making progress through the prepared material was the constant need to deliver short lectures filling in key historical information. As a result, in a course where the instructor had indicated in an early interview that she intended to lecture very little, seven of sixteen students complained in the final evaluation that there were too many lectures (demonstrating, it may be noted, that conditions #1 and #4 above are related). In contrast, six of thirteen instructors commented on insufficient language proficiency (condition #2), and these difficulties were concentrated in the more "difficult" languages (Japanese, Chinese, and Arabic.) Thinking skills (condition #3) were mentioned by only two professors.

In their journals students confirmed these findings. Many wrote of spending time in the library on recommended readings that provided background information on history, geography, and so on. Of eighteen diary writers in Comparative Politics of Western Europe, thirteen reported spending some time on refreshing or enlarging their knowledge of modern European history. The students were much harder on themselves in terms of language: all journal writers who were nonnative speakers of the language of instruction reported at least one occasion when their command of the language let them down and they either failed to communicate their point or opted to keep silent when they had something important to say. These extracts were written by students in the Francophone Africa class:

> Student 1: I found that I used more fragmented sentences and worse grammar when I spoke to the larger group. I guess because I felt less intimidated and more willing to take my time to formulate sentence structure and search for words in the smaller group.

> Student 2: I thought I knew the grammar of French, but I "blank" when I speak out loud. Meaning, I use simple vocabulary and grammar, when, in retrospect, I could easily have used the correct grammar. I do not have the native ability, though I have an intuitive grasp of what's right and what's wrong and have the knowledge to use it, but usually it's a passive knowledge.

Condition #3, thinking skills, is addressed only in one particular context: the difficulty of the nonnative speaker when faced with the close relationship of the target culture, its patterns of thought, and the language. Thus, in a Japanese class, a journal writer discusses the perplexing issue of how the Japanese (specifically, as represented by the instructor and four native-speaking students in the class) can be at once so logical and practical, yet so vague, indirect, and intuitive:

> The degree to which these fluctuations are reflected in the Japanese language—or should be reflected when spoken properly—is something I'm trying to grasp. I'm also trying to determine *when* to use which approach: in which situations it is kosher to be more direct or logical, straightforward. Most times, I try to be *clear* and grammatically correct (a challenge in itself), although I do notice that I tend, when speaking Japanese to use more qualifiers or statements which "discount" my main point, such as "hakkiri wakaranai keredo"[I'm not sure but...] or statements to elicit support: "ja nai desu ka/to omoimasen ka" [isn't it true that/don't you think that].

Another student in the same class consciously developed a strategy for expressing ideas:

> Be polite, use some qualifiers to soften what you say, but then say it anyway and follow with "don't you think" or "what do you think?" In a sense, it's using a more feminine, intuitive, relational approach to what you're saying, to communication. This is very appealing to me in any case, but I do want to know that I *am* clear, since I'm speaking a foreign language.

A third talks about a "Catch 22:" that the nonnative speakers try very hard to understand something which seems illogical to them, for example, a reading on foreign labor. However, the native speakers' attitude appears to be: " . . . we can't change, or our culture is very difficult to explain, but if you can't understand it, you can't play with us."

The lesson we have learned is this: an advanced level CBI program cannot be created without attention being paid to the appropriate preparation of students through the preceding levels of instruction.

Implications for the CBI Curriculum

In the light of the difficulties outlined above, the following may be offered as a template for a complete CBI curriculum at MIIS:

1) Intermediate/Upper Intermediate level language courses are based on the kind of subject matter (history, geography, basic facts of politics and government, etc.) which is prerequisite to IPS courses. Some proportion, say 25 percent, is devoted to the consideration of formal features of the language, especially discourse features related to patterns of thought.

2) Upper Intermediate/Advanced levels of language IPS introductory survey courses are taught in the foreign language. Language work is conducted outside class using teaching assistants (TAs) or partnership arrangements with native speakers; this work is required.

3) Advanced levels of language IPS seminars are taught in the foreign language. Optional language work is available through TAs or partnership arrangements with native speakers.

The Role of TAs and Native Speakers

When a group of MIIS graduate students in Applied Linguistics was given this whole issue as a curriculum project, they had the original idea of providing a rationale for the sequencing of CBI (they call it "gradual" CBI) through the application of Grice's (1975) cooperative principle for conversation (Clancey, Miller, Munson, Nobis, and Stauffer, 1990). They noted that it is evident that any successful classroom operates on the principle of cooperation between students and teacher and among students themselves. Grice himself points out that "the specific expectations or presumptions connected with . . . the foregoing maxims [of quantity, quality, relation and manner] have their analogs in the sphere of transactions that are not talk exchanges" (1975, 47). Hence, properly sequenced CBI should satisfy the maxim of quantity by providing an appropriate balance of language and content instruction. Thus, in the model above, this proportion has to be found to make the Intermediate/Upper Intermediate courses effective. Similarly, the maxim of quality would call for the conveying of significant information through the foreign language (rather than the accumulating of unwanted conscious knowledge about linguistic systems). The maxim of relation is satisfied by the relevance of well-sequenced CBI to the students' short-term needs (the requisite subject-matter knowledge for upcoming courses; the necessary level of language proficiency for the next level of CBI) and their long-term, professional goals. The fourth maxim, of manner, is satisfied by those facets of CBI instruction which motivate and interest students. However, in adjusting the fit of these conditions to the needs of a given group of students, there will always be a lack of congruence as far as any individual is concerned. These misadjustments might be characterized as follows:

Quantity: There is not enough, or too much language instruction in the course;

Quality: Students find the information about the language lacking in interest and want more content, or vice versa;

Relation: Students find content not relevant, either to IPS studies or to intended future profession;

Manner: The pedagogical problem that, frequently, there is either not enough, or there is too much, of certain features of the instructional process (i.e., documentary films, poems, small group discussions, guest lectures, and error correction.) This lack of fit cannot be remedied by the professor alone, however tireless and dedicated. There is thus a role for a teaching assistant or for native speakers of the language of instruction. The latter have clearly played a crucial part in classroom events, playing leadership roles in small- and large-group discussions or supplying the exact phrase when needed. However, properly organized native speaker/nonnative speaker interaction outside of class could provide a valuable compensatory service, through:

1) Giving help with readings before they are discussed in class;
2) Giving feedback to nonnative's use of the target language, perhaps using tapes of class sessions;
3) Giving feedback on early drafts of written papers;
4) Discussing aspects of the formal systems of the target language which might be causing difficulties; and
5) Exploring cultural norms for serious discussion and analytical thinking.

I use the term "partnership" above because international students who are native speakers in a Pew-funded course are nonnative speakers elsewhere and could use the same kind of help with their English. In summary, then, the Pew-funded experience, to date, provides a direction for the development of a more rigorous and complete CBI component for the IPS and IM programs at MIIS, together with ideas for a functional integration of the student community. We now look in more detail at the components of the curriculum: syllabus, pedagogy, and materials.

The Syllabus Level

In terms of subject matter, the selection and grading of topics is determined by the particular logic of that content area. Thus, for example, a course in contemporary politics of a country or region will include units on executive, legislative and judicial, branches of government, the constitution, the electoral system, the political parties, and so on. Of more relevance to the present purpose is the language aspect of course content. One aspect of the research program was the taping and transcribing of class sessions from each of the Pew classes. These transcripts were then examined for the nature and variety of the language use; we looked at syntax, vocabulary, and various aspects of discourse. One reason for this is the possibility of providing, in lower level classes, practice in using the language of the advanced CBI offerings.

After this analysis has been repeated on other transcripts from different Upper Intermediate/Advanced and Advanced level IPS and IM classes in French, the resulting list would be a valid and reliable input to a French course which prepared students for those courses. These expressions might be incorporated into the syllabus in various ways: 1) they might be grouped by function (additive, contrastive, causative) and compared, using examples of their use in written text; 2) they might be incorporated into listening and reading activities for recognition and comprehension; and 3) the transcripts themselves might serve as materials for the language activities, with students identifying these expressions and assessing their meaning. In similar fashion, these transcripts exhibit a surprisingly rich seam of vocabulary, which may be mined in different ways. From the same one hundred minutes of the French politics class, we pulled 242 technical words, part of the lexis of government and economics, and an almost equal number (226, in fact) of subtechnical items, words which might occur in any academic or serious nonfictional context.

While it might be argued that the role of a CBI course is, in a sense, to teach the technical vocabulary (which represents the facts and concepts and the core material), the value of the subtechnical vocabulary is its generalizability. Again, the wider the research net is cast, the more valuable will be the catch and the more useful this kind of syllabus specification.

Pedagogy

As part of the groundwork for the new courses, a survey was conducted to establish the salient characteristics of the instructional approach to the different kinds of IPS courses (introductory, survey, seminar and so on). The results showed almost complete uniformity: all students are responsible for reading assigned texts, additional material is presented by professors in a lecture format, and topics are discussed in a teacher-fronted, whole class context. (There are differences in the more quantitative courses, such as Economics, but they are not yet represented in the CBI program and are not discussed here.) In the later stages of a semester, student projects or seminar papers are the basis for in-class presentation and discussion. While the language faculty represented a more diverse approach to pedagogy, there was little in the planning phase to suggest that the new courses would be taught in a different fashion, apart from those changes imposed by the team-teaching formats of two of the models. The implications discussed here represent ideas that arose during the teaching of the Pew courses as responses to particular problems. These pedagogic responses are the use of small-group work, the jigsaw approach to reading, a process approach to writing, the correction of errors in the students' spoken language, and the use of authentic, varied, and abundant materials.

Small Group Work

The use of this technique—putting students in groups of three to five and setting a problem to resolve or an issue to discuss—arose as a response to two issues: class size and the need (in the Subsidiary Content Model, for example) to articulate material from one class session to another. Thus, the instructional team of Francophone Africa, faced with an enrollment of well over twenty students, regularly formed small groups and set a task based on the material of the day. Here is an example from the professors' log:

> The movie *Afrique Vivante* was shown. The class was then divided into five groups of four students each and given fifteen minutes to identify the cultural values of African village life that were identified in the film. They were to find one specific instance of each value in the film and one example from *L'Enfant Noire* (the novel being studied at that point.) After the break, the various groups reported the values they had identified and these were listed on the blackboard. From these various lists, the most common values were identified: Family, Community or Group, Nature, Work, Education/Instruction. These themes were then explored further in a discussion of *L'Enfant Noire*.

The reaction of students was generally positive. They valued the opportunity for participation and for using the target language under less stressful circumstances:

It's easier to talk in the small groups. I really feel that to be part of a small group and to be responsible for its successful presentation of viewpoint in class helps me to participate more... because the stress to perform and sound intelligent about the topic overrides the stress of my fear of making mistakes in my speech. In the large group, my fear, or feeling of intimidation becomes stronger and I tend to shut up.

Not only is there an effect in terms of quantity of participation: professors and students agree that the quality of work and ideas is superior in the small-group format:

The work in small groups continues to be very helpful. Much richer thoughts flow out of the groups as a general rule.

The interplay of group formats in Comparative Politics of Western Europe was valued by students both for the more effective management of material and for the opportunity to learn from others. It was certainly successful in helping to manage the complexities of this model.

Two problems with small-group work are found in the research record. The first is that success is directly correlated with the specificity of the instructions given: one cannot simply tell students to get into their groups and discuss something. They need clear guidance, normally a specific outcome. In the example quoted above, for instance, the student groups emerged with a list of values and two examples for each, one from the film, one from the novel. The instructor in overall charge of Comparative Politics of Western Europe often set the task through a worksheet chart, where the columns were the three countries (France, Spain, Germany) and the rows the particular facets of the issues of the day, for example, immigration and minorities:

	Spain	France	Germany
Identity/nature of immigrants/minorities			
Reasons for immigration			
Problems arising			
Government policies			
Your recommended solutions			

In the absence of such guidance, the results were disappointing. Here are two comments from the same student:

This group thing isn't working. Our discussion goes all over the place and no one seems to know what we are doing.

And six weeks later:

Today we were given specific questions to answer and the groups worked much better. I actually enjoyed the experience and participated a lot in the discussion.

The second issue is the preparation and capability of students to undertake small group tasks. A number of student diaries refer to unsatisfactory sessions in which their colleagues fail to take responsibility for the work of the group or where inappropriate interactive styles ruin a promising discussion by souring the atmosphere. The implication I draw is that even students of this maturity and world experience cannot necessarily be expected to function well in a small group setting without training.

Jigsaw Reading

It is an axiom of graduate education that students read a lot; all students are responsible for all the assigned reading for each class session as well as their own library research and background reading. As mentioned above, the survey of IPS instructors indicated this to be true at MIIS. However, the early diary entries in all courses are larded with complaints about the reading load. Even when instructors had consciously selected a relatively lighter load because of the language circumstances, students found it unmanageable:

Student 1: The readings are very long and dry. (German)

Student 2: The reading load is enormous and varies a lot in difficulty. This week I spent four hours on a ten page article. (Spanish)

Student 3: I'm spending as much time on the reading for this class as for all my other classes combined. (Japanese)

Instructor responses to these complaints were varied. Some lightened the load, making certain texts optional. Others urged greater concentration and application. One or two made suggestions for more effective reading strategies (see below). The most successful response, however, was to make some arrangement whereby responsibility for covering the reading material was distributed among the students. In *Movimientos sociales en América Latina,* for example, one pair of students was assigned to each of the set readings and given the responsibility of reporting the main points to their colleagues. In the Spanish section of Comparative Politics of Western Europe, students took turns week by week to lead the discussion from the texts of the day. Under such arrangements, students were better able to budget their time, giving concentrated effort to the material they were directly responsible for and using a more fluid approach (skimming for main points or scanning for interesting details) to the rest. In fact, there is anecdotal evidence from the journals that students actually read more (in the sense of looked at more pages) under such new arrangements. In turn, patterns of class participation were enhanced. When the instructor called for a summary or assessment of a particular article or chapter, students, rather than eyeing each other uneasily, knew whose turn it was to talk. Participation was reported as particularly satisfying when the small-group approach was combined with jigsaw reading, so that a particular team, having heard from each member about the reading they had studied closely, would then integrate this material through a specific task as in the example from Comparative Politics of Western Europe mentioned above.

In summary, I would express this implication as follows: that CBI instructors should maintain the breadth of reading they feel appropriate and should not exclude important texts on the grounds of excessive length or difficulty; and that, from the outset, they should organize the class so that individual students have a specified responsibility for a subset of the material and can make informed choices for the rest of their reading time. This, I believe, both alleviates the panic and inertia induced by a seemingly unmanageable reading load, and improves classroom participation by removing the circumstance that all students have "sort of" read all the material but no one has read any of it properly.

Approaches to Writing

Although ideas about writing as a process have been widespread for some time, college professors in the subject areas still focus on the product, the final draft of students' papers. This became an issue in the Pew courses in the following ways:

1) When students submitted only a final draft of a paper in the foreign language and linguistic errors were marked, they felt

resentful, suggesting that the instructor had not paid enough attention to their ideas and that their grade was based on how rather than *what* they wrote.

2) When students submitted a paper in the foreign language, some professors felt they could not do justice to the ideas because of their difficulty in picking through inaccurate or inappropriate language.

3) Students complained about the excessive amount of time which had to be devoted to writing papers in the foreign language; these comments were particularly strident in the Japanese and Chinese classes. In fact, in the case of the Japanese class, a solution was hacked out of the midst of the thorny problem. Faced with the papers written by American students, the professor extended the deadline and agreed to treat the papers as early drafts, commenting on language problems and areas of murky logic. Meetings with students resolved many of these difficulties and the final drafts could be fairly graded on the basis of content.

The implication I draw is that the writing process must be incorporated into the sequencing of a CBI class. This means that interim products (outlines, early drafts) are required by certain dates and receive feedback intended to resolve language-related difficulties. This process should involve peer response and editing processes, and I would also refer to the suggestions above involving TAs and the native speaking students. An obvious component of a native speaker/nonnative speaker partnership would be the reciprocal responding to drafts of papers written in the other's second language.

Error Correction

Some of the most virulently negative comments on their CBI experience were made by students who referred to occasions when their errors in spoken language were pointed out or corrected by instructors in class. Although some students felt that they could benefit from the correction of their errors, none enjoyed the experience. Although most of the students in *Politica e Cultura Italiana* welcomed the notes provided (after class, in private) by the language instructor, indicating language problems in their spoken discourse, only half the class felt that the process significantly improved their language skills.

I draw two implications from this: 1) correcting formal errors in class should be strictly avoided: it contributes little or nothing to the development of proficiency, and it has a strong adverse effect on the emotional atmosphere and on individual students' confidence and willingness to participate; and 2) whole class discussions, small-group work, and individual student presentations should be routinely taped and used as a basis for work with a TA or a native speaker or (in the Adjunct Model) in a language class.

Materials

Our experience to date has validated the original assumption that course materials should be authentic, varied, and abundant. While occasionally feeling overwhelmed and often struggling with its complexities, students clearly enjoyed dealing with entirely authentic materials and consistently rose to the challenge. Thus, for example, the members of the *Redemocratización en el cono sur* seminar greatly valued the fact that most of their readings were from the four countries under study (Brazil, Argentina, Chile, and Uruguay). At the same time their professor reported that they were clearly unprepared to deal with the style of political discourse in such writings and were unfamiliar with much of the background expected of the reader. However, I believe the remediation of such difficulties lies in the contribution of courses earlier in the CBI cycle and of learner training, not in abandoning the authentic materials criterion. I believe that the contributions of literature and of documentary and feature films have also been endorsed thus far. In the classes about Francophone Africa and the People's Republic of China, for example, the visual medium added a valuable dimension, and the ideas and examples were easily integrated with written and classroom discussions. Similarly, the short novels read and analyzed in the Francophone Africa course were an invaluable input of concepts, viewpoints, and illustrations, and they greatly enriched the nonfictional materials. Students stressed only one drawback of the films: the amount of class time they take up. When consulted, faculty seemed doubtful that enough students would attend screenings given at other times, although a sample of students all said they would find the time. Perhaps some suitable incentive should be sought, some version of academic popcorn.

Evaluation and Conclusion

Assessment

The assessing of individual progress in a second language on the basis of one fifteen-week/four-hours-a-week course is often tendentious at best, misleading at worst. In addition, the assessment waters have been muddied by the involvement of second language performance in the grading of subject-matter mastery. The following possibilities might be examined: that *language progress* be assessed over the two-year period of the degree program, using portfolio techniques and including an element of self-assessment; that such measures as an OPI rating be obtained on entry and at graduation; and that *CBI course grades* be based on subject-matter performance only, with resources available for language-related feedback on papers and assignments to facilitate an accurate representation of content mastery.

Teacher Preparation

While, on the one hand, it is a little awkward to discuss in-service training for a profession that lacks formal pedagogic training, it is, on the other hand, arguably about time that college professors had access to suggestions for varying and improving instruction. One implication I draw from the Pew experience at MIIS is that groups of instructors could profitably meet to discuss some of the following issues:

- Variation of the format of classroom instruction to include small-group discussion and other non-teacher-fronted alternatives;
- Team-building techniques to ensure the success of team projects and assignments and group work in class;
- The use of a jigsaw reading arrangement appropriate to the size of a given class and the amount of reading required;
- Definition of the background knowledge and language skills required to be successful in a given CBI course;
- Coping strategies for students who may lack either the required background knowledge or language skills;
- A process approach to foreign language writing skills;
- The role of formal error correction, and
- The development and maintenance of levels of student self-esteem, comfort, and confidence such that they perform in the FL to full capacity.

Learner Training

The counterpart to faculty development is learner training. The Pew experience provides abundant evidence that students in classes where a foreign language is the medium of instruction need help with reading skills, interactive listening skills, organizing and expressing ideas in writing, organizing their own learning, identifying and deploying successful language learning strategies, and seeking out and dealing with appropriate feedback on their performance. The Pew courses involved a briefing by the researcher at the outset, and this briefing came to include some of these elements. However, a much more systematic and detailed approach is needed. I feel that a clear implication of our work to date is the need for a twelve- to fifteen-hour training workshop for learners before the CBI course begins. The more such elements are incorporated into the lower levels of the CBI sequence, the less these workshops will eventually be necessary.

This chapter has surveyed a variety of models and discussed some implications that may be drawn from the development and deployment of the CBI courses at the Monterey Institute. My colleagues and their students would almost certainly draw some different conclusions and may well disagree with some expressed here. In addition, as these classes are retaught and others developed, circumstances and outcomes continue to change. However, I think we all agree on one thing: these courses have improved the programs offered to MIIS students, and my colleagues and their students should be congratulated on that very considerable achievement.

Endnote

1. This title was coined by Henry Clancey, Timothy Miller, Johanna Munson, Jennifer Nobis, and Stephanie Stauffer for a class project that constituted part of the needs analysis phase of this project. I cannot think of a better title and am grateful to them for granting me permission to use it.

Peter Shaw has taught language and has trained language teachers in Europe, Africa, Mexico, and California. He is currently Professor of Language and Educational Linguistics at the Monterey Institute of International Studies in Monterey California. Address: TESOL Department, Monterey Institute of International Studies, 425 Van Buren St., Monterey CA 93940 (E-mail: pshaw@miis.edu)

Part Six

In Retrospect

13

Content-Based Instruction:
Some Lessons and Implications

Stephen B. Stryker
Betty Lou Leaver

In the early 1980s when we first started to experiment with content-based instruction at the Foreign Service Institute, CBI in foreign language instruction was a rare phenomenon. Since that time, content-based approaches have appeared in many different settings and at all levels of foreign language education. In the previous chapters, we and our contributors have presented some of these approaches. The settings of these eleven case studies span the United States from coast to coast—New York City to Monterey Bay. The learners involved in these programs also cover a wide spectrum—from college freshmen to our country's senior Foreign Service Officers. These programs certainly have some major differences, but there are also some important commonalities. On the broadest philosophical level, we and our contributors all share a sincere commitment to creating an educational experience that connects our classrooms to the real world and provides our students with the opportunity to develop the skills to thrive on their own—that helps our nestlings spread their wings and fly away. Sternfeld (Chapter 3) uses a metaphor of "transformation" when he describes how his Italian CBI course aims at transforming his "caterpillars into butterflies." Each of the other authors, in his or her own way, articulates a desire to liberate learners from the boring old "crawl along" approaches and, instead, provide approaches that enable students to develop the coping skills, motivation, and self-confidence to spread their wings and soar beyond the classroom.

Many of today's foreign language teachers—certainly those of us who are proponents of CBI—see our central role not as deliverers of linguistic knowledge but as facilitators of communicative competence in learners. This "new goal" is to empower students to become autonomous learners. This happens most effectively when we tap into students' needs and motivations, help students to understand their own learning process, and allow them to take charge of their own learning from the very start.

We believe that CBI, more than any other "method," fosters these new roles and goals. CBI offers an opportunity to incorporate into one curriculum design (albeit with multiple permutations) all of the characteristics of the new paradigm for communicative language learning, while stressing the important role of foreign language in a shrinking global community.

The authors of the previous chapters have described eleven models in a range of settings that focus on the use of language in real-world tasks in cross-cultural settings. The adult students served in the nine foreign language programs were studying Arabic, French, Indonesian, Italian, Russian, Spanish, and Serbo-Croatian and ranged from "Novice" to "Advanced" on the ACTFL proficiency scale. The students described in the two foreign languages across the curriculum (FLAC) programs were students in a variety of disciplines who conducted their research in a foreign language.

These case studies provide models and methods for implementation of content approaches as well as insights into adult foreign language learning and acquisition processes. In this chapter we describe some of the characteristics of the models presented, discuss some of the insights provided by the authors, and summarize some of the implications for CBI.

We open our discussion by considering some ways in which the models address the three general criteria for CBI and the set of questions we postulated for each criterion in our introductory chapter.

Subject-Matter Core

The fundamental organization of the curriculum is derived from the subject matter, rather than from forms, functions, situations, or skills. Communicative competence is acquired during the process of learning about specific topics such as math, science, art, social studies, culture, business, history, political systems, international affairs, or economics.

Key Questions

- How can we build the necessary interdisciplinary foundation?
- How do we achieve the desired balance between language and content?
- Which subjects do we select and how do we sequence them?
- Who will teach the course, a language teacher, a content specialist, or both?
- How do we define and evaluate student learning outcomes?

All of the programs presented in this volume were organized around the study of subject matter rather than the study of grammar or language per se. However, the selection of subject matter and the manner in which it was presented varied widely depending on the objectives of each program and the needs of particular groups of learners.

Creating an Interdisciplinary Foundation

We and our former colleagues at the Foreign Service Institute, Ryding and Stowasser in Arabic (Chapter 5) and Chadran and Esarey in Indonesian (Chapter 10), chose "area studies" as our subject matter because the goal of FSI programs, in addition to language training, was to familiarize students with the geography, history, politics, economy, and culture of the area of the world to which they were assigned. This knowledge was as important to their professional and personal success in their assignments as was their proficiency in the language itself.

During the 1980s, when we were Language Training Supervisors at the FSI, the challenge of developing a curriculum based on the integration of area studies and language studies was greatly facilitated by the fact that there were already excellent area studies programs in place in the School of Area Studies. Collaboration between the School of Language Studies and the School of Area Studies was (and still remains) part of the institutional culture: all students and teachers in the Language School attended weekly lectures in English offered in the School of Area Studies, and those same topics were frequently discussed in the target language in follow-up classes in the School of Language Studies. Thus, the seeds for interdisciplinary cooperation had already been sown. They sprouted into the "area/language integration modules" that have been described by the FSI contributors.

The FSI programs were not the only models to combine the study of language with the study of area topics. Area/language integration was a major focus in Klahn's Mexican Topics course at Columbia University (Chapter 9) and Corin's Serbo-Croatian "conversion" course at the Defense Language Institute (DLI). At the DLI, however, traditional area studies shared priority with military themes, such as the organization and operations of the Army, and simulations in the field, such as the roadblock exercise that Corin describes in Chapter 4. Both these programs achieved an interdisciplinary foundation by finding language teachers who themselves were subject matter experts. Norma Klahn was a language teacher with the necessary content expertise, and Corin's team at the DLI were former academics, diplomats, soldiers, actors, and journalists.

Most of the other programs required a high level of interdisciplinary cooperation and coordination, as attested to by Klee and Tedick (Chapter

7), Straight (Chapter 11), and Shaw (Chapter 12). These authors observed that this interdisciplinary cooperation is in itself one of the benefits of implementing a CBI program. In these cases CBI did help to break down the "artificial barriers" between language and subject matter that were discussed in Chapter 1.

Balancing Language and Content

One of the first questions we must ask ourselves as we embark on a CBI curriculum is "What content do we teach?" Geography is often the topic of first choice. It is interesting to note that the FSI, DLI, and Columbia University programs emphasized the study of geography in the early phases of their CBI programs. Ryding and Stowasser (Chapter 5) say that they used geography as their main theme in the first two weeks of the FSI Arabic course because it 1) familiarized students with the topography and place names of the Middle East and Africa while 2) providing practice in hearing and reading Arabic words in familiar, understandable contexts.

Corin (Chapter 4) reiterates this view in his discussion of the use of geography in the first three weeks of the conversion course in Serbo-Croatian at the DLI. According to Corin, geography is a good beginning topic because it is highly visual, spatial, and contextual; it lends itself to the use of maps, charts, and realia, and the language tends to be descriptive in nature with use of the verb "to be," cognates, and proper names. We agree with Corin that geography is a logical choice to begin CBI because it is "cognitively undemanding and context-embedded language" (Cummins 1981) and as such, is especially suitable when the students' native language is not used to translate the meaning and the lessons must "speak for themselves."

Geography, however, is not the only way to start. Sternfeld's beginning Italian course (Chapter 3) uses aphorisms, proverbs and sayings from popular culture, and selections from children's literature. This emphasis on literacy skills reflects the goals of the program and the needs of the particular student population. Most students in the IM/ML Program are motivated to take foreign language courses only to fulfill a foreign language requirement and are not concerned about spoken fluency. Consequently, the Italian course places strong emphasis on literacy and "culturally broadening activities" rather than speaking skills. Sternfeld attempts to transform his "caterpillars into butterflies" by inviting them to become members of the "Italian Language and Literacy Club."

Vines (Chapter 6) uses the study of journalism as a vehicle for intermediate students of French at Ohio University. The content of her courses focuses on current events in the media as well as study of the media itself. Topics are often dictated by events and include current themes such as the environment, social problems, political elections, and AIDS. Vines developed a procedure for exploiting these topics that is representative of several others in this volume (the "CBI wheel" described by Stryker in Chapter 8, for example). She starts by selecting articles for which she prepares special vocabulary worksheets, then guides an introductory discussion on the topic. With this background, students view videos and prepare reports or lead discussions. Next, students go through a multistep procedure to research a topic, prepare and videotape interviews with native speakers, and, finally, write an article in French based on that interview. Students mentioned in their evaluations that the research-interview-reporting process was among the most valuable activities for improving all four language skills. Vines' strategy for getting her students to get out of the classroom and actually *do* something with the language provides a pedagogical model for any relatively advanced CBI course, not just for journalism students.

Klahn (Chapter 9) based her graduate Spanish course at Columbia University on the study of Contemporary Mexican Topics. She arranged thematic modules in a specific sequence that corresponded to the ACTFL guidelines and an "order of acquisition" suggested by these guidelines. For example, early topics included geography, history, and demography, which emphasize descriptive language accessible to students at the 1+/2 level. Topics from literature were held until students were near a 2+ level, and the more abstract topics, such as Mexican world view and U.S.-Mexican relations, were saved for last, when students were approaching a level 3. As in the scope and sequence of Vines' curriculum, Klahn's activities cover all four skills and are designed to become progressively more challenging over the semester. Aware that wrong choices can create frustration in students, Klahn was particularly concerned with careful sequencing of the content. For example, listening activities began with videotaped interviews on simple topics directed at a general audience and progressed toward more abstract films such as Buñuel's *Los Olvidados*. Reading activities started with descriptive narratives and news articles and evolved toward the more metaphorical language of poetry, songs, and editorials. Similarly, speaking and writing activities began with descriptive oral and written reports and moved toward more sophisticated interpretation, analysis, and debate on controversial topics. Newspapers, magazines, in-house videos, TV and film were the principal sources of content materials used.

Klee and Tedick (Chapter 7) describe not just a single course but an entire Spanish immersion program for language majors at the University of Minnesota. Intermediate language students study subjects such as "Politics and Cultural Expression," "Topics in International Relations," and "Foreign

Language News Coverage," rather than subjects like advanced phonology, morphology, syntax, or literature. Judging from the results that have been measured so far, the program is a success in meeting the dual goal of promoting language proficiency and new content knowledge.

In sum, it is crucial that, whatever the setting, the content of CBI courses be perceived as important, relevant, and useful to the learners. While economic theory and combat strategy might be a far reach for the typical university freshman (as well as totally irrelevant), they are reasonable topics for the Foreign Service Economics Officer and the Defense Attaché.

Content in FLAC

Content issues in foreign language across the curriculum differ somewhat from those described above. In FLAC programs the primary goal is not so much to learn a language as to *use* an already-known foreign language for the study of an academic subject. Certainly this basic concept is not new in a language/literature program (in which the two go hand in hand); however, it *is* new in an interdisciplinary setting.

Straight (Chapter 11) calls this interdisciplinary approach "language-based content instruction." He sees CBI more as a method of language instruction and FLAC more as a method of content instruction, although they do overlap in their fundamental approach. Both focus on meaning, move away from an emphasis on form, and require students to use language for understanding and self-expression—to test their linguistic wings.

As illustrated by the list of courses in Straight's Appendix A, FLAC programs can cover an infinite range of subjects. In the SUNY-Binghamton program, there are dozens of courses offering FLAC alternatives, both graduate and undergraduate, in more than twenty academic areas, from accounting to women's studies.

In the program at MIIS, described by Shaw (Chapter 12), graduate students who are already at an Intermediate level of proficiency take courses taught wholly or in part in a foreign language. Because the courses were designed for students in the International Policy program, they cover topics such as policy analysis, economics, and international relations. The courses are offered at Intermediate, High Intermediate, and Advanced levels. Students select, either by regional specialization or by topic, from courses such as "Social Movements in Latin America" and "Economic Development in the People's Republic of China." The goal of the program, in Shaw's words, is "to produce graduates who can do policy research in at least two languages." The near-equal emphasis placed on oral and literacy skills at MIIS sets this model apart from the SUNY-Binghamton models, in which reading is the principal skill.

Building the Scaffolding

The presentation of new information that students learn in their content courses varies greatly from program to program. Some of the programs depend on carefully designed scope and sequence that spirals and recycles content to facilitate student understanding. Others combine this strategy with the use of the native language to provide background knowledge.

The information presented in the FSI area/integration modules in Arabic, Indonesian, Russian, and Spanish, was not all new. FSI students had attended area studies lectures in English and were already familiar with at least some of the information. This procedure (reminiscent of the "preview-review" approach in bilingual education) greatly increased students' accessibility to new information and provided, in Ryding and Stowasser's term, "scaffolding" for students who could have been overwhelmed by so much input without background knowledge, especially in a language like Arabic.

In the beginning of the Basic Russian Program (Leaver, Chapter 2), students acquired background knowledge as they compared the differences in reportage between articles from the Russian press and the American press on the same topic. The Russian students were also given background readings in English, as in the case of the early presentations from *Mark Smith's Diary*. Teachers can exploit the knowledge base that students bring with them from other sources. Ryding and Stowasser (Chapter 5) explain that by linking native language content schemata (i.e., their area studies knowledge) to foreign language linguistic schemata (i.e., their emerging Arabic), students can build a foundation for processing new information through the medium of the foreign language. It is at this point that the scaffolding can be removed.

Student Readiness

Of course, most programs do not have the opportunity to construct content scaffolding through students' native language. Instead, any new information needs to be carefully selected so as to correspond to knowledge the students presumably already have and linguistic schemata from previous experience. For example, Corin's program for military personnel was built upon two basic assumptions: 1) that the student had transferable linguistic schema, i.e., another Slavic language, and 2) that the students had previous knowledge of military topics such as order of battle, rank and insignia, armored vehicles, first aid, arms, roadblocks, and interrogations.

Whether "scaffolding" is in place already or put into place through a prerequisite course in the student's native language we must deal with the important question of "student readiness" for a CBI program. If the students are not ready, in terms of both linguistic and cognitive schemata, they may be overwhelmed by the quantity of new information and may, ultimately, flounder. This problem was encountered in many of the programs presented in this volume. For example, in the FSI Spanish program, designed for students at an ILR level 2 proficiency, many students who entered that program with levels 1 and 1+ experienced frustration, and some even asked to be returned to a more structured, traditional classroom. In another example, Klee and Tedick found that students in their immersion program at Minnesota did well as long as their proficiency was at a certain "threshold." Students having a proficiency level lower than the ACTFL Intermediate High experienced "extreme frustration" in the Spanish immersion courses. One possible solution in a case like this is to lower the requirements and expectations of the students. The solution offered by Klee and Tedick is to ensure that students are given an "assessment battery" (described in Chapter 7) to determine their readiness to enter a High-Intermediate level program.

The concept of a "threshold," as used by Klee and Tedick (meaning, in this case, an appropriate level of readiness), does not imply that CBI is inappropriate for use at beginning levels of foreign language instruction. As we have seen in the cases of Italian, Russian, and Serbo-Croatian, CBI can be effective for beginning students as well. The key element in determining students' readiness is to ensure that the students' linguistic proficiency and cognitive schemata are adequate to perform successfully in the curriculum. The "fit" between students' readiness and the foreign language curriculum is, of course, important in any program, but it is especially important in CBI. If a gap exits, either missing schemata needs to be provided or students need to be kept from enrolling until they are "ready."

The Teachers

In order for CBI to work effectively and for students to be able to learn new subject matter while learning the language, the instructors must be more than just good language teachers. They must be knowledgeable in the subject matter and know how to elicit that knowledge from their students. This combination of skills is not often found in a single language instructor. A team-teaching approach offers definite advantages. The teaming pattern has varied considerably in our models. The FSI, DLI, and Monterey Institute of International Studies (MIIS) had teachers work in teams, often a content "expert" with a language instructor. In the FSI programs, the instructors acted as language teachers and "cultural informants," and guest lecturers were the "experts." In the DLI Serbo-Croatian conversion course, some of the instructors, who were also veterans of the military forces of the former Yugoslavia, acted as "experts." In courses at the MIIS, the content faculty taught their own subjects under the guidance of a language teacher, or vice-versa. In one unique variation—the Russian Advanced Course at FSI, mentioned by Leaver in Chapter 2 and the program in Uzbekistan mentioned in Chapter 1—the teachers were truly "facilitators of language acquisition," and the students themselves were the experts in a model reminiscent of a graduate studies program.

The multiteacher approach is not the sole formula for success. Single teacher approaches, as demonstrated by Sternfeld at the University of Utah, Klahn at Columbia University, Vines at Ohio University and Klee and Tedick at the University of Minnesota, can also be successful. Klahn notes that "an integrated course of this nature is difficult to deliver," because the instructor is required to integrate two fields that are traditionally separate departments at a university. The instructor, according to Klahn, must be knowledgeable about history, culture, literature and current events of the country and be an experienced language teacher and tester as well.

In cases in which a language teacher takes on a CBI course single-handedly but lacks the content knowledge, the acquisition of the necessary expertise is a major challenge. Vines, a French professor, became an expert on the French media by attending workshops and conferences and through reading on the topic, essentially "retraining" herself.

In answering their question "How do we best balance content and language learning?," Klee and Tedick underscore the importance of well-prepared instructors in the delivery of a successful CBI curriculum. They conclude that an instructor who is unwilling or unable to employ sheltered-content strategies can produce "devastating consequences." To avoid this, they have designed a series of training workshops on CBI methodology that all instructors are required to attend (see Chapter 7, Appendix A).

Shaw (Chapter 12), in his discussion of teacher preparation, identifies eight areas in which a teacher of sheltered content should have considerable expertise. Since these are essential skills for *any* CBI instructor, we highlight them below:

1) Varying the format of classroom instruction;
2) Using group work and team-building techniques;
3) Organizing jigsaw reading arrangements;
4) Defining the background knowledge and language skills required for student success;
5) Helping students develop coping strategies;
6) Using process approaches to writing;
7) Using appropriate error correction techniques, and
8) Developing and maintaining high levels of student self-esteem.

In addition to these specific pedagogical skills, CBI requires faith, high motivation, time, psychic energy, self-confidence, and multiple coping strategies on the part of the teacher.

Measuring Outcomes

When there is a dual focus on content and linguistic growth, defining and evaluating student learning outcomes becomes a more complicated task, both philosophically and pragmatically, than in traditional approaches. The questions concerning testing and evaluation that were discussed in Chapter 1 have no definitive answers yet. While "prochievement " tests are growing in popularity among CBI practitioners, there are still persistent questions concerning how to write and score them. Certainly the oral proficiency interview is the most valid and reliable test for oral skills, but it is also an expensive and time-consuming instrument. Although the oral proficiency interview may be one possible component of a comprehensive evaluation system, CBI requires a variety of measures. The best assessment system for CBI we have seen to date is presented by Klee and Tedick in Chapter 7. They provide a model for using a battery of tests that address student growth in all four language skills—listening, speaking, reading, and writing—as well as growth in content knowledge.

Use of Authentic Language and Texts

The core material—texts, videotapes, audio recordings, and visual aids—are selected primarily from those produced for native speakers of the language. Learning activities focus on understanding and conveying authentic messages and accomplishing realistic tasks using authentic language.

Key Questions

- How do we provide students with the appropriate authentic input?
- What are the appropriate activities and tasks to exploit this authentic input?
- How do we incorporate student schemata?
- What is the role of students' first language in coping with authentic language and texts ?

The use of authentic language and texts is one of the salient features of CBI. By "authentic" we mean that most or all of the language models and materials emanate from the culture being studied, rather than from sources especially prepared for students of the language. "Authentic texts" include books, newspapers, and magazines or any printed material from the culture. "Authentic language" takes many forms: a TV broadcast, a lecture, a fluent speaker conversing with another fluent speaker or a fluent speaker speaking to students in spontaneous conversation. All these represent what we would like to describe in the aggregate as "authentic input."

Providing Authentic Input

Typical authentic materials include newspapers, magazines, TV shows, radio programs, films, and the like. Some imaginative CBI instructors have even taken chapters from textbooks used to educate native speakers in K-12 public schools. For example, the Mexico Program at the FSI used excerpts from science, social studies, and history texts designed for use in Mexican grade schools. Sternfeld describes the use of a German world history text written for students in German high schools that is used in the German Immersion/Multiliteracy Program at the University of Utah. Similarly, the first-year French course in that same program uses a series of history books designed to be used in French elementary and high schools.

Using grade school or high school texts has a dual benefit. Such textbooks present simplified, yet authentic, input while providing students with insight into the world view of the culture being studied. For example, the students in the FSI Mexico Program were fascinated by the sharp contrast between the Mexican view of the Mexican-American War and the Treaty of Guadalupe and the version they had learned in the United States.

The use of "authentic materials," especially if the topics involve socioeconomics, politics, popular culture, or current events, eliminates the viability of using traditional textbooks in CBI, placing even more of a burden on instructors to find or produce relevant and interesting materials. Leaver, in describing the unsuccessful attempt in the FSI Russian Section to develop a CBI textbook, concludes that the most viable approach is to replace textbooks with an archive of authentic materials taken from a broad variety of sources, as was later done in the Slavic language programs at the DLI. In his discussion of materials for his "conversion course" at the DLI, Corin (Chapter 4) concludes that published textbooks are contrary to the very concept of CBI—and good language teaching in general. He lists a variety of materials including tourist guidebooks, technical journals, railway timetables, newspaper ads, radio broadcasts, and TV broadcasts (via SCOLA), and only rare use of "contrived pedagogical materials." He, as well as many of the other contributors, cites high levels of student motivation and outstanding test results as evidence that students can learn more from authentic materials than they can from a foreign language textbook.

Four-Handed Teaching

One of the unfortunate characteristics of most foreign language courses is that students are deprived of one of the most valuable sources of input for language acquisition in a natural setting—opportunities to hear native speakers interact with one another. In fact, in foreign language courses students rarely, if ever, hear two native speakers engage in real, spontaneous conversation. It has been our experience that the conversational exchanges that take place between two teachers in a "four-handed" teaching arrangement can help to provide this valuable source of authentic spoken input for students. By "four-handed" we mean that both teachers are in the room, conversing and interacting with each other constantly.

One characteristic of several of the CBI models was the effective use of "four-handed" team teaching. The success of the Russian and Spanish programs at the FSI and the Serbo-Croatian course at the DLI was linked closely to the presence and participation of two teachers in the classroom. Several of the students in the Mexico Program at the FSI commented in writing that the course would not have been nearly as effective had they not had the opportunity to be "constantly overhearing two native speakers interacting with each other." Klahn achieved nearly the same effect by having a series of Mexican guests in her class.

In sum, experience indicates that team-teaching implemented in the "four-handed teaching" mode can be an excellent source of authentic spoken input. (One caveat, however: it doesn't take the boss long to figure out that having two teachers in class will be twice the cost of having one, so the results better be impressive!)

Preparing the Materials

The time required to develop a library of "authentic materials," is significant—time in finding the materials, planning the scope and sequence of topics, updating the materials, and preparing activities to exploit them. Klahn, Shaw, Vines, Klee and Tedick, and Straight, all working with grant money, took weeks or months to prepare their materials. Preparation for the four-week Spanish Program at the FSI (about 120 instructional hours) required two instructors working full-time for six months, assisted by a professor of Mexican area studies from Georgetown University.

Moreover, the initial preparation of materials is only the beginning of the process. Since many of the themes in CBI deal with dynamic topics and current events, a portion of the materials has to be updated constantly, frequently using newspaper clippings from the very morning of class. Each of the contributors to this volume has made clear that the time and expense of materials development in a CBI course is a major challenge. Taking up this challenge requires a highly motivated and dedicated individual—or group of individuals.

"It's the Task, Not the Text"

If the selection and sequencing of the materials represents one of the most crucial decisions in a CBI program, an even more crucial issue is what the teacher does with those materials. Given authentic materials, students should be asked to accomplish authentic tasks, using higher order thinking skills and applying the cognitive skills they have acquired in content courses in their own language. Yet teachers sometimes feel daunted when giving materials prepared for native speakers to students who are at proficiency levels of 2 or lower. A typical teacher reaction is, "This material is too advanced for my students!" In this situation, the challenge to the teacher is to create a linguistically simple but cognitively challenging task that is at once realistic and interesting to the students. An imaginative CBI teacher should be able to use almost any piece of authentic material with students at any level successfully—by choosing the right task.

For example, Ryding and Stowasser (Chapter 5) in the Arabic course at the FSI used a process they call "recycling" of materials. A set of materials were used in the first few weeks with simple comprehension activities. The students were not expected to understand most of the text, nor were they to translate, but while listening to a text being read, they would 1) guess overall meaning from context, 2) listen for recognition of specific bits of information, and 3) acquire some basic vocabulary. Several weeks later, the identical set of materials were used with more advanced activities, which required students to locate and produce more specific information.

Corin combined the use of authentic materials and "task-based instruction" techniques throughout his Serbo-Croatian course at the DLI. For example, in a beginning lesson that used personal ads from a magazine, students were tasked with simply identifying the core information (name, address, age, gender, etc.). At a more advanced level, the same ads were used as models for students to compose their own personal ads seeking companionship. When the instructor read aloud the ads that the students had composed, students displayed "a most animated response" and "innovative language" in guessing who wrote which ad.

Several of the authors have concluded that the old idea of "graded texts" can be abandoned in CBI; however, thoughtful judgments must be made concerning the appropriateness of authentic texts—in both content and length. Bernhardt in "Proficient Texts or Proficient Readers?" (1986) points out that proficiency levels should be associated with student activities and not with the linguistic content of texts themselves. In other words: it's the task, not the text that counts. It is our firm conviction that almost any interesting and relevant authentic materials will work at any level of proficiency as long as the tasks that the students are required to perform are appropriate and meaningful; this, of course, is one of the basic tenets of effectively "sheltering the content."

Sheltering Content

For CBI to be successful, instructors must know how to shelter the content to make it accessible to the learners. Klee and Tedick related the case of one instructor (a graduate assistant) who strongly resisted the idea of sheltering content, thinking that it meant watering down the content of his course. Consequently, on the first day of class when he assigned 150 pages of reading in Spanish for the next day, there was a "near revolt" by the students. That teacher continued to resist using sheltered techniques and was reviewed negatively by the students. He violated all the guidelines for sheltering content: he assigned very long and dense readings, his class was entirely teacher-centered, his lectures were long and over the students' heads, he sought no feedback from students, used no cooperative learning techniques, and did not prepare reading guides. Fortunately, this extreme was not the norm. Most of the teachers were able to strike a good balance between language and content teaching. One teacher actually went a little too far in an effort to eschew the lecture mode. The students complained that there was not enough lecture from the teacher and they were not prepared to carry on discussion without more background information. Klee and Tedick conclude (as do most of the contributors) that the successful CBI instructors need to use a wide variety of sheltering activities that includes lectures, small- and large-group activities, student projects and presentations, invited speakers, and the use of all sorts of audio-visual aids.

The question of how much authentic text reading to assign is one of the crucial decisions in sheltering content. The key issue may not center on which readings to choose or how much reading to assign but what the students are expected to do with the reading. Shaw (Chapter 12) relates that many students at the MIIS complained about heavy reading loads. He suggests that readings might be "sheltered" by using jigsaw reading techniques, such as assigning sets of readings to pairs of students who are then given the responsibility of reporting to their colleagues in class. In a variation of this strategy, students are assigned specific portions of the readings and take turns leading a discussion on their assignment. He observes that students tend to read more under these conditions.

Shaw is a convincing advocate of the small-group format. However, he makes very clear that this format will only be effective if the tasks are clearly understood by the students. He notes that students felt more secure and that groups worked more effectively when they had specific tasks assigned and specific questions to answer.

We agree with Klee, Tedick, and Shaw—*it's the task!* The success of CBI programs depends on the ability to shelter content appropriately. When teachers complain that CBI is beyond the students' reach or that authentic materials cannot be used until the highest levels of proficiency, it is often because they have not yet learned how to shelter content.

The "Grammar" Question

Sometimes enthusiastic foreign language teachers embark on CBI experiments with the assumption that students can "acquire" grammatical competence in the foreign language while doing exactly the same kinds of activities that they would do in any subject matter class: reading articles, listening to lectures, presenting oral reports, working on individual or group projects, taking quizzes on the material, etc., without any special attention to formal grammar. However, many of us who, in our initial enthusiasm for CBI, minimized or removed the formal study of grammar, found that our adult students wanted—and needed—to deal with grammar in an explicit, deductive manner. This reality should be recognized before eliminating the study of grammar from any CBI program for adults and represents one of the more interesting "lessons learned" in these chapters.

Corin (Chapter 4) articulates this point clearly in his discussion of student learning styles and strategies. He points out that there are students—"analytical types"—who flourish in the traditional courses based on the study of grammar through exercises, translation, and memorization of vocabulary. This kind of student may encounter problems with the opposite (inductive) approach found in a CBI course. On the other hand, the global learner will thrive in this environment. The analytical learners in his conversion program experienced frustration when needing to communicate using structures they did not completely control. Corin thinks that much frustration could have been avoided if more analytical study had been built into the program from the beginning. When analytical study was initiated, including the formal study of grammar and translation of journalistic articles into English, there were "rapid and noticeable increases" in the accuracy of some students. Corin concludes that in holistic task-based and content-based programs, which give an advantage to global learners, teachers must assume responsibility for providing atomistic activities that appeal to and develop the skills of analytic learners.

Stryker and his team in Spanish (Chapter 8) learned this same lesson during the pilot phase of their Mexico Program. After having planned the near elimination of formal study of grammar they found that the students demanded, and benefited from, formal grammatical study and analysis. A formal grammatical analysis component was added to the module design. Stryker concludes that literate adult learners differ from child learners in that most educated adults perceive a need for the explicit study of grammar.

Tracy Terrell, who earlier in his career had discouraged the teaching of grammar in favor of the "acquisition process," argues exactly this same point in his 1991 article, observing that "explicit knowledge of grammatical relationships in the target language can be helpful to some learners in the acquisition process itself." (54)

In considering these experiences, it would appear that grammar does play a significant role in both adult language acquisition and language learning, and, therefore, it should be addressed in a CBI curriculum. The issue is not whether to teach grammar, but *how* and *when* to teach it. If we are sensitive to students' learning preferences and to their responses to the curriculum, we can use our own judgment on just how, when, and how much explicit grammar to teach.

The Use of English

The extent to which the students' first language should be used in the foreign language classroom is a hotly debated issue, not just in CBI but in second language acquisition in general. The use of the students' native language would clearly distress some "target language purists." Many CBI foreign language teachers are proponents of exclusive use of the foreign language in the classroom, and in the strictest cases, no use of the native language is allowed.

The Russian courses at the FSI, described by Leaver (Chapter 2), are representative of this extreme. The exclusive use of Russian was a requirement of the program, with all communication, including administrative memoranda, taking place in Russian. All teachers were native speakers of Russian, and some had little proficiency in English.

The philosophy of the Russian Section is that the teacher provides a model by maintaining a "persona" of one who speaks only the target language. If a teacher uses the students' native language to do some of the "essential communication," such as giving instructions, and bases much of the learning on translation, then the subliminal message is that the native language is for communicating "meaning" and the foreign language is the object of "study." Furthermore, students use their native language as a crutch, and the motivation to use the foreign language dissipates.

In less strict classrooms, where "immersion" is not necessarily as strongly advocated, teachers might use students' native language sparingly as a source of support for the foreign language in a variety of ways. One effective technique, practiced in some of the FSI programs and Sternfeld's Italian course, is not to *prohibit* the use of English but to let students at lower proficiencies use their native language to ask questions while the teacher responds only in the foreign language

A common technique in CBI classes is to use readings on relevant topics in the students' native language to support readings and activities in the foreign language. All the programs in this volume have done this to some extent, with FLAC, of course, reversing this: readings in the foreign language support the reading and study in the students' native language. In his Italian course, Sternfeld (Chapter 3) uses English language readings quite extensively to lay down schemata for his lessons, as well as to "stimulate students' reflection on the language learning process." He, however, speaks only Italian in his classroom. In all the FSI models, including Russian, there were cases in which readings on area studies topics were provided in English. Leaver (Chapter 2), taking an occasional step away from "pure immersion" in the Russian curriculum, used a task requiring a "contrastive analysis" of content and structure of English and Russian newspaper and television reports on the same events to provide students with "insights into the Russian ethos." Even in Klee and Tedick's Spanish immersion program (Chapter 7), in which all the courses are taught exclusively in Spanish, there are readings in English to supplement the required readings in Spanish.

When authentic printed materials are in languages in which the script is either not phonetic or does not correspond to the spoken language, a convincing argument can be made for introducing some content matter in English and using English as a "bridge" into the language. Arabic, for example, is diglossic. The written language differs so much from the spoken language that the two are not mutually intelligible. Ryding and Stowasser (Chapter 5) use this point to explain why Arabic instructors should start with "oral texts" (i.e., only spoken Arabic) and use only limited and simplified texts for beginning students of Arabic. Some Asian languages, notably Chinese, Korean, and Japanese, which are not phonetic, require students to learn many characters before they are able to begin deciphering written texts. While romanization can help, if students are ultimately to use authentic materials, they are going to have to cope with characters.

In such cases the purpose of using the students' native language in the classroom or for readings is to provide background knowledge— scaffolding—to help students build the schema essential for coping with authentic materials and facilitate the learning of new information. However, in no case was English used as a medium of classroom instruction classroom.

In conclusion, the use of a wide variety of authentic texts, in whatever combination of foreign language and the students' native language, has been a major factor in the success of all the CBI models presented in the previous chapters. Shaw (Chapter 12) eloquently summarizes our own feelings, when he notes that students benefit from, as well as enjoy, challenging authentic materials that are "varied and abundant."

Appropriate to the Needs of Specific Students

The topics, content, materials, and learning activities correspond to the linguistic, cognitive, and affective needs of the students and are appropriate to their professional needs and personal interests.

Key Questions:
- How do we make an accurate needs assessment?
- How do we ensure that students are cognitively, linguistically, and affectively prepared for the program?
- How can we accommodate the widest possible range of learner profiles?
- How do we deal with error correction to maximize learning and motivation?
- How can we use student input to ensure ongoing evaluation and adjustment?

A thorough assessment of students' needs, and an ongoing evaluation of the learning outcomes, should guide the choice of subject matter and the selection of authentic texts. CBI teachers need to be constantly aware of the interplay between the content of the course and the knowledge, skills, abilities, learning styles, and emotional states of the students.

Needs Assessment
The first step in meeting the needs of students is, of course, to determine what those needs are. Several of the contributors to this book describe the kinds of needs assessments they undertook. In general, information was obtained from future, current, and former students. Field analyses of jobs were done in those cases where language instruction could be fully correlated with job performance, as was the case at the FSI and the DLI, and to some extent the MIIS. Determination of student learning styles and affective variables should be an equally important part of a needs assessment. While the needs assessment may initially be little more than an educated guessing,

the assessment process must continue to monitor students' linguistic, cognitive, and affective growth as well as their responses to the curriculum. Flexibility and willingness to adjust or change are necessary qualities in a CBI instructor.

Cognitive and Linguistic Readiness

A CBI program requires constant monitoring of both teacher input and student output in order to determine students' linguistic and cognitive readiness. Shaw isolates four "key conditions" associated with identifying student readiness for activities in a CBI course : 1) requisite background knowledge; 2) adequate language proficiency; 3) minimal analytic and thinking skills; and 4) clear understanding of the instructional process. These key conditions imply the need for assuring students' readiness through assessment batteries, such as those as suggested by Klee and Tedick, as well as the need to provide a thorough orientation for students in what Shaw suggests be called "learner training workshops." Of course, workshops for CBI teachers are equally important so teachers know how to choose materials and tasks that match students' linguistic and cognitive schemata— or at least, know how to provide the scaffolding to develop the requisite schemata.

Learner Profiles

Designing an effective CBI course also involves consideration of student learning styles, adjusting instruction accordingly, and assisting students in developing an ever-wider range of learning strategies (Oxford 1990; Leaver and Oxford 1993). For example, Corin sensed the frustration felt by analytic students being taught through learning tasks that required more synthesis than analysis. To compensate, he added optional grammar practice drills on the computer, as well as translation. The analytic students profited from using these additional materials. Likewise, Stryker's team added blocks of grammar study and linguistic analysis in response to overwhelming demand from the FSI Spanish students (the majority of whom are analytic learners).

Students who need instruction that matches their learning style frequently are those who have limited learning strategies. CBI teachers, through the use of a broad spectrum of tasks, can assist students in developing greater learning style flexibility through the acquisition of a wider range of learning strategies. An example of this is the "4-MAT" approach used by Chadran and Esarey (Chapter 10). In this model each area studies lesson is divided into eight sections; each section addresses a different learning style, along with its attendant array of learning strategies. In choosing the 4-MAT design, Chadran and Esarey focus on two specific learning style domains: brain hemisphericity (which has two learner types: left-hemisphere dominant and right-hemisphere dominant) and the four Kolb learner types. Each class hour, then, includes activities and, thereby, learning strategies associated with eight different learning styles. Seven of the eight kinds of activities represent non-preferred styles and require students to develop a wider range of learning strategies in order to complete the assigned tasks.

Froumina and Khasan (1994) found that students who have a greater range of learning strategies also have a greater tolerance of ambiguity—one of the most valuable strategies that a second or foreign language student can develop. Ehrman (1996) lists tolerance of ambiguity as one of the essential learning characteristics required for what she calls "open country" classrooms, that is, classrooms characterized by open-ended conversations and tasks related to the use of authentic materials for reading and listening. In general, both CBI and FLAC programs tend to be "open country" approaches. For example, the kinds of tasks used by Vines in her French journalism course represent "open country" for students: students with a lower tolerance of ambiguity are helped in developing requisite strategies for dealing with such situations during the course through advance organizers, rehearsal, preparation of projects that are critiqued and returned for revision, and the opportunity to clarify (i.e., alleviate the ambiguity) through repeated trial and error. Students with low tolerance of ambiguity are further helped through such techniques as establishing an order in advance for questioning guest lecturers and pre-task research. Vines finds this combination to be motivating and successful for her students: " The results have been excellent. I never cease to be impressed by the amount of effort the students are willing to make, and they are proud of the results."

One of the reasons that students in Vines' class reacted with enthusiasm to "open country" research projects is that they themselves selected the research topics according to their own interests. Encouraging students to work with topics of their own choosing is a strategy repeated in all the models described in this book. For example, the Russian Advanced Course mentioned by Leaver not only required students to select the topics to be studied in the course but allowed students to determine how much time would be allotted to each topic; thus, each Advanced Course was different from previous courses. Even in the Russian Basic Program, students selected their own conference and research topics.

The strategy of involving learners in key decisions concerning the content and format of the course, helps to put the learners in charge of their own learning from the very start—even while still in the nest.

Encouraging Linguistic Risk-Taking

To take charge of their own learning, students need to develop coping skills. Tolerance of ambiguity is one of the vital coping skills. CBI in the hands of an expert can help learners to develop the needed tolerance for ambiguity and to develop strategies for coping with large quantities of unknown information. While some students are initially frustrated by this "global learning" process, they can, with practice and guidance, develop a wider range of learning strategies such as skimming and scanning skills, looking for context clues, guessing at meaning, and using conversation management techniques.

Unfortunately, the traditional practice of linguistically "spoon-feeding" students and always keeping the foreign language input to small, manageable chunks, is not necessarily conducive to developing the coping skills that are needed to function in the real world. If the input is artificially kept to only small chunks at a time, then the learner can easily choke, especially if the learner has become accustomed to depending on translation to get the meaning. In other words, a steady diet of a piecemeal, analytical approach will not foster the development of global coping skills or strategic competence in learners. Teachers who depend on such approaches (either as the result of training or lack of it) often discourage student risk-taking by paying too much attention to errors.

Error Correction

The development of learners' strategic competence, as well as motivation, can be retarded by teachers who, however well-meaning, overemphasize the importance of grammatical competence. Just as students can feel intimidated by a large quantity of authentic reading material, they can be equally intimidated by constant correction of their spoken or written errors. Shaw observes that the most "virulently negative comments" from MIIS students involved teachers who corrected students' spoken errors in obtrusive ways. Shaw recommends that overtly correcting errors be "strictly avoided" since it contributes "little or nothing to the development of proficiency and has a strong adverse effect on the emotional atmosphere and on individual students' confidence and willingness to participate."

On the other hand, there are some students, particularly the "analytical type" learners described by Corin, who want to be corrected and experience increasing insecurity when their hypotheses are not quickly confirmed. The most important question in error correction may not necessarily be *what* to correct or *when* to correct, but *whom* to correct. For example, field dependent learners (students who learn from context) and global students (those who focus on message rather than form) frequently misspeak, even when they have already acquired a grammatical form. Correcting their errors is, at best, annoying and rarely leads to more accurate production. However, correcting the errors of field independent learners (students who learn from dissecting text) and analytic students (those who focus on erudition of expression) does result in improved production. Our observation is that teachers who take into account the learning styles and affective needs of their students find themselves matching their correction techniques to individual student need. Stryker's team in the FSI Spanish Program, on the recommendations of students themselves, developed an interesting self-correction technique for addressing errors in speech. Each student made an audiotape of his or her own five-minute oral presentation, took the tape home, listened to it several times (often choosing to transcribe it), made notes on the errors, and came to class the next day to discuss those errors. Much of the grammatical analysis and "error correction" in the Mexico curriculum was accomplished through this procedure. The highly analytical students—most of the FSI students—loved this activity.

Related to the issue of appropriate error correction in speaking is the question of how to deal with errors in students' writing. When students are graded or evaluated on a single, final, written paper, which is later returned full of red marks, students feel resentful and instructors disappointed with the students' writing ability. This is clearly a lose-lose situation. Shaw has an excellent suggestion for dealing with this problem: the use of peer response and a multidraft editing process. This kind of "process writing" approach was used successfully in the FSI Russian programs described by Leaver (Chapter 2) for the preparation of student year-end term papers.

In sum, the ways by which a teacher corrects errors is one of the most crucial factors in the development of learners' self-confidence and, ultimately, their communicative competence. Unfortunately, too many of us can still remember being "shot down," or at least having our wings clipped, by an overzealous, and frequently intimidating, foreign language teacher.

Student Input

For CBI programs to meet the needs of students, there must be a mechanism for ongoing program evaluation and the flexibility to make adjustments based on student input. Many of the programs discussed in this volume made extensive but judicious use of student input. All of the authors demonstrated willingness to change and improvise; this was especially the case among the FSI and DLI instructors, who were, in many cases, making up the curriculum from day to day, depending on where the students were taking them. All of the programs requested and responded to student evaluations. In addition, Klee and Tedick and Shaw collected information from student journals and personal interviews. Major changes were made in several of these programs in response to student comments and recommendations. Involvement in the Russian curriculum at FSI did not end when the students left the program. Many former students continued to locate and provide materials for the CBI course to help the students who followed them.

Conclusions of the "Believers": The Advantages of CBI

Overall, the authors represented in these chapters—all of whom are unapologetic believers in CBI—have found that their CBI programs, although more difficult to design, implement, and maintain than traditional programs, have a worthwhile "payoff." We perceive that "payoff" to encompass three broad areas: 1) enhanced motivation and self-confidence, 2) enhanced foreign language proficiency, and 3) enhanced cultural literacy.

Enhanced Student Motivation

Student reactions to the CBI experiments in this volume and elsewhere indicate that if the program meets students' linguistic, cognitive, and affective needs, motivation is enhanced (noting, however, if the content is too far over their heads, their motivation will suffer). All of the authors note that CBI increased the level of students' interest. Corin observes that "more permanent, less ephemeral learning" can be achieved when there is genuine student interest. He found that the combination of content- and task-based instruction achieved this in his successful experiment in Serbo-Croatian at the DLI.

Stryker and Klahn both quote students who describe how much more they were motivated to learn Spanish when "real issues" became the focus of study instead of the "contextual vacuum and boredom" they had experienced with previous methods. Many students in the FSI Spanish Program expressed downright enthusiasm. Similar enthusiasm was noted in students who were interviewed on their experience in a Czech CBI course at the DLI. They said that the course was "fun," it helped them to "learn more with less pain," and created a situation in which they "couldn't help but to learn" (Duri 1992).

Lois Vines (Chapter 6) observes that her courses in French for journalism students at Ohio University have helped to stimulate enrollment in upper division French courses. Many of those who continue on are journalism and communication students who have been motivated by her journalism courses. Vines concludes: "Content-based courses in the French media have been very successful in motivating students and giving them self-confidence in their comprehension and speaking skills."

Enhanced Self-Confidence

Evidence presented in these chapters suggests that CBI can have positive effects on self-confidence and risk-taking. Leaver observes that in the Russian programs many students, by constantly using their new foreign language and cultural literacy skills to accomplish real tasks, appeared to develop more confidence in their ability to use the language. We suggest that CBI courses can foster the development of "strategic competence"— coping strategies and conversation management skills. A good example of the early development of strategic competence is illustrated in the anecdote related by Corin in which a student, after only four weeks of study, answered the telephone speaking in Serbo-Croatian and, without hesitation, successfully transcribed a message from a native speaker calling from Belgrade. Corin found the most striking aspect of this event to be that "the student reacted with no apparent surprise and no hesitation."

Leaver describes activities undertaken by the Russian Section that built upon and enhanced students' self-confidence to use Russian in a realistic, professional setting. For example, her Advanced Course students delivered lectures in Russian to the Washington area Russian community, Basic Program students assisted non-English-speaking immigrants with education, citizenship, legal, and general living issues, and students in both programs conducted a professional conference attended by the local Russian community. The self-confidence that resulted from these kinds of risk-taking activities created a willingness on the part of the students to take even greater risks—"success breeds success."

We see two important caveats here. First, students must be ready for the experience (i.e., ready to "test their wings"). If they are not ready, cognitively, linguistically, or emotionally, they may fail. Second, teachers must be willing to avoid excessive error correction, i.e., to find the right balance of freedom and control. Unfortunately, in many foreign language classrooms (including those that claim to be models of "teaching for proficiency" or a "communicative approach") students are, in fact, discouraged from taking risks by teachers who constantly interrupt to make corrections. Students in such an atmosphere soon lose their confidence and do not take risks for fear of failure, and, as success can breed success, failure can breed failure.

General Foreign Language Proficiency

Several of the programs described in this volume indicate that CBI can accelerate foreign language proficiency. The statistics presented for the FSI programs are particularly impressive. When CBI was introduced into the FSI Russian program, the percentage of students reaching speaking and reading levels of ILR-3 ("professional proficiency") in a ten-month period rose dramatically. Stryker observes that when the Spanish Section introduced CBI at the end of its twenty-four-week basic course, statistical results showed average increases in speaking and reading scores that were significantly higher than the norms for Spanish training. Similarly, Klahn observes that the Columbia University students, on the average, gained one full point on the ACTFL proficiency scale after just one semester of her intensive CBI course. The written comments in both the FSI and Columbia University Spanish programs indicated that the students themselves thought their proficiency had increased substantially. Chadran and Esarey indicate three areas of proficiency gain as measured on the FSI proficiency test: 1) higher scores than their predecessors in the final oral proficiency interviews, 2) significant improvement in the areas of breadth of vocabulary and general discourse competence, and 3) significant improvement in listening comprehension ability.

Students in Corin's Serbo-Croatian conversion course achieved unusually high proficiency levels for a ten-week program in a Slavic language. About 40 percent of the students reached an ILR level 2 in speaking and 5 percent reached level 3. Leaver observes that similar or better results were achieved in a DLI Ukrainian conversion course in 1992 in which 88 percent of the students reached an ILR level 3 in listening, reading, and speaking in four months of half-time study. In both of these cases, the students started at ILR level 0.

It is interesting and ironic to note that the very government agencies that spent so much time and money to develop content-based models and techniques—FSI and DLI—did not ever test for students' content knowledge. The only instrument used at FSI and DLI was the ILR oral proficiency test, which is not specific to any geographical area, subject matter, or content. Our own explanation for this irony (having worked as supervisors in those two institutions) is that the value of the content was simply taken for granted. Since the course content corresponded to the knowledge that students' professions required, it was seen as a logical vehicle for the teaching and learning of language.

Content mastery was addressed in the university programs, in which efforts were made to measure *both* the increase in language proficiency and the gains in content learning. Klee and Tedick, who designed and administered truly comprehensive assessments of the first two years of their Spanish immersion program, found that there were measurable language proficiency gains as well as gains in subject-matter knowledge.

Cultural Literacy

The outcomes of these experiments also suggest that a CBI curriculum, when focused strongly on sociopolitical and cultural information and cross-cultural literacy skills, can provide students with a significant short-cut to cultural literacy that might normally take months or even years of living "in-country" to achieve. The feedback received from Foreign Service personnel who studied in the FSI Spanish program and were posted to Mexico, was very favorable in this respect. One senior Foreign Service Officer, who was interviewed in 1988 in Mexico City, said that the most useful and valuable cultural information she learned during her six months at the FSI was from the CBI Mexico Program.

Similarly, students in the FSI Indonesian program reported that they felt more comfortable using Indonesian in work-related and cultural situations as a result of activities associated with the CBI modules. Chadran and Esarey report that the "culture shock" typically experienced by newly posted diplomats was reduced for graduates of the CBI program.

Leaver describes the reaction of one student who was posted to Leningrad as consul general. Having gone through the CBI Advanced Course in which he studied Russian political protocol, he reported that he was very comfortable conducting a meeting with members of the Executive Council (city council) of Leningrad and realized that excellent progress had been made. Without his CBI training, he commented, he would have been "devastated," thinking that no progress had been made, because he would not have understood the differences in Russian and American political thinking and behavior.

Through the "exit interviews" that Klee and Tedick used to evaluate the outcomes of their Spanish immersion program, they learned that most students felt that they had learned much about Latin American culture and society. One reported changing her views on American society and "discovering bias in U.S. news coverage."

Many Foreign Service Officers, in exit interviews from the area studies modules at the FSI, expressed a view that we paraphrase here: even if the CBI curriculum itself were not responsible for the significant proficiency gains that were measured (i.e., had the same gains been made in the regular program), the students still benefited greatly from the wealth of geographic, historical, political, economic, and cultural knowledge they gained in the program.

Requirements for CBI: Some Lessons Learned

The advantages of CBI described above have come at a cost—increased time, expense, and, in many cases, considerable logistical obstacles. These challenges have been described frankly by all of our contributors and include several conditions that must be met to establish and maintain a CBI program:

- Strong initial and continuing administrative support;
- Stable financial and physical resources;
- A faculty passionately dedicated to the philosophy of CBI;
- A faculty skilled in CBI strategies;
- Continued access to authentic materials;
- Students who are cognitively, linguistically and affectively prepared; and
- A system to assess and monitor program outcomes.

All of the authors have agreed that administrative support and leadership are essential for the initiation and the survival of CBI programs. Lack of support often hinders the development or continuity of CBI programs. Several of the successful programs described in the previous chapters have been either scaled down or eliminated due to lack of funding to maintain them. For example, of the programs described at the Foreign Service Institute, only the Indonesian program is still viable in the mid-nineties. The CBI modules in Spanish, Arabic, and Russian have been reduced to a minimum, due in part to the loss of continuing administrative support (i.e., funding cutbacks) and in part to the departure of the supervisors who were dedicated to the concept. Conversion courses at the DLI continue to be offered as the need arises.

The experiments at MIIS and Columbia University were initially financed by grants from the Pew Charitable Trusts. When the initial funds were expended, the multimodel program at MIIS atrophied. At Columbia University the CBI course Klahn established with grant funding is continuing in the hands of another instructor, and the course has been emulated in Russian. Many FLAC programs, as well as the current Spanish immersion program at Minnesota, were also funded by grants and, although they are still viable, their future without outside funding is not certain.

The faculty of all the programs described in this volume had strong dedication to the philosophy of CBI. As a result, they went to great lengths to acquire any new skills needed, e.g., Vines retrained herself as a content expert (Chapter 6) and Corin helped teachers acquire CBI teaching strategies (Chapter 4).

Access to a continuing supply of fresh authentic materials also represents both a challenge and a need. In some cases, innovation is required to establish such a supply. For example, Leaver (Chapter 2) relates how during the Cold War days, the FSI Russian Section relied on assistance from previous students who were assigned to the American Embassy in Moscow and on the cultural affairs staff of the embassy of the USSR in Washington!

The most successful students were those who had strong content knowledge and language proficiency at the level required by course tasks and materials and who understood the rationale for the course. Students who were prepared for the CBI programs succeeded and later became strong advocates of CBI.

While many of the programs described in this volume did not have strong assessment systems, so that the real successes of students were not adequately documented, most felt a need for them. In programs that retrenched under new management, we can but wonder whether a system that had recorded program outcomes in greater detail might have convinced some new administrators that the benefits exceeded the costs.

In Conclusion

When all the pros and cons are considered, content-based instruction offers a challenging but highly rewarding alternative to traditional foreign language approaches. We and all our contributors agree with Corin that, in the long run, CBI is "worth the payoff." We see that payoff coming when our students leave our classrooms empowered to become autonomous learners, or in other words, when our nestlings can fly from the nest and soar off across the horizon on their own wings.

∽∾ ∽∾

Stephen Stryker, Professor of English, TESOL Director, and Adjunct Lecturer in Spanish at California State University, Stanislaus, was Head of the Spanish Language Training Section at the Foreign Service Institute in Washington, D.C., from 1984 to 1990. Address: Department of English, CSU, Stanislaus, 801 W. Monte Vista, Turlock, CA 95382. (E-mail: stryker@toto.csustan.edu)

Betty Lou Leaver, President of the American Global Studies Institute in Salinas, California since 1993, served as Dean of the School of Central European Languages and Dean of the School of Slavic Languages at the Defense Language Institute from 1989-1993. From 1983 to 1989 she was Russian Language Training Supervisor at the Foreign Service Institute. Address: AGSI, 2 Rex Circle, Salinas, CA 93906. (E-mail: leaver@agsi.org, leaver@glasnet.ru)

Bibliography

Abrate, Jayne. 1987. "Commercial French in a Liberal Arts Setting." *Proceedings of the Fifth Annual Eastern Michigan Conference on Languages for Business and the Professions*. Unpublished document.

Adamson, Hugh Douglas. 1993. *Academic Competence: Theory and Classroom Practice: Preparing ESL Students for Content Courses*. White Plains, NY: Longman.

Aida, Yukie. 1994. "Examination of Horwitz, Horwitz, and Cope's Construct of Foreign Language Anxiety: The Case of Students of Japanese."*Modern Language Journal* 78: 155-168.

Aliev, Nizami and Betty Lou Leaver. 1994. "A New Age in Two Lands: The Individual and Individualism in Foreign Language Instruction." In: Anon., *Learner-Centered Instruction: Collected Articles by Faculty and Friends of the American Global Studies Institute*. Salinas, CA: AGSI Press.

Allen, J. P. B., James Cummins, B. Harley, and Merrill Swain, eds. 1987. *The Development of Bilingual Proficiency*. Toronto: Modern Language Centre, Ontario Institute for Studies in Education.

Allen, J. P. B. and Joan Howard. 1981. "Subject-Related ESL: An Experiment in Communicative Language Teaching." *Canadian Modern Language Review* 37: 535-550.

Allen, Wendy, Keith Andersen, and Leon Narváez. 1992. "Foreign Languages Across the Curriculum: The Applied Foreign Language Component." *Foreign Language Annals* 25: 11-19.

_____. 1993. "Foreign Languages Across the Curriculum." In: John W. Oller, ed., *Methods That Work: Ideas for Literacy and Language Teachers*. Boston: Heinle and Heinle.

Altman, Rick. 1989. *The Video Connection: Integrating Video into Languaqe Teaching*. Boston: Houghton Mifflin Co.

Anderson, JoAnn, N. Eisenberg, J. Holland, H.S. Wiener, with C. Rivera-Kro. 1983. *Integrated Skills Reinforcement: Reading, Writing, Speaking and Listening Across the Curriculum*. White Plains, NY: Longman.

Angelis, Paul J. 1982. *Language Skills in Academic Study*. Princeton, NJ: Educational Testing Service.

Anivan, Sarinee, ed. 1990. *Language Teaching Methodology for the Nineties*. Singapore: SEAMO Regional Language Centre.

Asher, James J. 1988. *Learning Another Language through Actions: The Complete Teacher's Guidebook*. 3d ed. Los Gatos, CA: Sky Oaks Productions.

Benesch, Sarah, ed. 1988. *Ending Remediation: Linking ESL and Content in Higher Education*. Washington, DC: TESOL.

Bernhardt, Elizabeth B. 1984. "Toward an Information Processing Perspective in Foreign Language Reading." *Modern Language Journal* 68: 322-31.

_____. 1986. "Proficient Texts or Proficient Readers?" *ADFL Bulletin* 18: 25-28.

Bilateral Language Conference Report. 1992. Washington, DC: USGPO.

Bloom, Allan D. 1987. *The Closing of the American Mind*. New York: Simon and Schuster.

Breiner-Sanders, Karen E. 1991. "Higher Level Language Abilities: The Skills Connection." In: June K. Phillips, ed., *Building Bridges and Making Connections*. South Burlington, VT: The Northeast Conference on the Teaching of Foreign Languages.

Brinton, Donna and Peter Master. In press. N*ew Ways in Content-Based Instruction*. Alexandria, VA: TESOL.

Brinton, Donna, Marguerite Ann Snow, and Marjorie B. Wesche. 1989. *Content-Based Second Language Instruction*. New York: Newbury House Publishers.
_____. 1993. "Content-Based Second Language Instruction" In: John W. Oller, ed., *Methods That Work: Ideas for Literacy and Language Teachers*. Boston: Heinle & Heinle.

Brown, H. Douglas. 1994. *Principles of Language Learning and Teaching*. Englewood Cliffs, NJ: Prentice Hall.

Brown, J. Marvin and Adrian S. Palmer. 1988. *The Listening Approach: Methods and Materials for Applying Krashen's Input Hypothesis*. White Plains, NY: Longman.

Buck, Kathryn, Heidi Byrnes, and Irene Thompson, eds. 1989. *ACTFL Oral Proficiency Interview Tester Trainer Manual*. Yonkers, NY: American Council on the Teaching of Foreign Languages.

Burger, S. 1989. "Content-Based ESL in a Sheltered Psychology Course: Input, Output and Outcomes." *TESL Canada Journal* 6: 45-59.

Burger, S., M. Chrétien, M. Gringas, P. Hauptmann, and M. Migneron. 1984. "Le Role Du Professeur de Langue Dans un Cours De Matiere Académique en Langue Seconde." *Canadian Modern Language Review* 41: 397-402.

Campbell, Christine M. 1996. "Language Testing Today: An Overview of the Most Commonly Used Test Types." *ACTR Letter* 12: 1-2, 4-6, 11.

Campbell, Christine M. and Jose Ortiz. 1987. "Dispelling Students' Fears and Misconceptions about Foreign Language Study: The Foreign Language Anxiety Workshop at the Defense Language Institute." Paper presented at the ACTFL Conference in Atlanta.

Canale, Michael. 1983. "From Communicative Competence to Communicative Language Pedagogy." In: J. Richards and R. Schmidt, eds., *Method: Approach, Design, Procedure*. Cambridge: Cambridge University Press.

Canale, Michael and Merrill Swain. 1980. "Theoretical Bases of Communicative Approaches to Second Language Teaching and Testing." *Applied Linguistics* 1: 1-47.

Cantoni-Harvey, Gina. 1987. *Content Area Language Instruction: Approaches and Strategies*. Reading, MA: Addison-Wesley.

Chamot, Anna U. and J. Michael O'Malley. 1986. *A Cognitive Language Learning Approach: An ESL Content-Based Curriculum*. Wheaton, MD: The National Clearinghouse for Bilingual Education.
_____. 1987. "The Cognitive Language Learning Approach: A Bridge to the Mainstream." *TESOL Quarterly* 21: 227-249.

Chomsky, Noam. 1965. *Aspects of the Theory of Syntax*. Cambridge, MA: MIT Press.

Christensen, Ben. 1990. "Teenage Novels of Adventure as a Source of Authentic Material." *Foreign Language Annals* 23: 531-537.

Clancey, Henry, Timothy Miller, Johanna Munson, Jennifer Nobis and Stephanie Stauffer. 1990. *With One Stone*. Needs Analysis Project, Monterey Institute of International Studies. Unpublished manuscript.

Cohen, Andrew. 1976. "The Case for Partial or Total Immersion Education." In: A. Simocs, ed., *The Bilingual Child*. New York: Academic Press.

Corin, Andrew. 1994. "Teaching for Proficiency: The Conversion Principle." *ACTR Letter* 20: 1-5.

Crandall, JoAnn, ed. 1987. *ESL Through Content-Area Instruction: Mathematics, Science, Social Studies*. Englewood Cliffs, NJ: Prentice Hall Regents.

Crandall, JoAnn, and G. Richard Tucker. 1990. "Content-Based Instruction in Second and Foreign Languages." In: S. Anivan, ed., *Language Teaching Methodology for the Nineties*. Singapore: SEAMO Regional Language Centre.

Crandall, JoAnn and Karen Willetts. 1986. "Content-Based Language Instruction: A CLEAR-Sponsored Seminar." ER*IC/CLL News Bulletin* 9 (2): 1, 7, 8.

Crawley, Sharon J. and Lee Harrison Mountain. 1988. *Strategies for Guiding Content Reading*. Needham Heights, MA: Simon and Schuster.

Cummins, James. 1981. "The Role of Primary Language Development in Promoting Educational Success for Language Minority Students." In: *Schooling and Language Minority Students: A Theoretical Framework*. Sacramento, CA: Office of Bilingual Bicultural Education, California State Department of Education.

_____. 1984. *Bilingualism and Special Education: Issues in Assessment and Pedagogy*. Clevedon, England: Multilingual Matters.

_____. 1989. *Empowering Language Minority Students*. Sacramento, CA: California Association for Bilingual Education.

Curran, Charles A. 1972. *Counseling-Learning: A Whole Person Model for Education*. Apple River, IL: Apple River Press.

_____. 1976. *Counseling-Learning in Second Languages*. Apple River, IL: Apple River Press.

_____. 1978. *Understanding: An Essential Ingredient in Human Belonging*. Apple River, IL: Apple River Press.

Curtain, Helena A. 1986. "Integrating Language and Content Instruction." *ERIC/CLL News Bulletin* 9: 10-11.

de Hainer, Emma V. 1985. "Learning Styles." Unpublished manuscript. Washington, DC: George Washington University.

_____. 1985. "Learning Styles: A New Approach to Teaching ESL." *WATESOL News*, 16: 1.

Duff, P. A. (forthcoming). "Innovations in Foreign Language Education: An Evaluation of Three Hungarian-English Dual-Language Programs." *Journal of Multilingual Multicultural Development*.

Duri, Jayne. 1992. "Content-Based Instruction: Keeping DLI on the Cutting Edge." *The Globe* 5: 4-5.

Early, M., C. Thew, and P. Wakefield. 1986. *Integrating Language and Content Instruction: An ESL Resource Book*. Victoria, BC: Publications Service Branch, Ministry of Education.

Edwards, H. P., Marjorie B. Wesche, Stephen Krashen, R. Clément, and B. Kruidenier. 1984. "Second Language through Subject Matter Learning: A Study of Sheltered Psychology Classes at the University of Ottawa." *Canadian Modern Language Review* 2: 268-282.

Ehrman, Madline E. 1996. *Understanding Second Language Learning Difficulties*. Thousand Oaks, CA: Sage Publications.

Ellis, R. 1987. *Second Language Acquisition in Context*. Englewood Cliffs, NJ: Prentice Hall International.

Eskey, D., D. Craft and M. Alvin. 1984. *Structuring a Content-Based Syllabus*. Houston, TX: TESOL.

Fein, D. and R. Baldwin. 1986. "Content-Based Curriculum Design in Advanced Levels of an Intensive ESL Program." *English for Foreign Students in English-Speaking Countries: Interest Section Newsletter* 4(1): 1-3.

Fichera, Virginia M. and H. Stephen Straight, eds. In press. *Using Languages Across the Curriculum: Diverse Disciplinary Perspectives.* (Translation Perspectives X.) Binghamton, NY: Center for Research in Translation, State University of New York at Binghamton.

Flowerdew, J. 1991. *Content-Based Language Instruction in a Tertiary Setting.* City Polytechnic of Hong Kong. Unpublished manuscript.

Freed, Barbara F., ed. 1991. *Foreign Language Acquisition Research and the Classroom.* Lexington, MA: Heath.

Frohm, E. 1992. "Content-Based Instruction." In: W. Rivers, ed., *The College Curriculum* . Lincoln, IL: National Textbooks Co.

Froumina, Yelena and Boris Khasan. 1994. "Attitudinal, Learning Style, and Gender Influences on Language Learning Strategy Selection in Siberian Students of English: Implications of Tolerance-Conflict, Analytic-Global, and Male-Female Differences." Unpublished manuscript.

Ganschow, Leonore and Richard Sparks. 1996. "Anxiety about Foreign Language Learning Among High School Women." *Modern Language Journal* 80: 199-212.

Garrett, Nina. 1986. "The Problem with Grammar: What Kind Can the Language Learner Use?" *Modern Language Journal* 70: 133-147.

Garza, Thomas J. 1987. *Russians Learning English: An Analysis of Foreign Language Instruction in Soviet Specialized Schools.* Ann Arbor: University Microfilms.

Gary, J.O. and N. Gary. 1981. "Comprehension-Based Language Instruction: Theory." In: Harris Winitz, ed., *Native Language and Foreign Language Acquisition.* 332-341. New York: New York Academy of Sciences.

Genesee, Fred. 1987. *Learning through Two Languages: Studies of Immersion and Bilingual Education.* Cambridge: Newbury House.

Giauque, Gerald S. 1987. "Teaching for Content in a Skills Course: Greek Mythology in French." *Foreign Language Annals* 20: 565-569.

Goroshko, Natalia. 1995. *Ten Content-Based Lessons in Russian.* Salinas, CA: AGSI Press.

Goroshko, Natalia and L. Slutsky. 1993. "Four-Handed Teaching." *Dialog on Language Instruction* (a Defense Language Institute publication) 9: 49-53.

Grandin, John M., Kandace Einbeck, and Walter von Reinhart. 1992. "The Changing Goals of Language Instruction." In: *Languages for a Multicultural World in Transition.* Lincolnwood, IL: National Textbooks Co.

Grice, H. Paul. 1975. "Logic and Conversation." In: Peter Cole and Jerry L. Morgan, eds., *Speech Acts*, vol. 3 (Syntax and Semantics). New York: Academic Press.

Grosse, Christine U. and Geoffrey M. Voght. 1990 . "Foreign Languages for Business and the Professions at U.S. Colleges and Universities." *Modern Language Journal* 74: 36-47.

_____. 1991. "The Evolution of Languages for a Specific Purpose in the United States." *Modern Language Journal* 75: 181-195.

Halliday, Michael A. and Ruqaiya Hasan. 1989. *Language, Context, and Text: Aspects of Language in a Social-Semiotic Perspective.* 2d ed. Oxford: Oxford University Press.

Hart, D., Sharon Lapkin, and Merrill Swain. 1987. *Early and Middle French Immersion Programs: Linguistic Outcomes and Social Character.* Toronto: Metropolitan Toronto School Board.

Hart, N. W. M., R. F. Walker, and B. Gray. 1977. *The Language of Children: A Key to Literacy.* Reading, MA: Addison-Wesley.

Hauptmann, Philip C., Marjorie B. Wesche, and Doreen Ready. 1988. "Second Language Acquisition Through Subject Matter Learning: A Follow-Up Study at the University of Ottawa." *Language Learning* 38: 433-475.

Heath, Shirley B. 1992. "Sociocultural Contexts of Language Development: Implications for the Classroom." In: Patricia A. Richard-Amato and Marguerite A. Snow, eds., *The Multicultural Classroom: Readings for Content-Area Teachers.* White Plains, NY: Longman.

Hirsch, Eric D., James S. Trefil, and Joseph F. Kett. 1987. *Cultural Literacy: What Every American Needs to Know.* Boston: Houghton Mifflin Co.

Hudson, Thom. 1991. "A Content Comprehension Approach to Reading English for Science and Technology." *TESOL Quarterly* 25: 77-104.

Hymes, Dell H. 1970. "On Communicative Competence." In: John J. Gumperz and Dell H. Hymes, eds., *Directions in Sociolinguistics.* 35-71. New York: Holt, Rinehart & Winston.

_____. 1971. *On Communicative Competence.* Philadelphia: University of Pennsylvania Press.

Johns, Ann M. 1992. "What Is the Relationship Between Content-Based Instruction and English for Academic Purposes?" *The CATESOL Journal.*

Johnston, Susan S. 1991. *Curriculum Development Process for Content-Based Language Courses in a Post-Secondary Setting.* Japan: Temple University, Unpublished project.

Jones, Beau Fly, ed. 1987. *Strategic Teaching and Learning: Cognitive Instruction in the Content Areas.* Alexandria, VA: Association for Supervision and Curriculum Development.

Jurasek, Richard. 1988. "Integrating Foreign Languages into the College Curriculum." *Modern Language Journal* 72: 52-58.

Jurasek, B. S. and Richard T. Jurasek. 1991. "Building Multiple Proficiencies in New Curricular Contexts." In: June K. Phillips and Judith Liskin-Gasparro, eds., *Building Bridges and Making Connections.* Middlebury, VT: Northeast Conference on the Teaching of Foreign Languages. 89-121.

Kelly, Louis G. 1969. *25 Centuries of Language Teaching: An Inquiry into the Science, Art and Development of Language Teaching and Methodology, 500 B.C. - 1969.* Rowley, MA: Newbury House.

Klahn, Norma. 1988. *Area-Language Studies: Program on Mexico,* plus 8 packets of materials. New York: School for International and Public Affairs, Columbia University.

Klee, Carol, Andrew D. Cohen, and Diane J. Tedick. 1995a. "Content-Based Instruction in Spanish, French and German at the University of Minnesota: The Development and Evaluation of a New Program." Long Beach, CA: American Association of Applied Linguistics.

_____. 1995b. *Research on the Undergraduate Foreign Language Immersion Program in Spanish.* Anaheim, CA: American Council on the Teaching of Foreign Languages.

Klee, Carol and Michael F. Metcalf. 1994. "Perspectives on Foreign Languages Across the Curriculum Based on the University of Minnesota Experience." In: H. Stephen Straight, ed., *Languages Across the Curriculum: Invited Essays on the Use of Foreign Languages throughout the Postsecondary Curriculum.* Binghamton, NY: Center for Research in Translation, State University of New York at Binghamton.

Knowles, Malcolm S. 1990. *The Adult Learner: A Neglected Species.* 4th ed. Houston: Gulf Publishing Company.

Kolb, David A., Irwin Rubin, and James M. McIntyre. 1979. *Organizational Psychology: An Experiential Approach.* 3d ed. Englewood Cliffs, NJ: Prentice Hall.

Krahnke, Karl. 1987. *Approaches to Syllabus Design for Foreign Language Teaching.* Englewood Cliffs, NJ: Prentice Hall.

Kramsch, Claire and Sally McConnell-Ginet, eds. 1992. *Text and Context: Cross-Disciplinary Perspectives on Language Study.* Lexington, MA: Heath.

Krashen, Stephen D. 1982. *Principles and Practices in Second Language Acquisition.* New York: Pergamon Press.

_____. 1993. "Sheltered Subject-Matter Teaching." In: John W. Oller, ed., *Methods That Work: Ideas for Literacy and Language Teachers.* Boston: Heinle and Heinle.

Krashen, Stephen D., Robin C. Scarcella, and Michael H. Long eds. 1982. *Child-Adult Differences in Second Language Acquisition.* Rowley, MA: Newbury House.

Krashen, Stephen D. and Tracy Terrell. 1983. *The Natural Approach: Language Acquisition in the Classroom.* San Francisco: Alemany Press.

Krueger, Merle and Frank Ryan, eds. 1993. *Language and Content: Discipline- and Content-Based Approaches to Language Study.* Lexington, MA: DC Heath.

Kulick, K. 1988. "Considerations in Teaching Adult Learners: Psychological, Physiological, and Pedagogical." Linthicum, MD: DOD-ACTFL Symposium.

Kurki-Suonio, Liisa. 1990. "Team-Teaching Experiment: History in English." *Language Centre News,* January.

Lambert, Richard. 1994. "Using Foreign Languages in Higher Education." In: H. Stephen Straight, ed., *Languages Across the Curriculum: Invited Essays on the Use of Foreign Languages throughout the Postsecondary Curriculum.* (Translation Perspectives VII) 55-62. Binghamton, NY: Center for Research in Translation, State University of New York at Binghamton.

Lambert, Wallace and G. Richard Tucker. 1972. *Bilingual Education of Children: The St. Lambert Experiment.* Rowley, MA: Newbury House.

Leaver, Betty Lou. 1984. "Twenty Minutes to Mastery of the Cyrillic Alphabet." *Foreign Language Annals* 17: 215-220.

_____. 1991. "From the New Paradigm to the Next Paradigm: Learner Centered Instruction." *Proceedings of the 1991 AATSEEL Vision 2020 Panel.* Tucson, AZ: AATSEEL.

Leaver, Betty Lou and M. Funke. (forthcoming). "Content and Grammar: Are They Separable?" *Modern Language Journal.*

Leaver, Betty Lou and Rebecca Oxford. 1993. *Learning Strategies: A Manual for Students.* Salinas, CA: AGSI Press.

Leaver, Betty Lou and Stephen B. Stryker. 1989. "Content-Based Instruction for Foreign Language Classrooms." *Foreign Language Annals* 22: 269-274.

Leaver, Betty Lou and Sophia M. Thompson. 1993. *Content-Based Instruction.* Salinas, CA: AGSI Press.

Linguistics Institute of Ireland. 1986. *Spoken Irish in Primary Studies.* Dublin: Linguistics Institute of Ireland.

Liskin-Gasparro, Judith. 1984. "The ACTFL Proficiency Guidelines: A Historical Perspective." In: *Teaching for Proficiency: The Organizing Principle.* Lincolnwood, IL: National Textbook Co.

Loaiza-Arango, Adalberto. 1993. "Language Related Attitude Changes and Academic Performance of Students in the Foreign Language Immersion Program at the University of Minnesota." Master's thesis, Department of Curriculum and Instruction, University of Minnesota.

Long, Michael H. and Patricia A. Porter. 1985. "Group Work, Interlanguage Talk and Second Language Acquisition." *TESOL Quarterly* 19: 207-227.

Macias, Clemencia and Bella Yerokhina. 1994. *Content-Based Instruction for Spanish: Ten Sample Lessons.* Salinas, CA: AGSI Press.

MacKay, R. and J. Palmer, eds. 1981. *Language for Specific Purposes: Design and Evaluation.* New York: Newbury House.

Makarova. G. 1990. "Individualization of Foreign Language Instruction for Non-Language Majors." Paper presented at the seventh MAPRIAL conference in Moscow.

Maly, Eugene. 1993. "Task-Based Instruction from the Teacher's Perspective." *Dialogue on Language Instruction* 9: 37-48.

McCarthy, Bernice. 1987. *The 4-Mat System: Teaching to Learning Styles with Right/Left Mode Techniques.* Barrington, IL: EXCEL.

Met, Myriam. 1991. "Learning Language through Content: Learning Content through Language." *Foreign Language Annals* 24: 281-229.

Metcalf, Michael F. and Diane J. Tedick. 1993. "Foreign Language Immersion Program: Proposal to the National Endowment for the Humanities." Institute for International Studies, University of Minnesota.

Migneron, Mariette and Sandra Burger. 1989. *Teaching Strategies for Immersion Courses.* Ottawa, Canada: Centre for Second Language Learning, University of Ottawa.

Milk, R. D. 1990. "Integrating Language and Content: Implications for Language Distribution in Bilingual Classrooms." In: R. Jacobsen and C. Faltis, eds., *Language Distribution Issues in Bilingual Schooling:* 32-44. Clevedon, England: Multilingual Matters.

Mitchell, E. 1987. "Teaching Scientific and Technical French at Napier College in Scotland." Proceedings of the Fifth Annual Eastern Michigan Conference on Languages for Business and the Professions. Unpublished document.

Mohan, Bernard A. 1986. *Language and Content.* Reading, MA: Addison-Wesley.

Moline, J. 1990. "On Making Foreign Languages Our Own." *Humanities* 11: 36-38.

Monaghan, Peter. 1992. "Monterey Institute Makes Language Fluency a Key Part of Its International Curriculum."*The Chronicle of Higher Education,* July 1, A33.

Morley, Joan. 1985. "Listening Comprehension: Student Controlled Modules for Self-Access Self-Study."*TESOL Newsletter* 19: (6) 1-33.

Morris, Michael A. 1997. "CAC and FLAC Compared." *Communication Across the Curriculum (Newsletter).* 4-6.

Morris, Michael A. and Margaret Dales-Sanhueza. 1997. *A Market Approach to Language and Cross-Cultural Learning.* Clemson, SC: Clemson University Center for Policy and Legal Studies.

Murrell, E. 1991. "French Outside the Literature/Language Classroom: International Relations in the 90's." Paper presented at the Eastern Michigan Conference on Languages and Communications for World Business and the Professions, Ypsilanti, Michigan.

Nagle, Stephen J. and Sara L. Sanders. 1986. "Comprehension Theory and Second Language Pedagogy." *TESOL Quarterly* 20: 9-26.

Nelson-Herber, J. 1986. "Expanding and Refining Vocabulary in Content Areas." *Journal of Reading* 29: 626-633.

Nikonova, S. M. 1968. *U istokov sovetskoi metodiki obucheniia inostrannym iazykam.* Moscow: Vysshaia shkola; Reprint 1994: Salinas, CA: AGSI Press.

Nunan, David. 1989. *Designing Tasks for the Communicative Classroom.* Cambridge: Cambridge University Press.

Oller, John W. 1988. "Review of *The Input Hypothesis*, by Stephen D. Krashen." *Language* 64: 171-173.

Oller, John W., ed. 1993. *Methods That Work: Ideas for Literacy and Language Teachers.* Boston: Heinle & Heinle.

Omaggio, Alice. 1986. *Teaching Language in Context: Proficiency-Oriented Instruction.* Boston: Heinle & Heinle.

Oxford, Rebecca. 1990. *Language Learning Strategies: What Every Teacher Should Know.* New York: Newbury House.

Patrikis, Peter C., ed. 1988. "The Governance of Foreign Language Teaching and Learning." Proceedings of a Symposium, Princeton, New Jersey, 9-11 October, 1987. New Haven, CT: The Consortium for Language Teaching and Learning.

Paulston, Christina B. 1974. "Linguistic and Communicative Competence." *TESOL Quarterly* 8: 347-362

Paulston, Christina B. and Mary N. Bruder. 1975. *From Substitution to Substance: A Handbook of Structural Pattern Drills.* Rowley, MA: Newbury House.

Peck, Sabrina. 1987. "Spanish for Social Workers: An Intermediate Level Communicative Course with Content Lectures." *Modern Language Journal* 71: 402-409.

A Plan for the Future: State University of New York at Binghamton. 1996. Binghamton, NY: Strategic Planning Council, SUNY at Binghamton.

Polio, C. 1988. "An Evaluation of the UCLA-Chinese Academy of Social Sciences English Language Centre." Los Angeles: University of California, Los Angeles. Unpublished manuscript.

Postovsky, Valerian A. 1974. "Effects of Delay in Oral Practice in Second Language Learning." *Modern Language Journal* 58: 229-239.

Prabhu, N. S. 1987. *Second Language Pedagogy.* Oxford: Oxford University Press.

Rardin, Jennybelle and Daniel D. Tranel. 1988. *Education in a New Dimension: The Counseling-Learning Approach to Community Language Learning.* East Dubuque, IL: Counseling-Learning Publications.

Rhodes, Nancy C. 1987. *Total and Partial Language Immersion Programs in U.S. Elementary Schools.* Los Angeles: Center for Language Education and Research, University of California, Los Angeles.

Rhodes, N. C. and Rebecca Oxford. 1988. "Foreign Language in Elementary and Secondary Schools: Results of a National Survey." *Foreign Language Annals* 21: 51-69.

Richard-Amato, Patricia A. 1996. *Making It Happen: Interaction in the Second Language Classroom: From Theory to Practice.* 2d ed. White Plains, NY: Longman.

Richard-Amato, Patricia A., and Marguerite A. Snow. 1992. "Strategies for Content-Area Teachers." In: Patricia A. Richard-Amato and Marguerite A. Snow, eds., *The Multicultural Classroom: Readings for Content-Area Teachers.* 145- 163. White Plains, NY: Longman.

Richards, Jack C. and Theodore S. Rodgers. 1986. *Approaches and Methods in Language Teaching.* Cambridge: Cambridge University Press.

Richards, Jack C. and D. Hurley. 1990. "Language and Content: Approaches to Curriculum Alignment." In: *The Language Teaching Matrix.* Cambridge: Cambridge University Press.

Rieck, Billie Jo. 1977. "How Content Teachers Telegraph Messages against Reading." *Journal of Reading* 20: 646-648.

Rubin, Joan. 1994. "A Review of Second Language Listening Comprehension Research." *Modern Language Journal* 78: 199-221.

Ryan, Frank L. 1994. "Languages Across the Curriculum: More Than a Good Idea." In: H. Stephen Straight, ed., *Languages Across the Curriculum: Invited Essays on the Use of Foreign Languages throughout the Postsecondary Curriculum* (Translation Perspectives VII) 47-54. Binghamton, NY: Center for Research in Translation, State University of New York at Binghamton.

Ryding, Karin C. 1990. *Formal Spoken Arabic: Basic Course.* Washington, DC: Georgetown University Press

_____. 1991. "Proficiency Despite Diglossia: A New Approach for Arabic." *Modern Language Journal* 75: 212-218.

_____. 1994. "Fostering a Learning Community for Arabic." *Theory into Practice* 33: (2) 23-28.

Salomone, A. M. 1993. "Immersion Teachers: What Can We Learn from Them?" In: John W. Oller, ed., *Methods That Work: Ideas for Literacy and Language Teachers.* Boston: Heinle & Heinle.

Samimy, Keiko Komiya. 1989. "A Comparative Study of Teaching Japanese in the Audio-Lingual Method and the Counseling-Learning Approach." *Modern Language Journal* 73:2:167-76.

Savignon, Sandra J . 1983. *Communicative Competence: Theory and Classroom Practice.* Reading, MA: Addison-Wesley.

Schleppegrell, Mary J. 1987. "The Older Language Learner." *ERIC Digest.* Washington, DC: Center for Applied Linguistics.

Schwartz, J., V. Bevan, and S. Lasche. 1987. "An Intensive Theme-Oriented Course in Advanced English for First-Semester German University Students in Diverse Subject Studies." *Fremdsprachenorientierte Studieneingangsphase* (Heft 6). Berlin: Free University of Berlin.

Shaw, Peter A. 1991. *Report on Content-Based Instruction Curriculum Development Project at MIIS.* Internal document. Monterey, CA: Monterey Institute for International Studies.

_____. 1996. "Voices for Improved Learning: The Ethnographer as Co-Agent of Pedagogic Change." In: Kathleen M. Bailey and David Nunan, eds., *Voices from the Language Classroom.* 318-337. New York: Cambridge University Press.

Shekhtman, Boris and Natalia Lord. 1985. *Mark Smith's Diary.* Arlington, VA: Foreign Service Institute.

Shih, May. 1986. "Content-Based Approaches to Teaching Academic Writing." *TESOL Quarterly* 20: 617-648.

Shohamy, Elana. 1990. "Language Testing Priorities: A Different Perspective." *Foreign Language Annals* 23: 385-393.

Short, Deborah J. 1989. *How to Integrate Language and Content Instruction: A Training Manual.* Los Angeles: University of California, Center for Language Education and Research.

Shrum, Judith L. and Eileen W. Glisan. 1994. *Teacher's Handbook: Contextualized Language Instruction.* Boston, MA: Heinle & Heinle.

Singerman, Alan J. and Richard C. Williamson, eds. 1988. *Toward a New Integration of Language and Culture.* Northeast Conference Report. Northeast Conference on the Teaching of Foreign Languages, Inc.

Smith, Frank R. 1988. *Joining the Literacy Club: Further Essays in Education.* Portsmouth, NH: Heinemann.

Smith, Frank R. and Karen M. Feathers. 1983. "Teacher and Student Perceptions of Content Area Reading." *Journal of Reading* 26: 348-354.

Snow, Marguerite Ann and Donna M. Brinton. 1988a. *The Adjunct Model of Language Instruction: Integrating Language and Content at the University.* Center for Language Education and Research, Technical Report #8. Los Angeles: UCLA.

_____. 1988b. "Content-Based Language Instruction: Investigating the Effectiveness of the Adjunct Model." *TESOL Quarterly* 22: 553-574.

_____. 1997. *The Content-Based Classroom: Perspectives on Integrating Language and Content.* White Plains, NY: Longman.

Snow, Marguerite Ann, Myriam Met, and Fred H. Genesee. 1989. "A Conceptual Framework for the Integration of Language and Content in Second/Foreign Language Instruction." *TESOL Quarterly* 23: 201-217.

Spolsky, Bernard. 1985. "What Does It Mean to Know How to Use a Language? An Essay on the Theoretical Basis of Language Testing." *Language Testing* 2: 180-191.

Spolsky, Bernard, ed. 1978. *Approaches to Language Testing.* Arlington, VA: Center for Applied Linguistics.

Stansfield, Charles W. 1986. *ACTFL Proficiency Guidelines for the Less Commonly Taught Languages: A Familiarization Project for the Development of Proficiency Guidelines for Less Commonly Taught Languages.* Hastings-on-Hudson, New York: Center for Applied Linguistics; American Council on the Teaching of Foreign Languages.

Star Mountain, Inc. 1991. *Perspectives in Foreign Language Education in the Soviet Union.* Sacramento, CA: U.S. Office of Personnel Management.

Stern, H. H. 1978. "Bilingual Schooling and Foreign Language Education: Some Implications of the Canadian Experiments in French." In: James E. Alatis, ed., *Georgetown University Roundtable 1978: International Dimensions Of Bilingual Education.* Washington, DC: Georgetown University Press.

_____. 1990. "Analysis and Experience as Variables in Second Language Pedagogy." In: Birgit Harley, ed., T*he Development of Second Language Proficiency.* Cambridge: Cambridge University Press.

Sternfeld, Steven R. 1985. *Foreign Language Education and the Psycho-Social Variables of Adult Foreign Language Acquisition.* Unpublished doctoral dissertation. University of Southern California.

_____. 1987. "Learner Expectations and the Promotion of Language Acquisition in the Classroom." *ITESOL Occasional Papers* 5: 26-42.

_____. 1988. "The Applicability of the Immersion Approach to College Foreign Language Instruction." *Foreign Language Annals* 21: 221-226.

_____. 1989. "The University of Utah's Immersion/Multiliteracy Program: An Example of an Area Studies Approach to the Design of First-Year College Foreign Language Instruction." *Foreign Language Annals* 22: 341-354.

_____. 1991. "Exploring Community in a Content-Based Foreign Language Classroom." *Crosscurrents* 18: 143-151.

_____. 1992. "An Experiment in Foreign Education: The University of Utah's Immersion/Multiliteracy Program." In: R.J. Courchêne, J. I. Glidden, J. St. John, C. Thérien, eds., *Comprehension-Based Language Teaching/ L'enseignement des langues secondes axés sur la compréhension.* 407-432. Ottawa: University of Ottawa Press.

Stevick, Earl. W. 1980. *Teaching Languages: A Way and Ways.* Rowley, MA: Newbury House.

_____. 1986. *Images and Options in the Language Classroom.* London: Cambridge University Press.

_____. 1990. *Humanism in Language Teaching: A Critical Perspective.* Oxford: Oxford University Press.

_____. 1996. *Memory, Meaning, and Method: A View of Language Teaching.* 2d ed. Boston: Heinle & Heinle.

Straight, H. Stephen. 1990. "Languages Must Be Taught 'Across the Curriculum' to Insure That Students Develop Functional Skills." *Chronicle for Higher Education,* 7 March.

_____. In press. Language Resource Specialists as Agents for Curricular Internationalization. (An Overview and Evaluation of SUNY-Binghamton University's LxC Program.) [Tentative title.] In: Virginia M. Fichera and H. Stephen Straight, eds., *Using Languages Across the Curriculum: Diverse Disciplinary Perspectives.* (Translation Perspectives X) Binghamton, NY: Center for Research in Translation, State University of New York at Binghamton.

_____., ed. 1994. *Languages Across the Curriculum: Invited Essays on the Use of Foreign Languages throughout the Postsecondary Curriculum.* (Translation Perspectives VII) Binghamton, NY: Center for Research in Translation, State University of New York at Binghamton. (Out of print; available on microfiche: ERIC Clearinghouse on Languages and Linguistics, Document ED 374 646.)

Suozzo, A. G., Jr. 1981. "Once More with Content: Shifting Emphasis in Intermediate French." *The French Review* 54: 405-411.

Swaffar, Janet K., Katherine M. Arens, and Heidi Byrnes. 1991. *Reading for Meaning: An Integrated Approach to Language Learning.* Englewood Cliffs, NJ: Prentice Hall.

Swain, Merrill. 1975. "Writing Skills of Grade 3 French Immersion Pupils." *Working Papers on Bilingualism* 7: 1-38.

_____. 1985. "Communicative Competence: Some Roles of Comprehensible Input and Comprehensible Output in its Development." In: Susan M. Gass and Carolyn G. Madden, eds., *Input in Second Language Acquisition.* 235-253. Rowley, MA: Newbury House.

_____. 1988. "Manipulating and Complementing Content Teaching to Maximize Second Language Learning." *TESL Canada Journal* 6: 68-83.

_____. 1991. "French Immersion and Its Offshoots: Getting Two for One." In: Barbara F. Freed, ed., *Foreign Language Acquisition Research and the Classroom.* 91-103. Lexington, MA: Heath.

Swain, Merrill and Sharon Lapkin. 1982. *Evaluating Bilingual Education: A Canadian Case Study.* Clevedon, England: Multilingual Matters.

_____. 1988, October. "Canadian Immersion and Adult Second Language Teaching: What's the Connection?" Keynote paper presented at the First OSU/MLJ Conference on Research Perspectives in Adult Language Learning and Acquisition, Ohio State University, Columbus, OH.

Terrell, Tracy D. 1986. "Acquisition in the Natural Approach: The Binding/Access Framework." *Modern Language Journal* 70: 213-227.

_____. 1991. "The Role of Grammar Instruction in a Communitive Approach." *Modern Language Journal* 75: 52-63.

Vacca, Richard T. and Jo Anne L. Vacca. 1989. *Content Area Reading.* Glenview, IL: Scott, Foresman.

Van Naerssen, Margaret. 1992. "Content-Based Language Instruction: Role of the Instructor in 'Sheltered' Courses." *Penn Language News* 14: 17.

Vignola, Marie-Josée and Marjorie Wesche. 1991. "Le Savoir-Ecrire en Langue Maternelle et en Langue Séconde Chez les Diplomes d'Immersion Française." *Etudes de Linguistique Appliqué* 82: 94-115.

Watkins, Beverly T. 1990. "Program at St. Olaf College Offers Student Incentives to Make Foreign Languages More Than a Requirement." *Chronicle of Higher Education* 38: A19-A21. (28 November)

Wesche, Marjorie B. 1985. "Immersion and the Universities." *Canadian Modern Language Review* 41: 931-940.

Widdowson, H. G. 1978. "Notional-Functional Syllabus 1978: Part IV." In: C.H. Blatchford and J. Schachter, eds., *On Tesol 78: EFL Policies, Programs, Practices*. Washington, DC: TESOL.

Wilkins, D. A. 1976. *Notional Syllabuses*. Oxford: Oxford University Press.

Williams, Mary, Madeleine Lively, and Jane Harper. 1994. "Higher Order Thinking Skills: Tools for Bridging the Gap." *Foreign Language Annals* 27: 405-426.

Willetts, Karen. 1986. *Integrating Language and Content Instruction (Education Report No. 5)*. Los Angeles: University of California, Center for Language Education and Research.

_____. 1989a. "Deutsch für Ingenieure: Das Rhode Island Programm." *Jahrbuch Deutsch als Fremdsprache*. Munich: Iudicium Verlag.

_____. 1989b. "Language and Engineering: The Next Step." *Proceedings of the Clemson Conference on Language and International Trade*. Clemson, SC: Clemson University.

_____. 1989c. "The University of Utah's Immersion/Multiliteracy Program: An Example of Area Studies Approach to the Design of First-Year College Foreign Language Instruction." *Foreign Language Annals* 22: 341-354.

_____. 1991. "The Evolution of Languages for Special Purposes in the United States." *Modern Language Journal* 75: 181-95.

_____. ed., 1988. *Language Learning and Liberal Education*. New Haven, CT: Consortium for Language Learning and Teaching.

Willetts, Karen and Donna M. Brinton. 1988. "Content-Based Language Instruction: Investigating the Effectiveness of the Adjunct Model." *TESOL Quarterly* 22: 553-574.

Willetts, Karen, Myriam Met, and Fred Genesee. 1989. "A Conceptual Framework for the Integration of Language and Content in Second/Foreign Language Instruction." *TESOL Quarterly* 23: 201-217.

Winitz, Harris, ed. 1981. *The Comprehension Approach to Foreign Language Instruction*. Rowley, MA: Newbury House.

Winitz, Harris and James A. Reeds. 1973. "Rapid Acquisition of a Foreign Language (German) by the Avoidance of Speaking."*International Review of Applied Linguistics* 11:295-317.

Wolf, Darlene F. 1993. "A Comparison of Assessment Tasks Used to Measure FL Reading Comprehension." *Modern Language Journal* 77:473-489.

Index